MICHAEL JORDAN

A Shooting Star

The Tar Heels' Michael Jordan jams home a slam dunk. (Courtesy of the *Durham Herald-Sun.*)

MICHAEL JORDAN

A Shooting Star

by George Beahm

Andrews and McMeel

A Universal Press Syndicate Company

Kansas City

For information, write: Andrews and McMeel, a Universal Press Syndicate Company, 4900 Main Street, Kansas City, Missouri 64112.

Attention: Schools and Businesses

Andrews and McMeel books are available at quantity discount with bulk purchase for educational, business, or sales promotional use. For information, please write to: Special Sales Department, Andrews and McMeel, 4900 Main Street, Kansas City, Missouri 64112.

Library of Congress Cataloging-in-Publication Data

Beahm, George W.
    Michael Jordan : a shooting star / by George Beahm.
        p.   cm.
    Includes bibliographical references.
    ISBN 0-8362-8048-2
    1. Jordan, Michael, 1963–   —Juvenile literature.
2. Basketball players—United States—Biography—
Juvenile literature. [1. Jordan, Michael, 1963–   .
2. Basketball players.   3. Afro-Americans—Biography.]
I. Title.
GV884.J67B43   1994
796.323'092—dc20
[B]   93-46005
                                                               CIP
                                                                AC

See page 160 for continuation of copyright notice.

To our nephews and nieces

—George and Mary Beahm

Contents

Four: Jordan and Basketball

Five: A Look Back

Six: Holding Court

Seven: Appendixes

Acknowledgments

I am deeply indebted to numerous individuals—far too many to acknowledge—for invaluable help on this book project.

To Wilson Chan, in the home office of the Chicago Bulls, for coordinating my numerous requests and allowing me the rare opportunity to research their Jordan files—a motherlode of information.

To the staffs at the Williamsburg Public Library and the Smithfield Public Library, for assisting with research. I especially want to thank Ms. Dorothy Rhodes at the Smithfield library for her patience while I researched the library's run of *Sports Illustrated*.

To the fine folks at Michael Jordan's/The Restaurant, for assistance on several matters: David Mazzorana, general manager; Molly Madden; and Gary Silver, retail store manager.

To Vizhier Corpuz of Nike, who provided much-needed information and photo resources that, otherwise, would have been impossible to obtain.

To Sean Bradley at Nike Town (Chicago, Ill.) for assistance and advice on "Air" Jordan and Nike apparel.

To Jan Hubbard from the National Basketball Association (NBA) for information and statistics on Michael Jordan.

To John Meyer, the managing editor of the *Wilmington Star-News*, for assistance with research and photographs.

To Harold Moore, director of photography at the *Durham Herald-Sun*, for assistance with research and photographs.

To Kristin E. Whitehurst, director of communications at Elmhurst College, for information and photo assistance.

To my agent and friend John White, whose counsel, support, and professional concerns were invaluable.

To Upper Deck and SkyBox, for providing much-needed trading cards for photo purposes.

To my small circle of friends that, always, were there with encouraging words during an admittedly difficult period in my life: Rusty and Maria Wornom, Steve Spignesi, and Colleen Doran.

To Jesse Hines, who has been my principal teenage adviser on this project, along with his brothers, Matthew and John, and his sister, Anne—all helped with research and materials. To Raymond Burrows, another nephew, for his unbridled enthusiasm and input on Jordan card collecting. To them and our other nephews and nieces, Mary and I are most grateful.

To my wife and life/business partner Mary Beahm, whose interest in sports exceeds mine, and who was my sounding board on the shape and substance of the book.

To my friends at Andrews and McMeel, who once again wanted to publish *well*, and knocked themselves out on this project: Patty Donnelly, who kept the lines of communication open; and to Jean Lowe, who (once again) shepherded this book through production. I owe a special debt of gratitude to my editor, Donna Martin, who helped shape this manuscript, focusing our vision of the book to give it clarity and theme—thanks, Donna. If they gave out publishing trophies, this team would win, hands down.

MICHAEL JORDAN

A Shooting Star

No bird soars too high,
if he soars with his own wings.

—*poet* **William Blake**

Introduction

by George Beahm

I think I owe kids the opportunity to show them a correct way or one way of being positive, of achieving dreams.
—*Michael Jordan*

I. Rare Air Up There

THIS IS A BOOK about dreams.

It's mostly about Michael Jordan's dreams, and how he realized them, but in a larger sense it's about *your* dreams.

Though there have been several books about Jordan, this one is different because it's written for his younger fans. Second, it's not written by a long-time Bulls fan knowledgeable about basketball; I come to this book with a new fan's enthusiasm. And, finally, it doesn't focus on Jordan with a "gosh wow" perspective, nor does it highlight the money that surrounds Jordan, which from my point of view is the *least* important thing about him.

This book, in short, is an unapologetic retrospective on Michael Jordan the basketball player, who in 1993 retired from the NBA as a player for the Chicago Bulls—the greatest sports figure ever, according to many.

Readers, or reviewers, who come to this book with the expectation of reading more "trash talk" about Jordan are bound to be disappointed. They seem incapable of distinguishing between Jordan the basketball player and the image they helped create of Jordan on a pedestal.

When you're on a pedestal, as Jordan found out, there's plenty of people wanting to knock you off.

There's also very little about Jordan's personal life, since he has been adamant about preserving what little remains of his privacy. In his own book, *Rare Air: Michael on Michael*, a photographic biography covering his on-court and off-court activities, Jordan shares with us his thoughts—10,000 words worth.

This book also does not dwell excessively on individual games, since these have been superbly covered over the years by *Sports Illustrated*. I cannot improve on their coverage. (This book, though, does cover the playoff games, reprinting *Sports Illustrated* coverage by Jack McCallum.)

Finally, this is not a book about Jordan and the Bulls; it's primarily about Jordan. (A book about the Bulls will undoubtedly be written, but this is not that book.)

To date, most of the books about Jordan are biographies, written by sports journalists from Chicago. Not desiring to cover the same, familiar ground again, I have instead chosen to look at the Michael Jordan phenomenon in light of what I think you, his younger fans, would find interesting. (See the appendixes for a complete list of biographies currently in print.)

This book, then, is a companion book that takes a chronological look at Jordan. Drawn in part from previously published pieces as well as new material, this book reflects my thought that we should celebrate Jordan: a superb on-court ballplayer and—despite what some in the media think—a role model kids will always look up to, long past the point of his retirement.

After the "Dream Team" brought home the gold medal from the Barcelona Olympic Games, two of the best players in the National Basketball Association retired, one voluntarily, the other involuntarily. Larry Bird of the Boston Celtics saw his jersey retired after a long, memorable career. Earvin "Magic" Johnson, of the Los Angeles Lakers also saw his jersey retired, his career cut short, after he discovered he had contracted the HIV virus. Before that time, however, when Bird, Johnson, and Jordan were active players, sportswriters speculated endlessly on who was the best player. With only Jordan remaining, however, the point became moot. And after Jordan announced his retirement, the consensus was that while Bird retired at the end of a lackluster season, and Johnson retired amid controversy in the league, Jordan left of his own free will, on his timetable, at the peak of his powers and the high point of his career—just as he always said he would. (We knew it was coming; we were just hoping he'd postpone it *one* more year.)

As John Edgar Wideman wrote: "As we envision soaring and swooping, extending, refining the combat zone of basketball into a fourth, outer, other dimension, the dreamy ozone of flight without wings, of going up and not coming down till we're good and ready, then it's Michael Jordan we must recognize as the truest prophet of what might be possible."

Though "Air" Jordan is grounded, he gave us nine years of memories that will live forever in the annals of sports history and, also, in our hearts and minds.

II. Play Like Mike

A few years ago I didn't know Jordan's name except through the television ads, but my nephews in nearby Smithfield, Virginia, changed that. All jocks, the boys when playing basketball all wanted to claim "being" Michael Jordan for the day, trying to imitate his fancy moves.

The more I watched them, and the more they told me about Jordan, the more curious I became until I, too, became a fan. The kids saw much to appreciate in Jordan (and his contemporaries, especially fellow Chicago Bulls teammates), an appreciation they shared with me.

Sports, I think, defines our culture better than any other field of endeavor, embodying American ideals: a sense of competition, a strong sense of individualism, and a shot at a worthy goal: trying to be the best you can be.

So, through Jordan and others like him, we see what we can be. Perfect? Absolutely not, for we are all-too human, subject to frailties. But we saw Jordan realize his dreams, and through him, we learn that all of us can dream, and perhaps one day live our dreams, if we want to.

Jordan's popularity cut across all boundaries: He appealed to young and old, male and female, black and white. His talent and personal charisma made him one of the most recognizable persons on the planet—no doubt helped by Nike and his participation as a Dream Team member at the Barcelona Olympic Games.

Though retired, Michael Jordan will still very much be with us. His commercial endorsements extend for many more years, so we at least will see him on TV. Beyond that, no one knows—not even Michael Jordan himself, who has tantalized us with the possibility of coming out of retirement, if he feels the urge. (Just do it, his fans are urging him, hoping he will give us another season or two of on-court Michael magic.)

Clearly, Jordan's message—whether intentional or not—is one that everyone wants to believe in: Give life your personal best, for by doing so you may attain your goals, find meaning in your life, and perhaps reap your just rewards.

That, I think, is what we should celebrate in Jordan, and in us, as well.

George Beahm
Williamsburg, Virginia
April 1994

Michael Jordan Chronology:

Personal and Professional

1963

• Born February 17 in Brooklyn, New York; the fourth child of James and Deloris Jordan.

1970

• Moves with family to Wilmington, North Carolina.

1975

• Named Dixie Youth Baseball Player of the Year, top player in Little League baseball (age 12).

• Named Most Valuable Player when baseball team wins state championship.

1977

• Attends D.C. Virgo Junior High School (Wilmington, North Carolina); plays three sports (baseball, basketball, football).

1978

• Attends Laney High School (Wilmington, North Carolina) as tenth grader. Plays basketball (no. 23) as a Laney Buccaneer.

• Quarterback for JV football team.

• Starting point guard for JV basketball.

1979

• Apocryphal story regarding Jordan being "cut" from the varsity team becomes part of Jordan legend.

1980

• Height shoots up to six-foot-three.

• Gives up football, concentrating on basketball.

• Named to the *Star-News* All–Hanover County team.

• Attends Five-Star Basketball Camp in North Carolina; wins five trophies for individual excellence first week; stays for second week and wins another four. Credited by Jordan as the turning point in his young life.

• Signs on to attend the University of North Carolina on basketball scholarship.

1981

• *Parade* High School All-American.

• Focuses on basketball, relinquishing baseball.

• Leads team to a Division II state championship.

• Graduates from Laney High School in June.

• Enters the University of North Carolina as a freshman in September.

1982

• Named Atlantic Coast Conference Rookie of the Year.

• Named to ACC All-Tournament team.

• Named to NCAA All-Tournament team at the Final Four.

- Named Atlantic Coast Conference Freshman of the Year.

- Makes the game-winning jumper at the 1982 NCAA championship against Georgetown, earning him the cover of local phone directory with "The Shot."

1983

- Selected first-team All-American.

- *Sporting News* College Player of the Year.

1984

- Begins playing golf, introduced to game by Davis Love III.

- Selected first-team All-American.

- *Sporting News* College Player of the Year.

- Wins Eastman Award as college basketball's player of the year (voted on by National Basketball Coaches Association).

- Leading scorer on U.S. Pan American team that wins the gold medal in Caracas, Venezuela.

- Cocaptain of U.S. Olympic team in Los Angeles, California; wins gold medal.

- Becomes a client of ProServ.

- Becomes a Nike spokesman; first Air Jordan shoes sold amid NBA controversy.

- May: Leaves North Carolina to turn pro.

- Is third pick in first round of NBA draft, selected by Chicago Bulls.

1985

- Named first-team All-Eastern Division.

- Schick Pivotal Player of the Year award.

- Named Seagram's Player of the Year.

- All-NBA second team.

- Named NBA Rookie of the Year.

- Completes college education at UNC, receives B.A. degree in geography.

- NBA All-Star team.

1986

- Sits out 64 games due to a bone fracture in foot.

- NBA All-Star team (selected, but sits out due to injury).

1987

- Named Seagram's Player of the Year.

- NBA scoring champion.

- NBA All-Star team.

- All-Star Slam-Dunk Champion.

1988

- NBA Defensive Player of the Year.

- NBA Most Valuable Player.

- All-NBA first team.

- NBA scoring champion.

- All-Defensive first team.

- NBA All-Star team.

- All-Star Game Most Valuable Player.

- All-Star Slam-Dunk Champion.

- Signs contract extension through 1995–96 season.

1989

- Named Most Valuable Player by *Basketball Digest, Basketball Weekly, The Sporting News.*

- All-NBA first team.

- All-Defensive first team.

- NBA scoring champion.

- NBA All-Star team.

- Marries the former Juanita Vanoy.

- With his mother, establishes the Michael Jordan Foundation, headquartered in Chicago, Illinois.

1990

- All-NBA first team.

- All-Defensive first team.

- NBA scoring champion.

- NBA All-Star team.

1991

- All-NBA first team.

- Named NBA Most Valuable Player.

- NBA scoring champion.

- NBA All-Star team.

- All-Defensive first team.

- Leads Chicago Bulls to first NBA Championship.

- Named NBA Championship Most Valuable Player.

- Selected as Sportsman of the Year by *Sports Illustrated*, commemorated in December 23, 1991, issue.

1992

- All-NBA first team.

- NBA Most Valuable Player.

- NBA scoring champion.

- Member of U.S. Olympic basketball team in Barcelona, Spain; wins gold medal.

- All-Defensive first team.

- NBA All-Star team.

- Leads Chicago Bulls to second NBA Championship.

- Named NBA Championship Most Valuable Player.

1993

- Michael Jordan's/The Restaurant opens in Chicago, Illinois.

- Leads Chicago Bulls to third NBA Championship.

- Named NBA Championship Most Valuable Player.

- All-Defensive first team.

- All-NBA first team.

- NBA All-Star team.

- NBA scoring champion.

- Father James Jordan murdered, August.

- Announces retirement, October.

One
The Early Years

It's Saturday morning. The other kids in the neighborhood have just started getting up, but the skinny kid with fire in his eyes walks confidently out to the backyard court, with a worn basketball in hand. His hands are too small to palm the ball, but one day—years from now—he hopes to be big enough to palm it as easily as he now holds a baseball.

In the backyard court, he waits for his older brother to join him. His brother's too fast, too good, and regularly beats him, but that, too, will change; one day, the younger brother will eclipse his older brother; *just wait and see*, he says to himself.

In his mind he's far away from the sleepy, coastal town of Wilmington, North Carolina, where his parents decided to put down roots, and where his father built a split-level house with the backyard court for the family. In his mind, fired by imagination, he's no longer a skinny kid but a grown man, towering six-and-a-half feet tall, playing in the NBA. Driving in, he eludes the defense, weaving in and out, setting up for a shot. Position, elevate, aim, and fire—two points!

He hears the appreciative roar of the crowd as he takes off, baseline, his right hand holding the basketball aloft; his arms are stretched out wide for stabilization, and his legs are splayed out for balance. It's almost as if he's an F-16 jet fighter zeroing in at a target, accelerating for the attack.

Soaring above the rim, hanging impossibly in the air, he dunks the basketball with a tomahawk jam that rattles the rim, as he lands, catlike, on the balls of his feet.

It's now tied three games to three, game seven of an NBA championship. It all comes down to one final shot—ten seconds on the clock. His team down one point, he takes an in-bounds pass and drives baseline; his brow is knit in concentration, his tongue protruding, as the defenders converge to double-team him, to block his shot.

Faking left, he goes right; blocked by another defender, he double-pumps a fake jump shot, watching with a smile as the defender rises in vain, arms outstretched; he elevates for the clutch shot—a jumper at the top of the key.

The crowd stands and roars its approval as the ball arcs toward the basket. The shot is . . . nothing but net! Two points! He's scored the game-winning shot, and wins the NBA championship!

The sun is finally up—a hot, yellow disk in the sky—and early shadows are thrown across the backyard court. He comes back down to earth, realizing he's not in the NBA—*not yet, anyway*—but instead in his own backyard, a million miles away from the NBA. Far away from the future crowds, the adulation, and the media, Wilmington, North Carolina, is where he learned to love the game. Just him and the net, and an older brother who neither gave nor asked for mercy.

As Jordan reminded us in his videotape, *Michael Jordan's Playground,* this is where it begins: on the playground or home court, with an older brother or other kids hungry for the ball, hungry to make the points, hungry to make a reputation as being the best of the lot.

No endorsements, no NBA salaries, no cameras flashing in your face; just a bunch of wide-eyed kids who grew up dreaming of the day when they, too, would soar higher than the rest. Kids with stardust in their eyes, and basketballs in hand. Perhaps one day some of them will step beyond the backyard court or school playground and into the larger world of professional NBA basketball where the demigods on Olympus have names like Cousy, West, Robertson, Chamberlain, Russell, Baylor, Frazier, Abdul-Jabbar.

Like Michael Jordan, his contemporaries—then just kids—named Earvin Johnson, Larry Bird, Charles Barkley, Clyde Drexler, and Dominique Wilkins dreamed of the day when they, too, would become skywalkers and ascend in flight on the power of their own wings.

A member of the North Carolina Dixie Team and selected as the Dixie Youth Baseball Player of the Year, a 12-year-old Michael Jordan stands at the plate. (Photo from the *Cape Fear Optimist,* courtesy of the *Wilmington Star-News.*)

1.

A Country Boy from North Carolina

MICHAEL JORDAN's father James Jordan was 18 when he met Deloris, then 15. "Someday," he said, "I'm going to marry you."

Deloris thought he was "a little fresh" and subsequently gave him a wide berth, but his persistence paid off; they started dating, and once she saw past his initially brash statement, she saw the basis for a friendship that, in time, caught fire.

After high school, they went their separate ways; Deloris went off to college, to Tuskegee Institute in Alabama, at the insistence of her parents, and James joined the Air Force. The courtship, though, continued and in the spring of 1957 when he proposed, she accepted; that fall they married.

Back then, it was an entirely different world from what it is today; back then, segregation in the South was a way of life; treated as second-class citizens, blacks found themselves judged not for who and what they were but instead by where they were on the color bar. White is right, but if you're black, get back—get to the back of the bus, come in through the back door at restaurants.

It's easy to see how, if you were black, your anger and frustration could turn to bitterness, but fortunately both James and Deloris Jordan were raised in color-blind neighborhoods, where everyone helped each other, and you were judged by *who* you were—a lesson the Jordans would later reinforce to their children.

The fourth of five children, Michael Jordan was born on February 17, 1963, in Brooklyn, New York, not in North Carolina as you might guess. James Jordan, attending a training school for General Electric in Brooklyn, subsequently took his wife and children back home to North Carolina, to a small coastal community, Wilmington, where he would begin work as a mechanic for GE. Likewise, Deloris Jordan began work at the United Carolina Bank in downtown Wilmington. They knew that life, with its ups and downs, came with no guarantees—only what you made of it; hard work, persistence, and determination, they knew, paid off. Their motto was simply: Don't wait for things to happen—*make things happen.*

In their careers, both James and Deloris Jordan made things happen. James Jordan went on to assume greater responsibilities as a dispatcher, foreman, and finally a supervisor; and Deloris Jordan, who started as a teller, worked her way up to head of customer relations.

Where, one asks, did Michael Jordan's athletic ability derive from? His athletic ability clearly came from both his parents. As a teenager, James Jordan loved basketball, and, as he recalled, "I was a pretty good player, but never had the height." As for Deloris Jordan, she's a natural, too. (If you've seen Michael Jordan's videotapes, you've seen his mother give him a few pointers—"Keep your eye on the rim," she says, as she fires off a shot that's nothing but net. "And now," she says, "some razzle-dazzle." She then makes a two-hand, reverse jam to drive the point home, while her famous son looks on and smiles knowingly.)

Basketball, in fact, was important enough to the Jordans that James had built a dirt court in the backyard, with goals at each end. As this was the only court in the neighborhood, it quite naturally attracted the neighborhood kids, who would come to compete.

For Michael, though, the real daily competition was his brother Larry, one year older than himself, who at five-foot-seven routinely dunked on his younger brother.

Michael Jordan takes to the air in a game against Hoggard High School, January 1981. (Photo by Dan Sears, courtesy of the *Wilmington Star-News.*)

Showing the aggressiveness that would take him to the pinnacle of professional sports, a youthful Jordan drives past a New Hanover defender in 1981, Jordan's senior year at Laney High School. (Photo by Dan Sears, courtesy of the *Wilmington Star-News.*)

Two defenders attempt to stop an airborne Michael Jordan in a 1980 high school game. (Photo by Dan Sears, courtesy of the *Wilmington Star-News.*)

In a brotherly spirit of competition, neither Michael nor Larry cut any slack; you played hard and won—or lost. (As Michael later recalled, "I learned a lot about being competitive from him.")

For Michael, that meant losing, which he hated, until he got the height advantage that finally gave him a much-needed edge.

As a teenager, Mike was an early Bo Jackson. You've probably seen the Nike ad in which much is made of Jackson's multisport ability. As early as 12, Mike knew baseball as a top player in Little League, as a pitcher and outfielder; later, at Laney High School, Mike knew football, as a quarterback on the junior varsity squad; and, of course, Mike knew basketball, as a starting point guard for the junior varsity.

Then five-foot-ten, Jordan's prospects as a sophomore JV player looked good, since he averaged 20 points per game. So when the call came down that there would be an opening for a JV player to join the varsity team in time for the state tournament, Jordan figured he had a shot at it.

The shot missed.

When the alphabetical list went up, Jordan and his teammates crowded around, eager to read it; they kept their fingers crossed. To his surprise, Jordan wasn't on it. As it turned out, the decision to pick Leroy Smith was based solely on height alone; Jordan didn't measure up physically to Smith, who stood six-foot-five.

Jordan did get to the regionals, but as a manager, carrying in the uniforms for the players. He watched the game from the bench, handing out towels while the varsity team played.

Adversity in life will either make your spirit—or break it. You'll either overcome it, or let it overcome you. For Jordan, this was a wake-up call, that it was now time to get serious—*really* serious—about basketball. He vowed that never again would he warm the bench and watch everyone else play. "I made up my mind right then and there that this would never happen to me again. From that point on, I began working harder than ever on my basketball skills."

That summer, between his sophomore and junior years, Jordan worked on his basketball game. Also, before he returned to school, Jordan—for no apparent reason—grew five additional inches, and now stood six-foot-three.

In basketball, height gives you a tremendous advantage, a fact made soon apparent as Michael began beating his talented brother Larry on the backyard court. Michael, on fire, made the varsity team and, in fact,

Michael Jordan grapples for a rebound in a January 1980 high school game. (Photo by Dan Sears, courtesy of the *Wilmington Star-News*.)

Michael Jordan, surrounded by two defenders, drives downcourt. (Photo courtesy of the *Wilmington Star-News.*)

began focusing on basketball, leaving football, and later baseball, behind.

It was as if Jordan realized the importance of focus—concentrating his energies and talent in *one* direction, instead of scattering them in several.

Jordan, clearly, was focused—sometimes *too* focused. At home, on the backyard court, he would play until his parents called him in; at school, the gym became a second home, which wasn't a problem until he got suspended for cutting classes.

As a junior, Jordan's star talents on the court began to emerge. Believing that if something is worth doing, it's worth *over*doing, Jordan frequently attended both junior varsity and varsity practices.

As Jordan's teammates soon discovered, Jordan not only set high standards for himself but for them, too;

he expected them to keep up, to give all they had, believing that a team was only as strong as its weakest link.

It was at this time that Jordan began making what would, years later, become a Jordan signature: spectacular, in-the-air movements that arrested people's attention. Similarly, near the end of the game, Jordan would insist on getting the ball because he had the confidence that, more than anyone else on the team, he could make the clutch shots.

You've probably heard that it's who you know that makes a difference in life. In truth, when you're starting out, it's who knows *you*. And, for Jordan, a tournament game with New Hanover High School served as his showcase: Near the end of the game, as Hanover took the lead, Jordan decided to take over. Exploding

Hero of Carolina's NCAA championship game, Michael Jordan autographs T-shirts for Special Olympians Brian Williams and Wayne Cherry as part of Michael Jordan Day (May 15, 1982) in Wilmington, N.C. (Photo by Wayne Upchurch, courtesy of the *Wilmington Star-News*.)

offensively, scoring the final 15 points of the game, Jordan won the game.

The spectators for that pivotal game included a University of North Carolina graduate, Mike Brown, who, after returning to the campus, suggested they should take a "look see" at the skinny kid from Wilmington. Coach Dean Smith sent down an assistant to check Jordan out.

During the summer between his junior and senior years, Jordan was invited to attend the Five-Star Basketball Camp, where the best high school prospects could show off their stuff. Among his contemporaries, Jordan was the standout, winning five trophies during a one-week session, then being invited for a second week, where he went on to win another four trophies—a rec-

ord. Looking back, Jordan said simply, "It was the turning point of my life."

Any questions he had about his own abilities—about his ability to compete not only with his peers at Laney and at surrounding high schools, but also with the best in the state—became moot, as southeast colleges began recruiting him.

In the end the homeboy from North Carolina decided to stay close to home. The University of North Carolina offered a basketball scholarship, which he accepted. Not yet a high school senior, Jordan would graduate knowing that, at least for the next few years, his future had been laid out for him—he would be a Tar Heel. The next goal, obviously, would be a shot at the NBA, but he'd have to prove himself in college ball first.

Now six-foot-five, Jordan redoubled his efforts. Even before school started, he would be at the Laney High gym, putting himself through his paces.

In June 1981, Jordan—focused, dedicated, with his eye on his college career—put his high school days behind him, not knowing what lay ahead. Would his destiny take him to pro ball in the NBA, or would he—like most of the college players—be good but not good enough?

One thing, though, was sure: If it was going to be the survival of the fittest, then Jordan would do every-thing in his power to make sure he came out on top; just as his parents had set goals, followed through, and achieved professional success in their careers, Michael would follow in their footsteps.

As his mother often reminded him, the road to achievement began with thinking you could, being mentally prepared.

Jordan was prepared.

The future lay ahead, bright and promising.

Michael Jordan, flanked by his mother, Deloris, and father, James, announces at a November 1980 press conference his decision to attend UNC at Chapel Hill. (Photo by Wayne Upchurch, courtesy of the *Wilmington Star-News.*)

Laney only hopes that you . . . expand your talents to make others as proud of you as Laney has been. Always remember Laney as your world.
—*from Jordan's high school yearbook,* The Spinnaker, *1981*

Michael Jordan at a UNC practice. (Photo courtesy of the *Durham Herald-Sun.*)

2.

The College Years

If you want to see what the University of North Carolina thinks of Michael Jordan, its most famous alumnus, go to the Dean Smith Center. The sense of history becomes obvious as you walk around the arena and view the full-color team photos from every year. Jordan, of course, was but one of many in the photos, looking like just another college player with stardust in his eyes.

But Jordan wasn't just another player—he became a shooting star. Downstairs, in an exhibition room, a moment in UNC sports history was captured in a black-and-white photo by Allen Steele, a UNC photographer: Jordan, wearing jersey no. 23, elevating for a jump shot, the ball carefully balanced for the follow-through, as a Georgetown player looks not at Jordan but at the basket, knowing he can't stop the shot. In the background, the clock has 17 seconds on it; the score—North Carolina 61, Georgetown 62.

That shot crystallizes how North Carolinians see Jordan—suspended in midair as a whole stadium of people watched breathlessly, seeing a shooting star with a clutch shot, the first of many to come.

Interestingly, it wasn't Michael Jordan—a freshman—who got all the attention; it was an upperclassman, an All-American named James Worthy looking to go pro. It was Worthy on whom UNC had pinned its hopes for the NCAA championship.

As for Jordan, things looked bleak, because in the final two weeks of the regular season he had gone into a shooting slump. The question was whether or not he could pull out of it in time to benefit his team, going into the NCAA tournament.

In the three pieces that follow from the Durham Sun, *we see Jordan coming out of the slump, Jordan in a game before the tournament, and Jordan making what has come to be known as "The Shot," securing his place in UNC basketball history and putting him on the map. Not bad for a player who failed to make the prestigious* Street and Smith *list of the top 300 high school prospects.*

Michael Jordan, and the basketball world, would never

be the same again. (Ironically, Jordan would, years later, meet his former teammates James Worthy and Sam Perkins on court—on the opposing team. Worthy and Perkins, with the Los Angeles Lakers led by Magic Johnson, were defeated in the 1990–91 NBA finals by Jordan and the Bulls.)

Michael Jordan listens intently to UNC coach Dean Smith during a 1982 game. (Photo by Dan Sears, courtesy of the *Durham Herald-Sun*.)

UNC's Jordan 100 Percent Again

by John Roth (1982)

Imagine being Dean Smith in 1982, coach of the top-ranked college team in the country, marshaling resources as you head toward the NCAA tournament, only to have one of your best players temporarily on the sidelines. The question: Will he be ready to play in the tournament—or not?

That was the fear Dean Smith faced, as Michael Jordan, then a freshman, finished the regular season only to go into the hospital 24 hours later, with possible complications.

Fortunately, Jordan recovered and would go on to make his mark in the tournament.

As for the unexplained 82 perimeter shots in this piece: That number wasn't picked randomly; it represented Jordan's focus on the current year, 1982.

JUST IN TIME for his annual stretch drive toward the NCAA Tourney, Dean Smith has all the gears in his Big Blue Machine back in working order.

If there were ever any doubts about it, they vanished yesterday afternoon when North Carolina freshman Michael Jordan checked out of the infirmary and into his first Atlantic Coast Conference basketball tournament.

Breathing life into an otherwise zestless affair, Jordan scored 18 points as the Tar Heels brushed aside Georgia Tech 55–39 in the tourney opener and awaited today's semifinal game with North Carolina State.

For Jordan, the performance signaled the end of a shooting slump that attacked the rookie over the regular season's final two weeks.

For the Tar Heels and their coach, the signal was louder and clearer. Having played without Jordan's offense for the past two weeks, they were only too glad to welcome him back—just in time for the roll they plan to be on when their focus shifts to the NCAA Tourney.

"I was happy to see Michael Jordan get off to a good start on the offensive boards," praised Smith. "He was just released from the hospital Thursday, but he still played very well. He hit some key shots for us down the stretch."

Actually, Jordan scored all but four of his 18 points in the first half. In the second, he and his teammates merely played out the finish so they could board their bus back to Chapel Hill.

Jordan was especially anxious for the return because he needed the rest. Last Sunday, less than 24 hours after

the regular season ended, Jordan was admitted to the hospital to have a boil removed from one of his tonsils. By Monday, fluid had built back up on the infected area and it had to be drained again.

"If it had built back up again by Tuesday," Jordan said, "they were going to take my tonsils out and I'd be out for the rest of the season. It was a day-to-day thing and I was worried about it."

Jordan stayed in the infirmary until Thursday, plugged up with intravenous tubes, occasionally allowed to ride an exercise bicycle to keep in shape. When he was finally permitted to check out for Thursday's practice, the inactivity showed. He couldn't hit a basket.

"Just going through shooting drills, all I hit was the rim, or air balls," he pointed out. "Coach Guthridge told me to go home and get some rest."

Jordan went home, but only after taking 82 perimeter jump shots at the conclusion of practice. It's a task he's gone through after each Tar Heel workout by the Carolina coaches when he went into a slump following the North-South Doubleheaders last month.

Eighty-two shots a day—no more, no less, no explanation.

"To keep my follow-through consecutive," Jordan said. "It helped me out a lot. Now all of our perimeter people do it."

During his "slump," which covered seven games, Jordan hit 28 of 62 field goals for 45 percent. He was, however, under double figures only once in that stretch and finished the regular season with a 13.8 scoring average and a .537 field goal percentage.

Against Georgia Tech, he was 8-of-13 and cashed in on the Yellow Jackets' refusal to guard him when he got the ball on the wing, which was a good bit of the time since he played in foul-plagued Matt Doherty's forward position for much of the game.

"He does the same thing whether he's playing guard or forward," Tar Heel forward James Worthy said. "He's free to go to the basket, free to penetrate inside."

About his so-called slump, Jordan admitted he was in one and that he'd been hesitant to take his shot, when open, the last seven games.

"It was something new to me," he said. "But I'm glad I experienced it now so I'll know how it feels in the future."

With Georgia Tech (10–16) sticking in tight on Worthy and center Sam Perkins, the two Carolina power men combined for only 16 points. But they had 20 rebounds and point guard Jimmy Black dealt six assists and that was about all the support Jordan needed.

Tech's Brooke Steppe was the only other player in

the game with more than 10 points. He had 14—and plenty of compliments for Carolina and its 25–2 record.

"They're obviously the number one team in the country and Dean Smith's the best coach in the country," he said. Looking ahead to a possible UNC-Virginia showdown, Steppe added, "Nobody on Virginia can match up with Jordan."

Nobody on Georgia Tech could either.

Jordan Lives up to Coach's Prophecy

by Al Featherston (March 22, 1982)

Early on, it was obvious that Jordan—given an opportunity—could score more points than Dean Smith allowed him. (As the joke goes: Who's the only person who can hold Jordan to under 20 points per game? Coach Dean Smith.)

In this piece, we see that although Jordan was a lowly freshman and, as such, low on the pecking order off court, on court Jordan was a rising star. James Worthy, Sam Perkins, and Jordan were the foundations on which the team was built.

Even in this early piece, right before the championship game, it was clear that Jordan was a powerful offensive weapon. Just as his high school coach had predicted, Jordan would help make the difference, enabling UNC to win the 1982 championship.

MICHAEL JORDAN was born to play for North Carolina.

The six-foot-five freshman guard has only been in Dean Smith's program for six months, but he already says all the right things.

Let Jordan score 20 points in a game and he'll thank Jimmy Black for all the nice passes. Ask him about his role on the team and he'll talk about teamwork and defense. Bring him to a press conference and he'll apologize for coming, then explain all the upperclassmen had classes.

It's all part of Smith's system. Freshmen wait their turn. All Tar Heel freshmen—the Phil Fords and the Ged Doughtons; the Michael Jordans and the Lynwood Robinsons—carry the projectors, give up their seats to seniors, and generally try to learn from the elders.

Off the court, Jordan, one of the nation's finest basketball players, has less status than Jeb Barlow, a rarely-used senior forward.

Ah, but on the court, there is a difference.

Jordan is one of three superstars Smith has blended with superb complementary talent to construct a Final Four team.

The Tar Heels are 30–2 and headed for New Orleans for a second shot at the NCAA title. Villanova, a 70–60 victim yesterday in the East Regional finals at Reynolds Coliseum, was the latest team to feel Jordan's bite.

Houston, the surprise winner in the Midwest Regional, will be the next step for Jordan and the Heels.

A year ago, Carolina got past Virginia in the NCAA semifinal game before falling to Indiana in the title contest. Surprisingly, Jordan didn't get to see the Tar Heels beat the Cavaliers in Philadelphia.

"I was playing baseball at the time," he said. "I got to see the final game, though.

"I wanted them to win so bad. I had already committed and I felt like part of the team. I was anxious to be here. I couldn't wait for my college career to start."

Carolina is the first team to win back-to-back Final Four trips since UCLA did it in 1975–76. Yet, few experts are surprised to see the Tar Heels in New Orleans. After all, UNC was picked number one in preseason by most polls.

However, Jordan's high school coach—Pop Herring of Wilmington Laney High—should be given credit for an even more amazing piece of forecasting. He picked Carolina for the Final Four back in November of 1980, when Jordan first committed to Smith's program.

"Add Michael to the people they already have, and Carolina ought to win the national title next year," he told a reporter at the time.

Remember—at that time, Carolina was picked somewhere in the middle of the ACC (Black was just an unproven point guard, James Worthy was coming off a serious ankle injury, and Sam Perkins was an enigmatic freshman).

In addition, Jordan was still relatively unheralded. He was coming off a strong summer camp showing, but was still a late bloomer.

The prestigious *Street and Smith's* didn't list him as one of the nation's top 300 prospects. And his commitment to UNC was overshadowed by Robinson's simultaneous decision to play for the Tar Heels.

"He's been watching me grow up since I was a little kid," said Jordan of Herring. "I guess he saw something in me I didn't know was there."

Four months after Herring's prediction, everybody else was saying the same thing—add a young superstar like Jordan to the established talents of Worthy and Perkins, throw in splendid players like Black and Matt

Doherty, season with a dash of Smith's coaching expertise, and voilà, the national championship is a lock.

Obviously, nobody is going to claim any titles yet—especially not the well-indoctrinated Carolina players—but no Tar Heel team has ever been to the Final Four with a better chance to win it all.

"We've worked hard all year to get where we are," said Jordan. "We're reaching our peak. Everybody's playing well. No slumps.

"This is a good chance to win it all. I'm not saying there won't be other chances, but since the chance is there, why not go out and win it?"

Victory came so easily in the East Regional, it's hard to believe Carolina can't handle Houston, then either Louisville or Georgetown.

Then again, Carolina won the West with ease a year ago, and it still took a brilliant performance from Al Wood (39 points) for the Heels to beat Virginia in the semifinal game.

"My role's a little bit like Al's role last year," Jordan admitted. "We do some of the same things. But his role was much, much bigger than mine."

Wood was the man Carolina looked for to take all the big shots. Now, the Heels go to Worthy in the clutch. However, Jordan is content to let the veteran carry the load, but he's ready to shoulder the burden when it comes.

There have been moments down the stretch when he seems to turn on offensively, and for those moments, he's the dominant player on the floor.

"It just happens when I feel I can beat my man," Jordan said. "It's just an instinct."

That instinct paid off in the ACC title game against Virginia, when Jordan beat Jeff Jones four straight times to bring Carolina from three down to a one-point lead it protected down the stretch.

Against Villanova, Jordan blitzed freshman Dwayne McClain during a brief spurt in the second half, scoring six of his team-high 15 points on three straight possessions.

Still, Jordan's most dazzling move occured in the game's early moments, when he launched a 12-foot baseline jumper over Villanova freshman Ed Pinckney.

The Wildcat's six-foot-nine rookie managed to get just a piece of the shot, causing it to miss.

But Jordan was moving toward the goal as soon as he had let the ball go, and he materialized under the basket when the shot came down. He went right back up with it, slipping the ball under the arms of center John Pinone.

It was a remarkable play, something a good player may pull off a couple times a season. Jordan had done it, not once, but *twice* in the previous game against Alabama.

That kind of skill had led observers to wonder what kind of scoring average Jordan might have compiled this season had he gone to a weaker team, where he would have been asked to get as many shots as possible.

His 13-point average is more a measure of Carolina's brilliance than a mark of Jordan's offensive abilities. He could have easily averaged 20 or 25 points a game.

"I'm not interested in scoring. I'm interested in winning," he said, like a true disciple of Dean Smith. Yet, it must be true—why else would he pick a school where he would have to sacrifice points for victories?

Jordan made the right choice.

Dean Smith Gets First NCAA Title

(An excerpt from the *Durham Sun*, March 30, 1982)

The morning after the Tar Heels' victory, the local paper ran the headline, "The Tar Heels Win It All!" One of the photos accompanying the story showed a jubilant Coach Dean Smith, surrounded by players and well-wishers cutting down the net from a basketball rim at the New Orleans Superdome.

In the following two pieces, we see "The Shot" as it happened, followed by an overview by Keith Drum, the Durham Morning Herald *sports editor, who summarized the game in the paper's March 30, 1982, edition.*

THE PLAY: BLACK inbounded the ball to Jordan—back to Black—to Jordan—to Black—to Doherty—to Black—to Jordan.

The shot was designed for Jordan.

"We wanted Michael to take it," said Dean Smith.

THE SHOT was clean—nothing but net.

The Hoyas got the ball with 15 seconds left but Fred Brown threw the pass into the wrong hands—into James Worthy's hands.

"I was surprised it was right to me," explained Worthy.

"I was going into the lane when I saw Fred pick up the dribble. When I got it, I figured I might be able to dribble the game away."

Wrong, James. Fouled, Worthy missed both free throws, but the Hoyas had only two seconds left. Two too few.

The national champion Tar Heels finished 32–2 but not without a struggle from a team that walked away ashamed of nothing. Georgetown did everything *but* beat North Carolina. The Hoyas actually got two more field goals, 27–25, than the Heels but they were out-gunned from the free throw line, 13–8.

Freshman center Patrick Ewing contributed to Carolina's first four field goals—by goaltending.

"He was blocking them and I was bringing them," said Worthy, who played a near-spectacular game, scoring 28 points, hitting 13 of 17 floor shots. He literally carried—and kept—the Heels in the game in the first half. He was 9-for-12 in the first 20 minutes as Georgetown took a 32–31 lead into the dressing room.

Smith had problems from the opening tip, containing the hyper Ewing and guard "Sleepy" Floyd.

"I was amazed at Ewing," said the Carolina coach.

"On [the] tapes we watched of him he had not shot that well."

Ewing did just about everything well, however, against UNC—he scored 23 points, pulled down 11 rebounds, hit 10 of 15 from the field, stole the ball three times, and blocked two shots.

Perhaps it was because he meant it or because of his friendship with Georgetown coach John Thompson, but Smith said, "I think I was outcoached tonight. Fortunately, I had the players to win it. There was tremendous talent on the court."

The win was sweet and nice for Smith.

Sweet because, as he put it, "I do think this is the *only* year we've gone to the finals that we should have won it. We were No. 1 preseason, most of the regular season, and I think we took everybody's best shot. Tonight I'm not sure we were the best team—but we were the lucky team."

It was nice, because, as Smith put it, "What's so nice is a highly intelligent writer from Charlotte once wrote that the reason we were not winning national championships is because of our system. Well, Georgetown plays the same system as we do—and we're both in the championship game."

The lead was never more than six points for either team, and that was early when Georgetown held a 12–6 edge on the Tar Heels.

The Hoyas relied mostly on balanced scoring, from Floyd (18 points) and Eric Smith (14), along with Ewing, while Carolina answered with Worthy's wonderous efforts throughout the night.

A Superdome crowd of 61,612 watched a harrowing final minute that came down to a shot that was *only* the biggest in Carolina's basketball history, or at least

since the 1957 team beat Kansas, and Wilt Chamberlain, in Kansas City for its only other national title.

Jordan's shot was soft, a typical jumper, a release which he'd used throughout a freshman season which saw him gain Atlantic Coast Conference Rookie of the Year honors.

The Hoyas did not consider a timeout after the shot.

"Had we called a timeout it would have given North Carolina an opportunity to set up a defense and I would have had no idea what defense Dean would be using," said Thompson.

"Besides, when Fred threw the pass, Worthy was out on the perimeter and that's where we wanted him to be."

Georgetown played the Heels man-for-man most of the game, "because we felt we could do it and they would hurt us more in the zone," continued Thompson.

"But Worthy was flooding the middle. There's no question we played against a great Carolina team and a great coach."

The game was intense from the start, from the first Ewing goaltend, to the Black-Floyd affair, to Doherty's missed free throws, all the way to Jordan's shot.

"It was the type shot we'd have wanted Jordan to take," said Floyd. "Fortunately, for them, it went in. I didn't think it was a high percentage shot."

Had it fallen short, Ewing was in position for the likely rebound, but Sam Perkins, who quietly scored 10 points and pulled down seven rebounds for UNC, had the edge had the shot gone long.

None of that, however, mattered because Jordan hit nothing but net—a shot that will *never* die in the memories of UNC basketball.

Oh what a night. Oh what a game. Only negative was the whole thing had to end.

But, when it did there was Dean Smith, crowded and drained, repeating himself time and time again, rehashing the shot by Jordan.

After all these years, Dean Smith fittingly, finally, had won the big one—his first.

UNC Beats Georgetown by One Point to Take Title

by Keith Drum (1982)

THE UNIVERSITY of North Carolina won the college basketball championship Monday night by beating Georgetown University, 63–62, in the final game of the National Collegiate Athletic Association tournament.

It happened on the 25th anniversary of Carolina's previous championship. That was in 1957 when Frank McGuire coached the Tar Heels to a perfect 32–0 season.

Dean Smith, who succeeded McGuire in 1962, had—until Monday night—won about everything else there is to win in college basketball without taking home the grand prize. UNC won the National Invitational Tournament and a dozen or so other tournaments over the years. And Smith coached the U.S. team to the 1976 Olympic gold medal.

But he had never struck gold in the NCAA tournament. His teams had been the runners-up three times.

Always the bridesmaid, repeated sportswriters and broadcasters across the country. On Smith's seventh trip to the Final Four of the NCAA tournament, his talented team took the monkey off his back before a national television audience and more than 61,000 spectators in the New Orleans Superdome.

It outfought an inspired Georgetown team that set a wild and woolly pace from the opening buzzer. The outcome was still not decided when Tar Heel freshman Michael Jordan of Wilmington hit a jumper with 15 seconds left in the game. That gave Carolina its final one-point margin.

Georgetown headed downcourt to try to regain the lead, but Carolina All-American James Worthy of Gastonia intercepted a pass and raced toward the Carolina goal. Worthy, who scored 28 points, was fouled with two seconds left in the game. He missed his two free throws and Georgetown got the rebound, but it was too late. The clock ran out and the celebration erupted on the court by the Carolina players and back home in Chapel Hill by the fans.

Worthy's 28 points were the most he had ever scored in a college game. Jordan added 16 for Carolina and led in rebounding with nine.

Georgetown's hulking Pat Ewing scored 23 points, and Eric "Sleepy" Floyd, who like Worthy is from Gastonia, scored 18 for the Hoyas.

Smith seemed emotionally drained at the end of the game. He could only say, "I'm very happy for our seniors."

The feeling was mutual. "I'm so happy. I wanted it so bad for coach," said senior guard Jimmy Black. "He's the man. The national championship is the one thing we never got for coach. Today, we went out and got it for coach."

The victory solidifies Carolina's number one ranking in the country, which it has held during much of this year on the basis of the Associated Press and United Press International polls.

The road to the historic championship was a long one. . . .

For the next two seasons, the Tar Heels would not be able to repeat their 1982 victory. In the 1982–83 season, without James Worthy, the extra offensive capability was lost, and although they won the ACC tournament, they were eliminated by Georgia in the third round of the NCAA tournament two weeks later.

The next season, North Carolina again made it to the third round of the NCAA tournament, losing to Bobby Knight's Indiana Hoosiers. In the wake of that defeat, speculation among basketball fans in North Carolina ran rampant, blaming the losses on what was perceived as restrictions inherent in Dean Smith's coaching system. History, however, would vindicate Smith, whose record speaks for itself.

For Jordan, who had developed into a more complete player, it was time to move on. Once considered a fast-breaking dunker whose on-court moves razzle-dazzled everyone, Jordan had worked on the more ordinary, but essential, aspects of his game: defense, ball-handling, and rebounding. When Jordan beefed up his jump shot, he had the arsenal of skills needed to play professional ball.

The only problem was that by declaring his eligibility for the NBA draft, he would miss his senior year and not earn his degree. Michael Jordan, his father, and Dean Smith felt it was time to make the transition, though his mother had her misgivings. Education, after all, would be there no matter what else happened, she reminded her son.

Typically, Jordan solicited advice from everyone he respected: friends, family, and colleagues. In the end, Jordan would make the decision himself, at the last second, and announce at a press conference on May 5, 1984, that although his UNC days were "the best of my life," it was time to move on.

It was also time to pick an agent to represent him. As it turned out, the hour-and-a-half presentation made by David Falk and his people from ProServ made the greatest impact on Jordan. Dean Smith later called ProServ to break the news.

At the time, the people at ProServ were happy but, like the Bulls to come, had no idea just what they had hitched their wagon to—a rising, shooting star. Rather than being just another pro ball player, Jordan would dominate the NBA in the years to come. As Falk recalled, "It was obvious that he was going to be marketable . . . but we didn't really have any glimpse that he would be the most prolific team sports personality of all time."

That short presentation would be the best time investment Falk's ProServ ever made.

Tar Heel Basketball History

In 1993 the University of North Carolina celebrated its 200th anniversary. In a special newspaper supplement in the Herald-Sun, *Eddy Landreth, "after consulting with university officials, decided . . . the 10 most important and memorable highlights in school history." The first, a "no-brainer," was the 1957 basketball team's national championship; playing an undefeated season (32–0), the Tar Heels beat Kansas—led by Wilt Chamberlain—in triple overtime.*

The second and third, however, are pieces of Jordan history.

The second-biggest event in UNC athletics took place in the summer of 1961. It was the day Dean Smith was elevated from Frank McGuire's assistant to head coach.

McGuire got the program on track, but Smith had taken it to a level few people in college basketball could dream of reaching. Smith turned the Tar Heels into the nation's most consistent and respected program.

And he has earned as much respect for the way he runs his program as for the results he gets.

No. 3. The national championship in 1982.

The '82 title gets a slight edge over the 1993 championship because it was Smith's first, and just the third in the ACC at the time.

This team lost two games all season and then won the title in another of the most thrilling final games ever, producing three great NBA stars—Michael Jordan, James Worthy, and Sam Perkins.

This season also vindicated Smith, who had taken an inordinate amount of flak for not winning the title before then.

In a trophy case celebrating UNC's basketball program from the '80s, in the sports award room at the Dean E. Smith Center, a Spalding NCAA basketball is displayed with (presumably) the net cut by coach Dean Smith after their 1982 championship victory.

Michael Jordan takes to the air to pass over Clemson's Chris Michael, during a game in the opening round of the ACC Tournament. (Photo by Dan Sears, courtesy of the *Durham Herald-Sun.*)

Michael Jordan is surrounded by a trio of defenders, with a fourth on the way, in a game against NC State. (Photo courtesy of the *Durham Herald-Sun*.)

Michael Jordan goes up for a dunk as a defender looks on. (Photo by Hugh Morton, courtesy of the *Durham Herald-Sun.*)

Michael Jordan catches a Duke defender off guard. (Photo courtesy of the *Durham Herald-Sun.*)

With an Olympic gold medal and NCAA national championship to his credit, Michael Jordan watches as Laney principal Kenneth McLaurin retires Jordan's jersey in an August 1984 ceremony. (Photo by Charlie Archambault, courtesy of the *Wilmington Star-News.*)

Michael Jordan presents his Olympic gold medal to his mother, Deloris, during a ceremony in his honor at Thalian Hall at UNC at Chapel Hill in 1984. (Photo by Charlie Archambault, courtesy of the *Durham Herald-Sun.*)

3.

Drafted in the NBA

It all relied on the toss of a coin. . . . It really is funny how things turned out.

—*Michael Jordan, on the coin toss that determined his future*

ON MAY 23, 1984, executives from the Portland Trail Blazers and the Houston Rockets met at NBA headquarters in New York City to toss the coin—not just any coin, but a hundred-year-old coin that would give one of them the right to pick first in that year's draft.

The coin was flipped. Portland called tails. The coin came to a rest—heads up. The Houston Rockets would have first pick, and they didn't hesitate, choosing that year's favorite rookie, Hakeem Olajuwon of the University of Houston.

Portland, which had second pick, wasn't looking for another guard; they had two already, in Jim Paxson and Clyde Drexler, and so they picked Sam Bowie, an All-American center from Kentucky.

Chicago, which had third pick, took Michael Jordan, not realizing that they had gotten the diamond in the rough—a diamond that shone brightly on the '84 Olympic team that brought home the gold. Years later, as the Bulls public-relations director put it, "They thought we had picked a solid player who would turn out to be good for the team, but not the greatest player in the league."

The Bulls

Getting Jordan was the only consolation after a miserable 1983–84 season in which the Bulls won only 27 of 82 regular-season games. Far from lovable, the Bulls sold few tickets for their home games—averaging less than 7,000 in attendance. Chicago sports fans were down in the dumps, and rightly so. The Bulls were very stoppable.

Everyone knew that Olajuwon was the man with the potential to turn a ball club around; nobody expected the same from Jordan, who had his mind fixed on the idea of bringing Chicago an NBA championship.

The first indication Chicago had gotten that Jordan was a diamond in the rough came during the 1984 Summer Olympic Games, held in Los Angeles. Playing with future Dream Teamers Patrick Ewing (whom he had confronted, and defeated, in the 1982 NCAA championship victory over Georgetown) and Chris Mullin, Jordan captured everyone's attention.

The American team, composed of college players, won all eight games, with an average margin of victory of over 32 points.

Jordan—a leaping, scoring machine—was ready to show his stuff in the NBA.

Michael Jordan displays his new jersey during a 1984 press conference. (Photo by Phil Velasquez, courtesy of the *Chicago Sun-Times.*)

Two
The Bulls

Though he's got about a dozen cars—including luxury cars built for comfort and speed—his vehicle of choice for the Chicago winters, where treacherous ice and snow coat the roads, was probably his trusty Chevy Blazer, equipped with four-wheel drive.

Ahead was the Chicago Stadium, an old, venerable structure that has housed countless games, where basketball history had been made. (Soon, like Jordan, it too will become part of basketball history, as the new stadium is erected in time for the 1994–95 season.) Making his way through the crowds, the cameras, the ever-present reporters, he parked and quickly moved through a sea of kids and adults shouting his name, screaming for autographs; in one hand he held a gym bag, and in the other a Sony Walkman, his headset on to drown out the crowd noise.

At such times—if he signed autographs at all—he signed and moved, never stopping, knowing that to do so would mean a convergence of people that would multiply in numbers so great that he could never get free. Long ago he learned the skill of signing autographs and moving on, with a trail of people following him up to gate no. 23, where only players and members of the media are allowed.

In his mind he focused on the game. Blocking everything out, visualizing the task at hand, he knew that when the ball went up, it was showtime.

Fame meant nothing on the court. There was no past, and if you didn't play full-tilt boogie, there would be no future. There was only the present, because there was always a young gunslinger out there, looking to make a reputation at his expense.

The audience: a capacity crowd, with millions of viewers tuning in across the country. The reality: every move scrutinized, photographed, analyzed, and reduced to numbers—statistics that define the performance. After all, style points don't count on the scoreboard—just points scored, rebounds made, shots blocked, balls stolen, and the percentage of shots and free throws made.

Beyond the hype, the hysteria that surrounded him, he knew the truth: Every night the world expected him to live up to impossibly high expectations. Jordan as the leading scorer in the NBA, the team leader who took the Bulls to three consecutive NBA championships, and—whether he liked it or not—the NBA's goodwill ambassador.

When the games finally ended for him, he knew the truth: Statistics never lied.

BOB GREENE
HANG TIME

Days and Dreams

with

Michael

Jordan

The cover to *Hang Time* by Bob Greene, an insider's look at Jordan on and off court.

4.

Jordan's Pregame Warm-up

by Bob Greene

Of all the things I'd taken away from all those Stadium nights, maybe that was the most important: the knowledge that, if you look closely enough, amid the merciless and bitter there's always the chance you may find comfort and the promise of something good.

—*Bob Greene, on his days and nights at the Chicago Stadium, watching Jordan play basketball (from* Hang Time*)*

Like most sports stars—entertainers, really—Michael Jordan kept a professional distance from reporters. A very few—Ahmad Rashad among them—know Jordan personally, but for the most part journalists saw Jordan during locker-room interviews and press conferences only.

A columnist for the Chicago Tribune, *Bob Greene confesses in* Hang Time *that he paid no attention to basketball or, indeed, the Bulls, though they were the home team. That changed, though, when one of Greene's columns caught the attention of someone at the Bulls' office. Greene's heartfelt piece told of an abused four-year-old boy caught up in the court system, a victim of circumstance. Like most kids in Chicago, the boy was a Bulls fan and, when offered tickets to a home game, eagerly accepted; just to be at the game was enough, but to his surprise, he was treated as an MVP—most valuable person—by the Bulls and, especially, by Jordan.*

Jordan's affinity for children—rarely reported, since it lacks the juiciness of gossip—is a side few people see, but it shows Jordan's heart, which compelled Greene to look at Jordan more closely.

What Greene wrote—after spending, at Jordan's invitation, many hours off court, at home and road games—was an intensely personal, intimate book, Hang Time: Days and Dreams with Michael Jordan.

For Jordan fans, Greene's book is a rare treat. Letting Jordan speak for himself, Greene is a chronicler, content to report what is said. The book is terrific reading, and I commend it to your attention.

The excerpt that follows is from chapter five, and gives an inside look at what happens before game time—showtime, as Magic Johnson likes to call it.

WHEN I ARRIVED the temperature inside would be uncomfortably cold. The lights would not be all the way up; parts of the interior of the Chicago Stadium would be in shadows.

The vendors would be there, and the ushers, and maybe a few uniformed Chicago police officers. They would all be getting ready for their night of work.

And in this setting—frigid and dimly lit and quiet—Jordan would emerge from the stairs that ran up from the basement and, usually by himself, he would walk onto the court, dribbling a ball to test the surface.

He would do this almost every night. That was why he arrived so early; for him to practice after the building had been opened would be impractical, because too many people would crowd around to call to him and ask for autographs and take pictures.

In these moments Jordan would not be wearing the famous Bulls uniform with the numeral 23 on the front and back. In these moments he was just a person in a pair of gym shorts and a T-shirt. And he would start shooting. One. Two. Three. Four. Five. Six. Seven. Eight.

He would switch to a different position on the court. There would be no fooling around. He was up here in the empty arena for a reason. He was aware of something: All of the endorsements, all of the television commercials, all of the magazine covers, all of the interviews . . . all of that was absent in these moments, and paradoxically it was these moments that made all of that possible. Sometimes—considering the apparent ease with which Jordan dominated opponents—it was tempting to temporarily lose sight of just how skilled those opponents were. That Jordan could so often leave those superlative professional athletes flat-footed and embarrassed as he glided past them was merely testament to just how singular he was.

And he knew that everything that had come to him in his life stemmed from this, from moments like these in the locked arena. Once they were all kids learning how to loft a basketball into the air. Nine. Ten. Eleven. Twelve. Thirteen. Jordan, by himself in the empty Stadium, would fire the ball. The best basketball player in the world. In all likelihood the best basketball player who ever lived. Fourteen. Fifteen. Sixteen. Seventeen. The ball would keep dropping through the net.

Much has been made of the story that, as a sophomore in high school, Jordan was cut from his school's basketball team. It's part of the legend. But think about it for a minute. It wasn't a legend for him then. He was a boy who was told that he wasn't good enough. Eighteen. Nineteen. Twenty. Twenty-one.

Often Jordan would ask one of the Bulls ball boys to help him in these moments. Jordan would stand near the out-of-bounds line, with his back toward the basket. The ball boy, cued by a nod from Jordan, would fire him the pass. Jordan, catching the pass, would wheel and jump and face the basket and shoot. The ball would come down. Jordan would already be facing the ball boy again. Another nod. Another throw. Jordan, with not a sound from the vacant stands, would go into the air. I found myself hoping that the ball boys realized how important their memories of these late afternoons would be to them some day.

When it was time for the building to open up, Jordan would head back downstairs to the locker room. The next time he would emerge, he would be in the familiar clean white Bulls uniform, and the music would be playing, and the arena would be packed with a standing-room-only crowd, and the voices would be screaming in tribute from the moment of the first communal glimpse of him.

For me, no matter how exciting the game might turn out to be on a given night, the trip to the Stadium would already have been worth it. By the moment of the tip-off, I would already have seen things to make me glad I was there. Probably it was because of this:

In the course of my work I saw so much of the world that was low-spirited and mean and shoddy and common. I saw so much that was wretched. But in these

hours in the deserted Stadium, watching Jordan in solitude honing his craft, I saw something that was almost beyond excellence. It was like nothing I had ever seen in my life, and it was changing the way I looked at the world, and each game day before the sun went down I headed off to witness it anew.

• *Jordan's pregame ritual never varied. In the locker room he would put on his North Carolina baby-blue shorts underneath his Bulls pants, get his ankles taped, and put on a new pair of Nike shoes, lacing them up tight. (At home games, he always put resin on his hands, walked over to the announcer Johnny Kerr, and slapped them in front of him, creating a resin cloud in Kerr's face. Appropriately, when Jordan announced his retirement, it was Kerr who, with resin on his hands, walked up to Jordan, seated at the press conference table, and slapped his hands together. "You got me," Jordan said, grinning broadly.)*

Air Jordan shows grace even with his feet on the ground at the free throw line in a 1989 game. (Photo by Brian Jackson, courtesy of the *Chicago Sun-Times.*)

5.

An Interview with Michael Jordan

conducted by John Edgar Wideman

When it's played the way it's spozed to be played, basketball happens in the air, the pure air; flying, floating, elevated above the floor, levitating the way oppressed peoples of this earth imagine themselves in their dreams, as I do in my lifelong fantasies of escape and power, finally, at last, once and for all, free. For glimpses of this ideal future game we should thank, among others, Elgin Baylor, Connie Hawkins, David Thompson, Helicopter Knowings, and of course, Julius Erving, Dr. J. Some venerate Larry Bird for reminding us how close a man can come to a perfect gravity-free game and still keep his head, his feet firmly planted on terra firma. Or love Magic Johnson for confounding boundaries, conjuring new space, passing lanes, fast-break and breakdown lanes neither above the court nor exactly on it, but somehow whittling and expanding simultaneously the territory in which the game is enacted. But really, as we envision soaring and swooping, extending, refining the combat zone of basketball into a fourth, outer, other dimension, the dream ozone of flight without wings, it's Michael Jordan we must recognize as the truest prophet of what might be possible.

—*John Edgar Wideman, in "Michael Jordan Leaps the Great Divide" (Esquire, November 1990)*

MICHAEL JORDAN: What do I like about basketball? *Hmmm.* That's a good question. I started when I was 12. And I enjoyed it to the point that I started to do things other people couldn't do. And that intrigued me more. Now I still enjoy it because of the excitement I get from fans, from the people, and still having the same ability to do things that other people can't do but want to do and they can do only through you. They watch you do it, then they think that they can do it. Or maybe they know it's something they can't do and ironically, that's why they feel good watching me. That drives me. I'm able to do something that no one else can do.

And I love competition. I've earned respect thanks to basketball. And I'm not here just to hand it to the next person. Day in and day out I see people take on that challenge, to take what I have earned. Joe Dumars, for one—I mean, I respect him, don't get me wrong. It's his job. I've got something that people want. The ability to gain respect for my basketball skills. And I don't ever want to give it away. Whenever the time comes when I'm not able to do that, then I'll just back away from the game.

We've always been given credit for our athletic skill, our bodies. You've been blessed with exceptional physical gifts, and all your mastery of the game gets lost in the rush. But I believe your mind, the way you conceive the game, plays as large a role as your physical abilities. As much as any other player I've seen, you seem to play the game with your mind.

The mental aspect of the game came when I got into college. After winning the national championship at North Carolina in 1982, I knew I had the ability to play on that level, but there were a lot of players who had that ability. What distinguishes certain players from others is the mental aspect. You've got to approach the game strong, in a mental sense. So from my sophomore year on, I took it as a challenge to try and outthink the defense, outthink the next player. He might have similar skills, but if I can be very strong mentally and really determined mentally, I can rise above most opponents. As you know, I went through college ball with Coach Dean Smith, and he's a very good psychological-type coach. He doesn't yell at you. He says one line and you think within yourself and know that you've done something wrong. . . . When I face a challenger, I've got to watch him, watch what he loves to

Illustration to videotape box, *Air Time.*

do, watch things that I've done that haven't worked. . . . How can I come up with some weapon, some other surprises to overpower them?

You don't just use someone on your team to work two-on-two. Your plan seems to involve all ten players on the court. A chesslike plan for all four quarters.

I think I have a good habit of evaluating situations on the floor, offensively, defensively, teammate or opponent. And somehow filling in the right puzzle pieces to click. To get myself in a certain mode or mood to open a game or get a roll going. For instance, the last game we lost to Detroit in the playoffs last spring: We're down 20, 18, 22 points at the half. Came back to 11 or 10 down. I became a point guard. Somehow I sensed it, sensed no one else wanted to do it or no one else was going to do it until I did it. You could see once I started pushing, started doing these things, everybody else seemed like they got a little bit higher, the game started to go higher, and that pushes my game a little higher, higher, higher. I kept pulling them up, trying to get them to a level where we could win.

Then, you know, I got tired, I had to sit out and rest. Let Detroit come all the way back. It hurts a little bit, but then again I feel good about the fact that I mean so much to those guys, in a sense that if I don't play, if I don't do certain things, then they're not going to play well. It's like when people say it's a one-man gang in Chicago. I take it as a compliment, but then it's unfair that I would have to do all that.

I can dictate what I want to do in the course of a game. I can say to my friends, Well, I'll score 12 points in the first quarter . . . then I can relax in the second quarter and score maybe six, eight. Not take as many shots, but in the second half I can go 15, 16, quick. That's how much confidence I have in my ability to dictate how many points I can score and be effective and give the team an opportunity to win.

I don't mind taking a beating or scoring just a few points in the first half, because I feel the second half I'm going to have the mental advantage. My man is going to relax. He feels he's got an advantage, he's got me controlled, that means he's going to let down his guard just a little bit. If I can get past that guard one time I feel that I've got the confidence to break him down.

Your style of play comes from the playground, comes from tradition, the African-American way of playing basketball.

Can't teach it.

When I was coming up, if a coach yelled "playground move" at you it meant there was something wrong with it, which also meant in a funny way there was something wrong with the playground, and since the playground was a black world, there was something wrong with you, a black player out there doing something your way rather than their way.

I've been doing it my way. When you come out of high school, you have natural, raw ability. No one coaches it, I mean, maybe nowadays, but when I was coming out of high school, it was all natural ability. The jumping, quickness. When I went to North Carolina, it was a different phase of my life. Knowledge of basketball from Naismith on . . . rebounds, defense, free-throw shooting, techniques. Then, when I got to the pros, what people saw was the raw talent I'd worked on myself for 11, 12 years *and* the knowledge I'd learned at the University of North Carolina. Unity of both. That's what makes up Michael Jordan's all-around basketball skills.

It seems to me we have to keep asserting the factors that make us unique. We can't let coaches or myths about body types take credit for achievements that are a synthesis of our intelligence, physical gifts, our tradition of playing the game a special way.

We were born to play like we do.

Players like you and Magic have transformed the game. Made it more of a player's game, returned it closer to its African-American roots on the playground.

You know, when you think about it, passing like Magic's is as natural, as freewheeling, as creative as you can be. You can call it playground if you want, but the guy is great. And certainly he's transcended the old idea of point guard. You never saw a six-eight, six-nine point guard before he came around. No coach would ever put a six-eight guy back there.

If you were big, you were told to rebound, especially if you were big and black.

Rebound. Go do a jump lay-up, be a center, a forward. A man six-eight started playing, dribbling in his backyard. Said, I can do these things. Now look. Everybody's trying to get a six-nine point guard.

For me, the real creativity of the game begins with the playground. Like last night, watching young guys play, playing with them, that's where the new stuff is coming from. Then the basketball establishment names it and claims it.

They claim it. But they can't. The game today is going away from the big guy, the old idea everybody's got to have a Jabbar, Chamberlain. The game today is going toward a versatile game. Players who rebound, steal, block, run the court, score, the versatile player who can play more than one position. Which Magic started. Or maybe he didn't start it, but he made it famous. This is where the game's going now.

Other people name it and claim it. That kind of appropriation's been a problem for African-American culture from the beginning. Music's an obvious example. What kind of music do you like?

I love jazz. I love mellow music. I love David Sanborn. Love Grover Washington, Jr. Rap . . . it's okay for some people. But huh-uh. Not in my house.

Do you listen to Miles Davis?

Yeah.

He talks about his art in a new biography he wrote with Quincy Troupe. When Miles relates jazz to boxing, I also hear him talking about writing, my art, and basketball, yours.

I know what you're saying.

Right. There's a core of improvisation, spontaneity in all African-American arts.

I'm always working to put surprises, something new in my game. Improvisation, spontaneity, all that stuff.

Michael Jordan drives past defenders. (Photo courtesy of the *Durham Herald-Sun*.)

6.

On Chicago's West Side, Poverty Surrounds the Bulls

by Michael Abramowitz and David Aldridge (1992)

When you tune in on a Chicago Bulls home game, you see a pristine world from inside the stadium—a view of reality that is in stark contrast to the surroundings that lay just outside, where instead of dreams, there are nightmares; instead of hope, there is despair; and instead of lifting you up, life slam-dunks you daily.

HOURS BEFORE Michael Jordan would electrify 18,000 fans in Game One of the NBA finals, His Royal Airness negotiated his black BMW 850i through back streets around Chicago Stadium. Driving unmolested there was almost harder than slicing through the Portland Trail Blazers defense.

"It's Michael! It's Michael!" Jermaine Day, 12, and a gaggle of small boys yelled. Surrounded by youngsters straining for a word or glance from their millionaire idol, Jordan's car slowed to a crawl.

Within seconds, security guards began shooing away the crowd and ushering Jordan into the parking lot, without a word from the young prince to his young admirers. "There were too many people out there," said Day, an insightful sixth grader, as he watched Jordan disappear into the bowels of the stadium.

The scene, familiar for Jordan and his Chicago Bulls teammates, was jarring because the home court of professional basketball's champions and hockey's Blackhawks, a frequent destination these days for the rich and powerful, is in one of the city's poorest, most desolate neighborhoods.

Day and many youngsters who gather near the stadium come from nearby Rockwell Gardens and Henry Horner Homes, among the most notorious projects operated by the Chicago Housing Authority. The Homes, two blocks from the stadium, are light-years away in atmosphere.

A recent visit there revealed a powerful stench of urine in hallways, elevators that rarely worked, and stairways so dark that a flashlight was needed in midday. Gangs such as the Renegade Vice Lords, Disciples, and Four Corner Hustlers battle to control the decrepit buildings.

"It's just a big, old junkyard now," said Beatrice Winters, an 18-year resident and the only one on her floor. "We're scared to come out in the hallways, even in the daytime."

Much of this Near West Side area was a thriving commercial corridor until many shops were torched during riots in 1968. Despite gentrification of some surrounding areas, private investment has largely bypassed the stadium neighborhood.

There is no bank, no drug store, no supermarket. "You can't get a loan. You can't get insurance. You can't get nothing," said Ricky Hendon, a young alderman representing the stadium ward.

On the Near West Side, the median household income is $9,750 a year, making it the sixth poorest of Chicago's 77 neighborhoods, according to a recent Census Bureau report in the *Chicago Sun-Times*.

The contrast is not lost on Jordan and some of his teammates. The Bulls have almost no contact with the inner city other than on game nights, like an increasing number of professional sports teams. The Bulls practice in Deerfield, an affluent northern suburb, and almost no one in their organization lives in the city.

"It's sad," Jordan said, "but it really puts you in tune with some of the athletes in the limelight. The kids in this neighborhood get a kick out of seeing us come through here 41 times a year. They establish a relationship with us, and that means a lot for them and it could possibly help them a lot. I give four guys tickets to all the games. I stop and talk to them coming in and talk to them when I leave."

Jordan has been known to stop a few blocks from the stadium after games and talk to youngsters awaiting him. He tells them to "stay in school" and sometimes offers his game towel, said Darnell James, 12, who said he has talked with Jordan.

But neighborhood residents said that only guard Craig Hodges and forward Cliff Levingston make frequent appearances in the projects and local schools. Other players such as Horace Grant and Scottie Pippen also are visible.

Although the Michael Jordan Foundation provides many scholarships for blacks each year and his philanthropic endeavors are legion, people want him to be even more visible.

"I see Michael in the suburban shopping malls," says Al Clark, a former professional football player and principal at Cregier Vocational School. "I don't see him where it counts, for free. I don't care about Michael selling some shoes. Give me some time. And don't talk about basketball. Talk about, did he get his degree? Tell 'em to stay in school. Tell 'em to listen to their mother. . . . The kids would walk out with glassy eyes."

Hodges says of his teammate, "We've got the most visible person on the planet in Chicago. His mission is bigger than mine. I don't know whether or not he understands that, but I'm sure in due time he will because he has powers.

"And it's not just Michael," said Hodges, who runs a youth organization that works in the inner city. "It's all of us . . . because we still haven't done what we're capable of doing."

Jordan said many people are unaware of what he does for others because he does not seek such publicity. "I'm not going to make a public announcement that I'm buying these kids seats, and I enjoy stopping every day and talking to the kids," he said. "That's something I do out of the kindness of my heart. I don't need people to know that. . . . As long as I feel good about it, that's all that counts."

Bulls owner Jerry Reinsdorf said Jordan is criticized unfairly. "What about all the other things Michael does?" he asked. "He gives hundreds of thousands of dollars to charity. He goes to children's hospitals on his own. He talks to kids, all without publicity."

Acknowledging that the Bulls have a responsibility to the community, Reinsdorf said, "You can't just focus on one neighborhood. We're doing a lot in the neighborhood, but there are limits. The neighborhood doesn't own the Chicago Bulls."

He referred to a recent agreement by the Bulls and Blackhawks with community groups on construction of a new, $175 million arena across the street from the aging stadium. The two teams said they would build re-

placement housing for 19 families displaced by construction and finance building another 75 homes in the first private investment in the neighborhood in years.

Reinsdorf, a real estate millionaire and also majority owner of the Chicago White Sox baseball team, said the new stadium could be the catalyst for the Near West Side's long-delayed renaissance. "It just takes a few new houses, and it starts to fill in," he said.

Even jaded neighborhood activists have been impressed with the Bulls' willingness to provide seed money for business development near the stadium.

Earnest Gates, vice president of the Interfaith Organizing Project and a Near West Side resident, contrasted the behavior of the Bulls and Blackhawks with that of football's Chicago Bears, who once contemplated building a stadium in the neighborhood but, he said, never cooperated with the community.

The Bears, he noted, have never attained the heights they attained with victory in the 1986 Super Bowl.

The Bulls have soared since beginning to work with their neighbors. "I believe justice has a way of winning out in the end," Gates said, smiling.

Bulls star Michael Jordan is the center of attention as the Bulls host their fifth annual Charity Kids Christmas Party in 1989 at the Multiplex in Deerfield, Michigan, where more than 125 underprivileged children participate in the festivities. (Photo by Phil Velasquez, courtesy of the *Chicago Sun-Times*.)

7.

Building the Team

Observations by Rick Telander, with commentary by George Beahm

The good thing about having a team like the Bulls in 1984 was that there was no place to go but *up. In* Sports Illustrated Presents: The Chicago Bulls *(1993), Rick Telander explained that the Bulls took ten steps to the top, picking the right mix of management talent and player talent, using Jordan as the nucleus of the team.*

1. "On March 26, 1985, 13 days after buying the Bulls, Reinsdorf hires Krause." After he purchased the Bulls franchise in 1985, Jerry Reinsdorf looked within his ranks and found Jerry Krause, who was asked to find players to complement Jordan.

2. "On June 18, 1985, the Bulls acquire Charles Oakley." Oakley, a six-foot-nine member of the Cleveland Cavaliers, would represent the "toughness" that Krause was looking for. (Oakley would later be traded for Bill Cartwright.)

3. "On August 1, 1985, the Bulls hire Al Vermeil to be their strength-and-conditioning coach." Vermiel helped the Bulls pump up—necessary for building endurance and stamina for the bruising kind of ballplaying that would be trademarks of teams like the New York Knicks.

4. "On October 29, 1985, the Bulls get Paxson." A former member of the San Antonio Spurs, John Paxson would be the man behind the three-point line, ready to take the ball in case Jordan—typically double-teamed—couldn't shoot. (In the 1991 finals as well as the 1993 finals, Paxson would prove his worth.)

5. "On June 22, 1987, the Bulls acquire Scottie Pippen." Acquired by Krause, who spied the talented six-foot-seven Central Arkansas player, Pippen would be the player most like Michael Jordan—a perfect complement.

6. "On June 22, 1987, the Bulls draft Horace Grant." This added the rebounding talent they needed, as well as someone who could keep up with Jordan and Pippen.

7. "On June 27, 1988, the Bulls trade for Cartwright." Trading Oakley for Bill Cartwright to play the center position gave much-needed defensive strength to the Bulls.

8. "On June 27, 1989, the Bulls draft Armstrong." Krause picked B.J. Armstrong because he wanted another three-point shooter on the team. (B.J. would later replace Paxson, who would serve as his back-up.)

9. "On July 10, 1989, the Bulls promote Phil Jackson from assistant to head coach, the first move toward building a good coaching staff."

10. "The Bulls acquire a decent bench."

8.

The First NBA Championship: Shining Moment

by Jack McCallum (1991)

After seven long years, as Jordan piled up individual achievements, one after another, everyone conceded that while Jordan was an outstanding individual talent, the true test of talent would be if he could lead his team to an NBA championship, which he finally accomplished in 1991 as the Bulls defeated the celebrated Los Angeles Lakers.

Jordan was no longer considered to be in a different league, so to speak, than his contemporaries Magic Johnson (of the Lakers) and Larry Bird (of the Celtics).

In time, Jordan would rise above his contemporaries, by winning the championship two more times in succession—something Johnson and Bird did not accomplish.

It was a Kodak moment, a photo that came to define that first championship: Jordan in the locker room, his eyes closed, the championship trophy held against his forehead, as time stood still for him, as he reflected on the long and winding road leading up to that moment.

AFTER ANSWERING every bell for the Chicago Bulls this season, including the ultimate one that tolled for the Lakers in Los Angeles last week, Michael Jordan was apologetic for getting a late start on the first day of his summer vacation. "Alarm clock malfunction," said Jordan last Saturday morning, sliding into a booth at a restaurant in the Chicago suburb of Deerfield, not far from Jordan's home. "Can you believe I missed my first tee time? The official beginning of the golf season?" He shook his head in amazement.

Jordan was scheduled to play a second round that afternoon at one o'clock, and his breakfast companion suggested that maybe, just maybe, he was too tired for 36 holes, considering the events of the preceding few days: an NBA championship on Wednesday followed by an all-night victory party in Los Angeles, a mini-homecoming ceremony on his lawn on Thursday, a motorcade and rally in downtown Chicago on Friday,

and an overall emotional catharsis that, in scope and intensity, surprised even Jordan.

"Too tired for golf?" said Jordan on Saturday, genuinely perplexed. "You're kidding, right?"

And so this is Michael Jeffrey Jordan in late spring of 1991—an indefatigable 28-year-old still enchanted with games. But he is somehow different, somehow transformed. The Bulls' first NBA title, secured with a 108–101 victory over the Lakers in Game Five of the finals at The Forum, didn't earn for Jordan—as it did for such teammates as Scottie Pippen, Horace Grant, and John Paxson—much more fame. Jordan has had an astounding measure of that since he came into the NBA in 1984. Neither will the title do much for his bank account, as it will for Pippen's; last Friday Pippen received a five-year contract extension worth $18 million. Jordan will average about $3.7 million per year from the Bulls over the next five years (undoubtedly the best deal for a franchise in all of sport), and his earning power off the court (in excess of $10 million a year) defies credulity. He says he expects to reduce, not increase, his off-the-court commitments.

"The difference," said Jordan, tapping his chest, "is in here."

The feeling of inner peace means no more moments of doubt, however fleeting, no more wondering if he was a true winner like Magic Johnson, Larry Bird, or Julius Erving, all of whom have played on teams that won NBA titles. "I think people will now feel it's *O.K.* to put me in the category of players like Magic," said Jordan, pushing around waffles on his plate. "Personally, I always felt that in terms of intensity and unselfishness, I played like those type of players. Some people saw that, but many others didn't. And the championship, in the minds of a lot of people, is a sign of, well, greatness. I guess they can say that about me now."

It would be hard to say anything less after Jordan's

masterly performance throughout the five games of the finals, the last four of which were Chicago victories. He scored with metronomic consistency, averaging 31.2 points—a 36-point effort in Game One was his high, a 28-point night in Game Four his low—and a .558 shooting percentage from the floor. (By contrast, Magic, who recognizes a good shot better than anyone, averaged 18.6 points and .431.) Jordan also averaged 11.4 assists, 6.6 rebounds, 2.8 steals, and 1.4 blocked shots. And his energetic defensive play, along with that of Pippen and Grant, the other two members of what assistant coach Johnny Bach calls the Wild Bunch, was the key to the series.

In sum, Jordan turned in what was probably the finest all-around performance in a five-game finals series, of which there have been 11 in NBA history. Jerry West, for example, had more points (33.8 average) in the five-game 1965 finals between his Lakers and the Celtics, but Jordan set five-game records for assists (57 to Bob Cousy's 53 in 1961) and steals (14 to Terry Porter's 10 in 1990). And few guards have grabbed more rebounds, Magic being one of them: He got 40 rebounds in the series to Jordan's 33. When NBA officials collected the ballots for MVP near the end of Game Five, several members of the media asked, "Are you serious?" Jordan won unanimously.

The Bulls were also helped by a sound game plan. Coach Phil Jackson sniffed out the Lakers' true weakness—the lack of a penetrator who can consistently break down the defense off the dribble—and massed his defensive strength to double- and sometimes triple-team L.A.'s post-up players. The Lakers could muster no counterpunch, and time after time they mindlessly threw the ball into the post, only to have Sam Perkins, James Worthy, or Vlade Divac—their vision "occluded," as Bach put it, by the pressure—dribble frantically out to the corner, taking precious seconds off the 24-second clock. L.A. coach Mike Dunleavy finally confused the Bulls somewhat by giving playing time to the young and talented Elden Campbell and Tony Smith in Game Five, but that strategy was more or less forced upon him by injuries to Worthy and Byron Scott. There is no doubt that the Lakers, in contrast to the healthy Bulls, were tired and somewhat battered after an enervating six-game Western Conference final against the Portland Trail Blazers. But there is no doubt that Jackson decisively outcoached Dunleavy when it counted.

Best of all for the Bulls, Jordan's performance, while sometimes show-stopping, was never showy. (Well, ignore, if you can, the moment late in Game Five when he blindly tossed in a 12-foot bank shot over his shoulder as he walked to the foul line.) That gave plenty of room for the talents of Pippen, who scored a game-high 32 points in the clincher, and Paxson, who shot a remarkable .653 from the field for the series, mostly on radarlike jumpers from the perimeter. In Game Five, Paxson broke the game open when he scored 10 points in the final four minutes, mostly on long, clutch jumpers. Grant, a gutsy power forward in a small forward's body, epitomized the Bulls' team effort; he didn't attempt a single bad shot in five games and averaged an economical 14.6 points on .627 shooting. No wonder the Bulls' .527 team shooting percentage tied the 1989 Pistons for the best in NBA finals history. And no wonder Jordan insisted that the other four starters, Pippen, Grant, Paxson, and center Bill Cartwright, be included in the now traditional "I'm Going to Disney World" commercial filmed shortly after Game Five, for which they divided $100,000.

But, clearly, this was Jordan's show—"a tribute to Michael," as Jackson put it. It may have started out as the Magic and Michael finals, but Jordan had left the ol' purple-and-gold warrior in the dust by the time the final buzzer sounded. Magic knew it, too. He calmly answered question after question about Jordan in the locker room and never showed a trace of jealousy or pique, a tranquillity forged at least in part by his nine finals appearances and five championship rings. Those who had visited the Chicago locker room reported Jordan's teary reaction to winning the championship and asked Johnson if he, too, had felt so emotional after his first title, way back in the rookie year of 1980.

"No, I didn't react that way, but there's a good reason for the difference," said Magic. "I was so young [20], so unschooled in what it took to win an NBA championship. So I know exactly what Michael is feeling now because I felt that way later in my career, when it took so much more effort and sweat to win it."

Over breakfast on Saturday, Jordan said that Magic's analysis was correct.

"After we won the NCAA championship in my freshman year I felt happy, but not all that emotional," said Jordan. "I remember seeing Jimmy Black and a few of the other guys really crying, and I'm thinking, What's going on? This is *supposed* to happen, right? You come to college and win a championship.

"But in the pros I've seen it from the opposite side. All the struggles, all the people saying, 'He's not gonna win,' all those little doubts you have about yourself. You have to put them aside and think positive. I am gonna win! I am a winner! And then when you do it, well, it's just amazing."

Still, even Jordan was surprised by the tidal wave of emotion that struck him as he entered the locker room after Game Five and knelt for the team prayer. He sobbed, at times almost uncontrollably, as his wife, Juanita, and father, James, sat beside him, massaging his arms and shoulders. He had almost stopped crying when a friend led a smiling woman into the circle. "Michael, it's your mother," the friend said. And he broke down again as Deloris Jordan kissed him, patting his cheek, and retreated into the background. "I figured he'd react that way because it took so much hard work," said Deloris. Recalling the moment, Michael again seemed touched. "You go through that as a kid," he said. "Your mother comes over to console you about something, and that makes you cry even more. But my mom? She handled herself like a movie star."

Which is how Jordan was treated when he arrived back in Chicago at four P.M. Thursday. At least 100 well-wishers from his neighborhood and beyond—"Seems like everyone in Chicago knows my address," he said afterward—had turned his front lawn into a minicarnival. Letters, telegrams (one from North Carolina coach Dean Smith), balloons, posters, and drawings were tacked to his front door, and there were flowers and plants—"Enough to open up a florist shop," he said—piled up on his porch. He shook his head. "Sometimes I can't believe my life is so crazy," he said.

As for the Bulls' immediate future, Jordan, predictably, had his opinions. Over the past few seasons he had been outspoken in his criticism of general manager Jerry Krause, and although early in the playoffs he said he was willing to eat his words if the Bulls won the title, he didn't sound quite so repentant on Saturday.

"I don't regret anything I said [about Krause], because I was honestly expressing my feelings at the time," said Jordan. "Our bench was not playing very well and I thought we needed help. Fortunately, they responded. But I think next year we'll have to build on it to stay strong."

The big questions among the frontline players are Cartwright and Paxson, both of whom are unrestricted free agents. The Bulls are expected to make Cartwright an offer, though it remains to be seen if he will accept one instead from a team closer to his northern California roots, such as Golden State or Sacramento. "I think it's going to be up to Bill," said Jordan.

There is no such ambivalence in his feelings about Paxson. "Pax signed his own contract with his play in the finals, and if they don't sign him, I will be one upset Bull," said Jordan. "Anybody playing beside me is going to have to knock down those shots that Pax did in the finals. We've always communicated well on the floor, but in the finals it was really something. I *always* knew where he was as soon as I got double-teamed. And I know how he wants the ball—waist-high and in rhythm. He gets it too high or too low, he doesn't shoot it. I want Pax around, that's for sure."

And Jordan will probably get him. Krause had made no move on Paxson as of last weekend, but the feeling is that the general manager will make a solid offer and that Paxson will accept it. The championship season was the first in the 25-year history of the franchise, and Chicago fans will not take kindly to a major breakup. As Jordan finished his breakfast on Saturday, a middle-aged man approached his table sheepishly. "I don't want to bother you for an autograph, Mr. Jordan," he said, "but I just have to thank you for what you've done for Chicago."

Indeed, the 1991 finals will go down as a championship won for a city that has given the NBA some of its finest moments over the years. And it will go down as the series in which the Bulls' supporting cast at last shrugged off its tag of "the Jordanaires." But make no mistake about it—the victory belonged most of all to Michael Jordan, who, for now at least, sits atop the basketball world, higher even than Magic. And for those who felt that Jordan was already the king, consider the 1991 finals his coronation.

Cover to *Beckett Tribute: Michael Jordan*.

9.

The Second NBA Championship

by Jack McCallum (1992)

Immediately after the Bulls won their first NBA championship, the question became whether or not they could repeat. After all, anyone can win one championship, but winners repeat and three-peat. They take a licking and keep on ticking.

BEFORE THE LOS Angeles Lakers won back-to-back championships in 1986–87 and 1987–88 and the Detroit Pistons did the same in 1988–89 and 1989–90, there had not been a repeat winner in the NBA for two decades. It had been, in fact, an annual story for journalists who cover the NBA. Why couldn't anyone repeat?

For those close to the league, however, there was an easy answer to that question. It was just too damn difficult to find the same blend of desire, motivation, and team chemistry that earned a team its first championship. The Bulls team that prepared for the 1991–92 season provided a number of crystal-clear examples of what can happen to sidetrack a defending champ.

Distractions? That didn't quite describe it. After the Bulls won the championship in 1991, Michael Jordan was easily the most famous athlete in the world, and he was spreading himself incredibly thin. One moment he was hosting "Saturday Night Live," another he was in North Carolina for a ceremony at which a highway was named in his honor, another he was filming a commercial for one of the numerous companies for which he was a spokesman, another moment he and Scottie Pippen were being introduced as charter members of the first U.S. Olympic basketball team to include NBA stars. And all that, of course, had to be fit in between his regular 36- and 54-hole golf orgies.

Even the Olympic announcement was not without its controversies. Though Jordan vehemently denied it, there were reports that he had lobbied to keep his Piston nemesis, Isiah Thomas, off the team, and he

took some heat for that. And the inclusion of Pippen, only lately an elite player, on the Dream Team was criticized by some observers, particularly those who remembered him as Mr. Migraine.

Then, too, word had begun to spread late in September about an upcoming book that was said to be extremely critical of Jordan. Written by Sam Smith, who had covered the team for the *Chicago Tribune*, it was called *The Jordan Rules* and reportedly contained detailed complaints from other players about preferential treatment given to Jordan. Those complaints seemed to be borne out in early October when Jordan missed what was called a "mandatory" team trip to the White House, where President George Bush congratulated the Bulls for winning the NBA title. Jordan said he was with his family, but anyone who knew Jordan knew that his "family" included a seven-iron.

The troubles continued in training camp. Jordan was late in reporting and testy when he did. The book, released on November 13, 1992, was indeed somewhat anti-Jordan. Some of the Bulls backed off the criticisms they had made of Jordan in the book, but only partially. Relations remained particularly strained between Jordan and Horace Grant, who was considered by most members of the media to be the most forthright member of the Bulls.

In short, no one would've been surprised if the defending champs came out of the gate stumbling.

Instead, they came out smokin'. There were many reasons for this, but they all boiled down to one: The Chicago Bulls of 1991–92 were far and away the best team in basketball. Early in the season the team quickly established a pattern. The Bulls would arrive in a new town, where Jordan and his teammates would be asked about the revelations in *The Jordan Rules*. They would answer that the book was either inaccurate or exaggerated, and then they would go out and tear up the home team. An early-season West Coast road trip set the tone for the whole season. Chicago beat the Golden State Warriors, Seattle SuperSonics, Denver Nuggets, L.A. Clippers, Portland Trail Blazers, and Sacramento Kings, all in a row. O.K., Jordan seemed to be saying, you dis me off the court and I'll dis you on the court.

The Bulls spent most of the season chasing the NBA's all-time best record of 69–13, set by the 1971–72 Lakers. They finally fell two games short, at 67–15, but were clearly the class of the league going into the play-offs. Jordan was again the shining star with a league-leading 30.1-point scoring average, but Pippen, who averaged 21.0 points, 7.7 rebounds, 7.0 assists, and 1.9 steals per game, was as good a second banana as the game had to offer. Grant also had an outstanding season, and B.J. Armstrong, who had had trouble making his own take-it-to-the-hoop skills fit in the same back-court with Jordan, had begun to establish himself. Armstrong's 9.9 (oh, let's just call it 10) scoring average for the regular season was a career best. Out in Portland the talented Trail Blazers were putting together an outstanding record of 57–25 in the West, but almost no one noticed them because of the Bulls' supremacy.

Would the playoffs go just as easily for the Bulls?

No. Things never go smoothly when everyone thinks they will.

The Bulls took care of the Miami Heat in three games, which hardly prepared them for the suddenly dangerous New York Knicks, whom they had beaten 14 consecutive times going into the postseason. The Knicks shocked Chicago with a 94–89 victory in Game One at Chicago Stadium, then won Game Four at Madison Square Garden by a score of 93–86 to even the series at 2–2. For the Bulls, the series brought echoes of those terrible days of futility against the Pistons a few years earlier. The Knicks slowed down the tempo, talked trash, and banged Jordan and Pippen around in an effort to break their will.

"A forearm, a hip, two hands in the back—they do anything as far as position goes," said Chicago front-courtman Scott Williams. And Jordan seemed to be nothing more than disgusted. "Their methods are no different from what Detroit's used to be," he said after Game Four. On the sideline even Bulls coach Phil Jackson grew frustrated. He was ejected near the end of the third period of Game Four for repeatedly giving an earful to the referees about the Knicks' physical style.

The Bulls regained the edge with a 96–88 victory in Chicago, but by now an enervating and dangerous seven-game series seemed inevitable. Sure enough, a seemingly tired Jordan missed 16 of 25 shots—22 of

them from the perimeter—as the Bulls lost Game Six at the Garden 100–86. Knick guard Gerald Wilkins, who was probably getting too much credit for "stopping" Jordan, even proclaimed before the decisive seventh game in Chicago that the Knicks had hounded Jordan into becoming a "mistake player."

Gerald, *that* was a mistake. Chicago simply blew out the overmatched Knicks 110–81 in Game Seven as Jordan scored 42 points.

Still, the seven-game series left people divided about what the outcome meant. There were some observers who felt that the Knicks series proved the Bulls were vulnerable. But there were just as many others who felt it proved that whenever he had to, Jordan could simply elevate his game and take the Bulls along with him.

The entertaining six-game Eastern Conference finals against the Cavaliers would make no one change his or her opinion. The Bulls won the first game 103–89 and then decided—what the heck?—let's take Game Two off. They fell behind by a mind-numbing 20–4 at the start (this was in Chicago, don't forget) and lost 107–81. Just as quickly, they turned it around in Cleveland, building a 26–4 lead after eight minutes and winning Game Three, 105–96. And then they promptly got blown out again, 88–85 in Game Four.

The series seemed to be a contest between two teams that didn't quite know themselves. The Cavs were obsessed with criticism from the media referring to the team as a bunch of "marshmallows" and "cream puffs." Before Game Three, in fact, Cavalier officials used the scoreboard in Richfield Coliseum to show a scene from the movie *Ghostbusters* in which the giant Stay-Puft Marshmallow Man tramples everything in its path. When the game started, however, the Bulls went out and trampled the marshmallows.

Though they were infinitely more self-confident than the Cavs, the Bulls still couldn't seem to muster the collective killer instinct of true champions, that steely-eyed desire to stomp on everyone and everything that gets in the way. Old problems surfaced too. Both Jordan and Jackson pointed to failures of the bench after the Game Four loss and Armstrong took exception. "I totally disagree with that," he said. "If Phil and Michael want to point to the bench, then I think it's something that needs to be talked about in-house instead of going to the media." And Pippen, after a desultory second-half performance (three shots, zero points) in Game Four, expressed uncertainty over his role in the offense. "I just didn't get the opportunities," he said. "I guess there were other guys out on the court that were more important."

Still, the Bulls got it back together for Games Five and Six, winning 112–89 at Chicago and then wrapping up the series with a 99–94 win in Cleveland. Beyond sending the Bulls into their second straight finals, Game Six was particularly gratifying for Jackson because Jordan, who did not have a great shooting game for three quarters, was propped up by the solid all-around efforts of everyone else, particularly Pippen, who was still hampered by a badly sprained right ankle suffered in the Knicks series. And then, in the fourth period, Jordan took over with 16 points to assure the win.

The individual battle that everyone was waiting for in the finals matched the league's best shooting guards, Jordan and Portland's Clyde Drexler, who was considered Jordan's near-equal on pure athletic ability. In fact, it wasn't close to an even match, and both players knew it. Jordan was far superior to Drexler as a shooter and ball handler and had more grace under pressure—not to mention more off-the-court endorsements and all-around star appeal. The two players mirrored in many ways the Bulls-versus-Blazers series. There was much to like about the Blazers, much championship potential in their roster, but they seemed to have a fundamental weakness when it came to mental toughness.

Game One in Chicago Stadium began with a shrug. Not a shrug as in "Who cares?" but a shrug as in "Who knows? Even I can't explain it." That's the look that Jordan flashed at his buddy Magic Johnson, who was sitting courtside as an NBC commentator, after Jordan converted the last of his six three-pointers in the first half. Jordan finished the first 24 minutes with an incredible 35 points to all but finish off the Blazers, who ultimately went down 122–89. Before the series began, when Jordan was asked to compare his game with Drexler's, one of the things he said was "Clyde is a better three-point shooter than I choose to be." So in Game One he chose to show up Drexler in that department, too. Drexler seemed to almost physically disappear from the Chicago Stadium floor, taking only 14 shots and making just five of them. Jordan, meanwhile, turned into a passer in the second half and finished with "only" 39 points. That was a calculated move and a wise one, since it enabled the proverbial "supporting cast" to share in the triumph.

Drexler had already fouled out when the Blazers rallied to win Game Two by 115–104 in overtime. Game Two was as shocking a loss as the Bulls experienced in the postseason. Being unprepared to play, as they were in, say, Game Two of the Cleveland series was one thing; blowing a nine-point lead in the final 4:09 at home was something else again. Most disturbing was Jordan's lack of composure down the stretch—after being whistled for a foolish reach-in foul, he was hit with a technical after screaming at referee Jess Kersey.

Drexler finally put together a solid performance (32 points, nine rebounds) in Game Three in Portland, but none of his teammates were there to help him. The Bulls' 94–84 win was a strange one because no one on the team really played well. But perhaps the game's ugliness could be attributed to the swarming Chicago defense, which can throw teams so out of kilter that the game suffers along with it.

Did someone say "suffer"? That's what Bulls fans were doing after Game Four fold-o-rama by Chicago that paralleled the team's collapse down the stretch in Game Two. This time Chicago was up 80–74 with 7:42 left when it suddenly went flat and lost 93–88. Flattest of all was Jordan, who went scoreless over the last 10 minutes and later mentioned (complained, really) that he was tired because Pippen's foul troubles had kept him on the floor for 44 minutes.

So now the series was tied 2–2 even though the Bulls had dominated all but about 10 minutes of the four games. Couldn't this team that won 67 games during the season do *anything* the easy way in the playoffs?

Game Five would almost certainly decide the series. Win it, and the Bulls would have two chances to get the title back in Chicago. Lose it, and the Blazers moved into the driver's seat.

One of the game's first plays set the tone for what would follow. With the score tied 2–2, Jordan streaked back on defense, broke up a Blazer fast break, then came back down and drilled a three-pointer. The Blazers could not begin to match the Bulls' ferocity and lost 119–106 to send the series back to Chicago.

Would the Blazers even bother to show up? Whaddya think, Bulls by 20?

No such luck. Continuing its pattern of doing things the hard way, Chicago trailed 79–64 going into the fourth period, which began with four reserves (Armstrong, Williams, Bobby Hansen, and Stacey King) on the floor with Pippen. Anyone for a Game Seven? But then began the most incredible comeback in finals history. Hansen, who wouldn't even be with the team the following season, hit a three-pointer and made a key steal. King made three free throws and a jumper. Pippen hit a layup. The Blazers double-dribbled, traveled, and threw bad passes. Jordan, after checking back into the game, took over down the stretch with three jumpers, two baseline drives, and two clutch free throws.

When the dust cleared and the Blazers were able to

shake the cobwebs from their brains, the Bulls had a 97–93 win and were dancing on the scorer's table, fists and champagne bottles held high. The Trail Blazer's Danny Ainge seemed to sum up these Bulls when he said, in a subdued losers' locker room: "I don't think they're a great team. Let's just say they're a very good team with one great player."

Fair enough, Danny.

But how about if they were to win *three* straight titles?

• *For Pippen and Jordan, there would be no respite, no long summer break to kick back, take it easy, and get ready for the upcoming preseason, as the challenge of a three-peat loomed. Instead, as McCallum pointed out in his piece, Pippen and Jordan, selected for the first "Dream Team" of NBA athletes to play in the Olympics, spent their summer in La Jolla, California, then went on to Portland, Oregon, and finally to Barcelona, where they helped the team win Olympic gold. It would be Pippen's first time, Jordan's second, at the Olympics; for Pippen, it was a new experience, but for Jordan the real pleasure was likely in the opportunity to play for a common cause with the players that he respected on court, and enjoyed off court as friends.*

10.

A Hero for the Wired World

by David Halberstam (1991)

IN SOME mysterious way the word has gotten out. The Chicago Bulls bus, the bus that *he* rides on (which is as close as most of these fans will ever get to the street where he lives), is to leave the Westin Hotel in Seattle at five P.M., and by 4:20 the crowd has begun to gather in the lobby, concentric rings of fans or, more properly, worshippers: They are more white than black, more young than old, more male than female, but they cut across every ethnic and demographic line. It seems almost ceremonial, a certain hum of anticipation rising each time the elevator opens. Finally at 4:50—for he likes to be the last man on the bus—the door opens, and out he comes, in his Michael Mode: His smile-and-sign-and-move-and-smile-and-sign-and-keep-moving drill is flawless. He is the seigneur—swift, deft, graceful, never rude—in the splits of the second in which he at once enters and departs their lives. "I actually saw him *live*," a boy says. Fame is indeed fleeting for those whose closest connection to it is to stand and work the 60 yards from the Westin elevator to the team bus.

I have not seen fame like this in almost 30 years. I think of the time, in 1960, when I was the one reporter in the country allowed to ride the train bearing Elvis Presley back to Memphis from the army, and I think of John Kennedy in that same year, when he campaigned in California, and I watched the teenyboppers and saw the first reflection that in a television age, politics had become theater. I do not cover rock concerts, but I presume Mick Jagger and others who play at his level deal with this all the time. In a pretelevision age, Joe DiMaggio had fame like this and was comparably imprisoned, though his fame was limited largely by the boundaries of the 48 contiguous states.

There is an even greater dimension to the fame of Michael Jordan. He is one of only two black American athletes who, almost 45 years after Jackie Robinson broke into baseball, have finally become true crossover heroes—that is, they receive more commercial endorsement deals from the predominantly white, middle-class purveyors of public taste than do white athletes (the other is the pre-HIV Magic Johnson; the jury is out on Bo Jackson now that he's a mere one-sport man). But unlike Johnson, Jordan has created a kind of fame that exceeds sports; he is both athlete and entertainer. He plays in the age of the satellite to an audience vastly larger than was possible in the past and is thus the first great athlete of the wired world.

His good looks—indeed, his beauty, for that is the right word—are a surprise to older white Americans, who by cultural instinct grew up thinking that Gary Cooper and Gregory Peck and Robert Redford and Paul Newman were handsome but did not see beauty in a young black athlete with a shaved head. Jordan has given us, then, among other things, a new definition of American male beauty. Not surprisingly, in many households it has been the children who have taught the parents about him and about his fame, artistry, and beauty.

About a year ago New York governor Mario Cuomo gave a speech bemoaning the disappearance of the athlete as hero in America. Where have you gone, Ted Williams and Joe DiMaggio? he asked. A friend of mine named Dick Holbrooke, a former U.S. State Department official, wrote him that comparable heroes still existed, but that their names were Michael Jordan and Magic Johnson and that today's children were inspired by the grace and ease with which they carried their fame. Cuomo called back and said, I stand corrected.

Jordan, infinitely disciplined, product of a very strong, very ambitious family, knows innately how to handle this staggering role—to deal with the media, to know what to say and what not to say and when to hide and when to go public, and to smile always. He is the first new-age athlete. And he is the right athlete at the right time. He plays the right sport, for its purpose is

Michael Jordan autographs a basketball that was among the prizes for participants in Jordan's third annual Celebrity Golf Classic for Ronald McDonald Children's Charities in 1989. (Photo by Rich Hein, courtesy of the *Chicago Sun-Times.*)

easily comprehensible even in a country where basketball has not yet taken root. Had the satellite been pervasive 20 years earlier, Pele, also playing an international sport—soccer—on a level above even the best players of his day and with a charm that radiated easily across national boundaries, might have been first. Perhaps Muhammad Ali might have been first, but he was politicized by his conversion to Islam and the Vietnam War. Besides, Ali's considerable charm notwithstanding, boxing was never the ideal sport for the young, with whom all idolatry of this kind must start. Ali, far more graceful than most boxers, conquered his opponents by stylishly punching them senseless; Jordan meets his opponents and conquers by gracefully soaring over them.

More, he does this for an audience that greatly exceeds that of the ballet. This is sports as ballet, something utterly new and modern, its roots African-American, ballet as a contested sport. No one, after all, ever guarded Baryshnikov. When we talk in Jordan's hotel room, I talk to him about Baryshnikov and Nureyev and their beauty and grace, and he listens, curious, patient, intrigued by these stories of potential rivals, and when I am through, he asks only one question about Baryshnikov: "How tall is he?" Short, I answer, quite short—low center of gravity. I detect a small smile, a category-four smile, almost invisible, a smile of private victory: Michael's pleasure as he thinks about posting up Mischa.

Jordan's is the most original of performances. What thrills the fans—and the other players and his coaches—is that almost every night there is something unique in his moves. It is not, says Bulls coach Phil Jackson, that Jordan's hang time is so great; there may well be others in the league with greater hang time. What sets Jordan apart, Jackson says, is what he does in the air, the control, the vision, the ability to move his body after he has seemingly committed it. If Jordan, Jackson notes with a certain delight, is the lineal descendant of those great basketball innovators who went before—Elgin Baylor, Connie Hawkins, and Julius Erving, each learning from and expanding upon the accomplishments of his predecessors—then the most exciting question is, What is the *next* great player going to be able to do?

Ever since the coming of the communications satellite, there has been an inevitability to all this—that there would be an athlete of Jordan's surpassing international fame, that he would most likely come from soccer or basketball, because they are the most readily understandable of international games, the games that essentially explain themselves. Since America is the home team in the wired world, it would likely be an American sport. But American football has too many rules and cloaks its players in uniforms that deny individuality. Baseball has complicated rules too and seems, in contrast with basketball, a languid sport to the uninitiated, building slowly over an entire season. That left basketball. It was therefore almost a given that the first athletic superstar of the wired world would be a black American basketball player who played above the rim.

The last great export of America in the postindustrial international economy may be entertainment and media. We as a country are now to the rest of the world what New York was to the rest of the nation when New York was merely a domestic media capital. (Consider the relative fame and success in endorsements of, say, Joe DiMaggio and Mickey Mantle of New York compared with Stan Musial of St. Louis and Hank Aaron of Milwaukee-Atlanta.) We do not, as a nation, merely reprocess the talents of others through our powerful communications system; like any good isolationist society, we tend to export, first and foremost, our own deeds, concerns, and talents.

Jordan's fame is of a kind that builds on itself. Images in our world beget additional images. Having seen one dazzling image, we hunger for another. We fear only boredom. Because Jordan's athleticism is so great, the camera seeks him out every night. And because the camera singles him out, he in turn receives the endorsements, particularly the immensely skillful Nike commercials. What we finally come to is not merely the sale of sneakers but the creation of a myth, a movie in continuum, made up of brief commercial bites—the Michael Jordan story: Chapter 1, Michael soaring into space; Chapter 2, his palship with Mars Blackmon (even mocking Jordan's own lack of hair). In the end, he is a film star as well as an athlete.

The decision to broaden the story, year by year, was made by Jim Riswold, who writes the Nike commercials. He had heard early in Jordan's career that Bill Russell, not a man lightly given to compliments about other players, had told James and Deloris Jordan that their son was an even better *person* than he was a basketball player. We will proceed, Riswold thought, to show that. And he has. The Michael Jordan story, as told by Nike, has become such a cultural event that the release of a new commercial is preceded by great secrecy. We are allowed to know only that a new Michael commercial is soon to appear on a television channel near you. Then there is a screening for journalists. *A screening of a commercial for journalists!* Of the next episode, to be unveiled at the Super Bowl, all we are allowed to know is

that it portrays Michael with another American icon, someone older from outside sports. (The smart money is on a carrot-eating wabbit of cartoon ancestry.)

Jordan is a reflection of what the world has become and of the invisible wires that now bind it. CNN, the network of the satellite, has been in operation for little more than a decade; the rise of the NBA as an international sport has taken place largely in the past five years. Some 75 nations received some combination of regular-season and playoff games in 1990–91, and that figure is up to 88 this season. The internationalization of the sport, of course, has dovetailed almost perfectly with Jordan's pro career. He had been half hidden in college in the controlled North Carolina offense. Nike had signed him in '84, thinking it was getting one of the better players of the year. It did not know that it was getting the greatest athlete in the world. He was immediately able to showcase his abilities at the Los Angeles Olympics, while the world watched. From then on, the legend built.

When Nike bid to represent Jordan, his agent, David Falk, insisted that he not sign on as just another basketball player endorsing a sneaker, but that he have his own line. In time Nike agreed, and Air Jordan was created. Nike, which had come upon stagnant times in the sneaker wars, thought the Air Jordan line might do about $10 million in business the first year. Instead, despite the attempts of the NBA commissioner to ban the Jordan shoe, Nike sold $130 million worth of Air Jordans.

Thus began the legend (and the dilemma) of the young man who is the most talented athlete in basketball but whose fame and income transcend the game, making him entertainer as well as player. For everything in a media age must entertain; that Jordan can do so is his great value. He is not just the ultimate player; he is the ultimate show.

It is about more, of course, than scoring and smiling. Being a Pied Piper is not enough. He is a warrior, a smiling warrior to be sure, and that too comes through to the fan. There is an intensity to his game, a feral quality, and an almost palpable desire to win. Great athletes are not necessarily nice people, in the traditional definition of nice, which implies a certain balanced, relaxed attitude toward life. They are, at least in their youth, obsessed by winning, by conquering others. Jordan is, for all the charm and the smiles, the athlete personified, egocentric and single-minded, tough and hard—hard on himself, on teammates, on opponents—fearless and unbending, never backing down, eager to put his signature on an opponent, looking for new worlds and teams to conquer.

A logo for the Michael Jordan 1994 calendar.

There are endless testimonials to this intensity: Michael wanting and needing to win at everything he does—pool, cards, video games; Michael staring for hours at a blank television set late at night after missing a critical foul shot in the final seconds of a playoff game against Cleveland; Michael, in the finals against the Lakers last spring, hurting his toe, which then swelled up badly, and trying to play in a special shoe that gave him more room but also limited his ability to cut, coming over to the Bulls bench early in the game and saying to the trainer, "Give me the pain," which translated meant give me my regular shoe, and I'll play in pain.

He had hated the reputation, which he bore in his early years in the NBA, that he was a great player, perhaps the greatest player ever to play the game, but that he would never be able to win a championship ring. This was so, it was said, because the Bulls offense, like it or not, would revolve too much around him, and in

the playoffs, at the highest level of the game, he would, in this most team-oriented of sports, subtract rather than add by playing into the hands of the defense. He became, year by year, a more complete player. But what also became clear about him—as it was clear about Di-Maggio—was that he was the ultimate big-game player, the bigger the game, the better he played, and the better and tougher he played in the final quarter, and even more, in the last four minutes, when everyone else was exhausted. All of his skills came together last year in the finals, giving him the championship some said he would never attain.

Now, with that championship under his belt, he pushes for a second and for wider victories. His teammates at Nike and Gatorade are thinking now of Europe. His teammate NBA commissioner David Stern is thinking of the rest of the planet. Their time is clearly coming. The phenomenon of the athlete as global figure grows

Michael Jordan is the center of attention as reporters and photographers surround him at a practice session. (Photo courtesy of the *Chicago Sun-Times.*)

at an accelerating rate. The Olympics loom ahead, and when Michael leads the U.S. team in the gold medal game just outside Barcelona on August 8, some 2.5 billion viewers in 170 countries will likely tune in.

And this is just the beginning. The stadium is now the world. Sports, particularly soccer and basketball, are ever more international (in soccer, only America lags behind the world, and that is partly generational; younger Americans are already more connected to the game than their parents were). The commercial impulse for more international competition can only grow—the shoe companies and the soft drink companies are increasingly international, and they hunger for this limitless audience.

As for Michael, he is contemplating other fields. We are sitting in Jordan's hotel room, and he is talking about playing another sport. It is hard to tell when he is entirely serious and when he is daydreaming. Some-

times the daydreams sound very real. Bo Jackson, he is saying, made it possible to be a two-sport man, opened it up for me. He clearly would like to compete against Jackson's achievement. Besides, all that jumping is hard on the knees. Football, he says . . . I could be a wide receiver. Almost nothing I couldn't catch. "But I won't go over the middle."

Then he goes on to baseball. He ponders a career there, for he loves the game and would still like to give it a try. At 28, could he hit the curveball? The question is tantalizing.

In the meantime, as his fame grows, his right to privacy shrinks. Almost everywhere he goes in the world now, he draws large, demanding crowds. Paris, cool to basketball, disdainful of Americans, was a surviving safe haven, a place where he could walk around with ease and relative anonymity. But the next Olympics, he knows, may cost him even Paris.

11.

A Galaxy of Shooting Stars:
The 1992 Men's Olympic Basketball Team

I could sense the anticipation, the hunger to see an NBA Olympic team when I was in Europe two years ago. But this was even more incredible than I had imagined. I don't think anyone thought we would get that kind of reception we got. It was wild, wild from the start.

—*Michael Jordan, from* 100 Years of Basketball

THE GAME had ended, and the 1972 men's Olympic basketball team retired to its locker room to celebrate winning the gold against a more experienced and formidable opponent, the USSR.

The celebration, however, was premature. Citing a timeout by the Soviet coach that had gone unnoticed, officials resumed the game. Failing to rise to the occasion, the Soviet team missed the basket, as the U.S. team began celebrating again—again prematurely. As it turned out, the game clock hadn't been reset properly, so the game—for the third time—resumed. This last time, a court-length pass enabled the Soviet team to score a basket and win the game, 51–50.

Outraged, the U.S. team left for the States, refusing to accept its second-place silver medals. To date, no team member has accepted his medal—we won the gold, they insisted, not the silver. The defeat was all the more galling because, until then, the U.S. had dominated in men's basketball in the Olympics.

Though the U.S. team would go on to win the gold in 1976 and 1984, and the bronze in 1988, the country that invented the century-old game had never seen its best basketball players—the 300 men that comprised the NBA team rosters—hit the hardcourt in international Olympic competition. As Dream Team coach Chuck Daly explained in *America's Dream Team*, "The

United States was the only country whose professional players were not allowed to compete in the Olympics, and that was wrong."

In 1989 the International Basketball Federation removed restrictions that prevented NBA players from competing in the Olympics. Finally, the Olympics would host the best basketball players in the world. Olympic competition in men's basketball would, finally, see the entry of an American team that would set the standard of excellence—an entry long overdue.

Unlike in previous years, the team coach would have no say in who was picked for the team; to select the first "Dream Team," a group of 13 coaches had the unenviable task of picking a dozen players from the NBA, with the certainty that some of the picks would be controversial.

Shooting For Gold
1992 U. S. Olympic Team

Commemorative art poster celebrating the U.S. men's basketball team at the 1992 Olympic games in Barcelona.

The men chosen were:

- #4, Christian Laettner (Forward/Center, Minnesota Timberwolves)
- #5, David Robinson (Center, San Antonio Spurs)
- #6, Patrick Ewing (Center, New York Knicks)
- #7, cocaptain Larry Bird (Forward, Boston Celtics)
- #8, Scottie Pippen (Forward/Guard, Chicago Bulls)
- #9, Michael Jordan (Guard, Chicago Bulls)
- #10, Clyde Drexler (Guard, Portland Trail Blazers)
- #11, Karl Malone (Forward, Utah Jazz)
- #12, John Stockton (Guard, Utah Jazz)
- #13, Chris Mullin (Forward/Guard, Golden State Warriors)
- #14, Charles Barkley (Forward, Phoenix Suns)
- #15, cocaptain Earvin "Magic" Johnson (Guard, Los Angeles Lakers)

The coaching staff consisted of head coach Chuck Daly and three assistant coaches: P.J. Carlesimo, Mike Krzyzewski, and Lenny Wilkins.

Indeed, for everyone, this was, in every sense of the expression, a Dream Team: incandescent shooting stars that would streak across Olympic firmament. For NBA fans—national and international—this was a dream come true: their favorite players on the court, playing not against each other but against a common foe. For the players, this was a unique opportunity to play not for their respective teams but, together, for their country. For the U.S. basketball community at large, this was an opportunity to showcase its best players, bringing them to a worldwide audience estimated in the billions. And for the international basketball community at large, this was an opportunity to finally see world-class, competitive basketball at the Olympic games—the best of the best.

On the commercial front, this would be the biggest licensing opportunity in Olympic history. As David Burns, of Burns Sports Celebrity Services, explained: "No doubt about it, this is the biggest, most expensive marketing deal in the history of sports." According to Jack McCallum, writing for *Sports Illustrated*, 14 companies were "official team sponsors" and 26 more signed on for licensing agreements: pins, posters, buttons, action figures, wall decals, carrying bags, pennants, and even breakfast cereal (Kellogg's)—all emblazoned with the logo of USA Basketball. Costs ranged from $2 (for a button) up to $65 (for a set of "starting lineups" action figurines); in addition, you could literally dress yourself in USA Basketball clothing, from a $15 T-shirt to a $150 sweat suit. (Other apparel included sneakers, mesh shorts, sweatshirts, jerseys, cotton shorts, and a cap.) An estimated $30 million was projected in sales for Dream Team memorabilia, according to McCallum.

So, having rested quite a while, then God created the Dream Team.

And He saw that it was good, verily, real good, a team made in His own image, considerably better even than the '27 Yankees.

And the Dream Team gathered by the salt sea at a place the name of it called La Jolla, which was like unto a golf resort; but mornings there was *some* practice.

And the players, who had been taken away from their sneaker companies, became a dozen even.

The numbers of them were the sons of Nike most; Michael, though, was first among them all upon the earth.

But also came the sons of Converse.

These were the elders Magic and Bird, who had both lived many seasons but prospered still.

And it came to pass that the Dream Team would travel to the land of Oregon and there set upon the pitiful hoopsters of the other tribes of the Americas who had likewise been called to try for the Olympics.

But yea, it is *written*; it would be a slaughter.

The Dream Team would fall upon their rivals' guards, but also they would smite their rivals' centers and even their rivals' power forwards.

So the Dream Team would go then for yet more practice at a place by the great Sea called Monte Carlo.

They actually go *practice* in Monte Carlo?

Yea, behold, even there; and the Dream Team would at last arrive at the city of Barcelona, where they would finish the chores given them, even as the fans of all the other lands *begged* for mercy.

But from the Dream Team there would be None.

And NBC was well pleased.

—Frank Deford, from "Team of Dreams," Newsweek (July 6, 1992)

For Michael Jordan—as with other team members—the flood of merchandising and tie-in products conflicted with previous agreements. Nike, for instance, owns his apparel rights, which meant that Jordan could not and would not wear the Converse basketball shoes; likewise, Jordan initially refused to wear the Reebok suit medalists wore while accepting Olympic medals. (In the end, Jordan compromised and did wear the suit, but draped an American flag over a shoulder to obscure the Reebok logo; the other five Nike men on the team simply turned their collars up, obscuring the logo.)

For the public at large, however, the commercial aspects of the Dream Team were secondary to seeing their favorite players compete in an international arena.

For Jordan, the Dream Team—assembled at a time when the nation was beset with national and international distractions—took on a larger dimension, becoming a symbol of what the United States could achieve. As Jordan told *Newsweek*, "We've got to regain our sense of pride, our dignity. Some way—even if it's just basketball. We can at least show the world that *we can take control of something.*"

Clearly, Jordan didn't share the opinion of commentator and former college coach Al McGuire, who in the February 18, 1991, issue of *Sports Illustrated* was quoted as saying, "An NBA all-star team will *not* win an Olympic gold medal."

La Jolla, California

With only five days to prepare before the beginning of the Basketball Tournament of the Americas, to be held in Portland, Oregon, the Dream Team assembled in La Jolla, California. Coming off the regular season, the Dream Teamers would be giving up their summer—their free time—to play for free, for the privilege of representing their country.

The only concern—compatibility on and off the court—proved to be a nonissue, as Coach Chuck Daly wrote in *America's Dream Team*:

> There was no sign of a clash of egos in La Jolla, much to the relief of the coaching staff. These players, most of whom had never spent any extended time together, got along well, spending much of their free time in foursomes of golf, going into town for dinner, or playing cards.

In addition to intra-team scrimmages, the Dream Team honed its edge against a Developmental Team comprised of eight college players. Ironically, the Developmental Team handed the Dream Team its first—and only—defeat. In a 20-minute scrimmage game, the college players scored 62 points against the Dream Team's 54 points.

A rude awakening, the defeat made the point: You can't afford to be complacent, *especially* when you're the Dream Team. It would be a mistake they would not repeat.

Basketball Tournament of the Americas

Held from June 27 to July 5 in Portland, Oregon, the Basketball Tournament of the Americas would trim down the Olympic competitors from nine teams to four. Brazil, Canada, Cuba, Mexico, Panama, Puerto

Rico, the United States, Uruguay, and Venezuela would battle it out for the slots.

Capitalizing on the intense media coverage, USA Basketball published a six-page color insert in *USA Today*, giving all the details about the Dream Team and the Basketball Tournament of the Americas. Just in case you hadn't gotten the word, USA Basketball, in its insert, enthused:

> It has been called the Dream Team, the greatest collection of basketball talent ever assembled. Ever before a single dunk was slammed, the mission facing the USA Basketball team that for the first time features NBA superstars was clear: Bring home the gold medal!

To which Coach Chuck Daly, tongue-in-cheek, responded, "If we don't do that, we might as well stay in Barcelona and not come home again—or retire to the country that beat us!"

The Tournament of the Americas was less a tournament than a rout. Predictably, the visiting teams—without exception—were awestruck by the Dream Team. As Daly pointed out, the Cuba coach remarked, "You cannot cover the sun with your finger." More a photo opportunity and a media event than a real competition, the Portland games, if nothing else, gave the Dream Team the opportunity to play by FIBA rules, instead of the NBA rules to which they were accustomed.

As far as the team was concerned, the real benefit was the inevitable bonding that resulted as the players spent additional time together on and off court. In Barcelona, the competition would be greater—as would the stakes—and they would have to win as a team, not as individual superstars.

Barcelona, Spain

Traditionally, Olympic athletes stay in the designated Olympic village. The idea is that it promotes international goodwill. But when the Dream Team members inadvertently created mob scenes wherever they appeared in the village, it was clear goodwill had to take a back seat to practicality—a fact soon apparent to nearly everyone, except some in the media. Even Monte Carlo, normally blasé with the prospect of celebrities in town, had been unprepared for the media circus that surrounded the Dream Team when it arrived there for a final Olympic warm-up.

In the end it proved necessary to put the Dream Team in its own hotel, which became a media magnet, as well as the site for round-the-clock vigils from fans who *had* to get a glimpse of their heroes.

As the team left the hotel, thousands crowded the streets, taking pictures and waving. (As the games progressed, roads were blocked off to allow safe and easy passage, police escorts were essential, and—concerned about a terrorist attack—a helicopter provided air escort.)

The day before the opening game, the Dream Team gave a press conference, with over a thousand members of the media on hand, peppering the players with questions. Predictably, the same tired questions came up: Why weren't they staying in the village? And don't you think it's somewhat unfair to have professionals at the Olympics?

The Dream Team had more important things to think about—namely, the games ahead, including the first one with Angola.

In retrospect, the Barcelona Games were, for the most part, a repeat of what had happened in Portland. The Dream Team came, saw, and conquered, including Brazil's team, which had talked trash back in Portland, asserting that the U.S. team was coasting and they'd be put in their place. Instead, the Dream Team put away Brazil, 127–83, a record high for any U.S. team in the Olympics. So much for trash-talking!

If anything symbolized the Dream Team, it was a seven-story-high, black-and-white Nike billboard on the side of a building in downtown Barcelona—Michael Jordan, suspended in air, his back to the backboard, with a basketball that was dunk-bound.

Like the billboard, the Dream Team towered above its competition, leaving them in the shadows. Nothing illustrated this point more vividly than seeing U.S. TV coverage of the Dream Team go from full-game coverage to news updates as it became obvious that the Dream Team would *always* win; the only question was by how much. As the former Soviet Union coach Alexander Gomelsky observed, "The Dream Team does not make games. They make spectaculars."

From the beginning, it never was a question of the Dream Team not winning the gold; the only real question was what team would take the silver as the consolation prize.

After Barcelona

After the Olympics, the members of the Dream Team—brought together for a brief moment in time—went their separate ways. In four years, there will be a new Dream Team of established NBA stars and newcomers from the college ranks. Of those on the Dream Team, both cocaptains, Larry Bird and Earvin "Magic" Johnson hung up their jerseys and retired, citing health reasons. For those remaining, the games continued, as they geared up for another season.

Beyond bringing home the gold, the Dream Team accomplished on a larger scale exactly what had been expected by the international basketball community: A new standard had been established, and henceforth competing teams would play with upped antes. Being good simply wasn't good enough; you had to be the *best*.

Think about it: Without the NBA competition, international basketball at the Olympics would stagnate. Spirited competition—the lifeblood of any sport—is what keeps the game alive and the players sharp; without it, it's just another game.

Dream Team II

At the 1994 World Championships in Toronto, on August 4–14, Dream Team II will compete with 15 other nations. The coach will be Don Nelson of the Golden State Warriors.

Though undeniably a talented group, when compared to the first Dream Team, the new team—as Magic Johnson told *USA Today*—"is similar to our team . . . but not good enough to beat our Barcelona team."

The members include:

- Derrick Coleman, New Jersey Nets
- Joe Dumars, Detroit Pistons
- Tim Hardaway, Golden State Warriors
- Larry Johnson, Charlotte Hornets
- Dan Majerle, Phoenix Suns
- Alonzo Mourning, Charlotte Hornets
- Shawn Kemp, Seattle SuperSonics
- Mark Price, Cleveland Cavaliers
- Steve Smith, Miami Heat
- Dominique Wilkins, Los Angeles Clippers
- Shaquille O'Neal, Orlando Magic
- Reggie Miller, Indiana Pacers

The Dream Fulfilled

by Coach Chuck Daly *with Alex Sachare*

The following is an excerpt from America's Dream Team: The Quest for Olympic Gold *by Coach Chuck Daly with Alex Sachare. Turner Publishing, Inc., 1992. Hardback, 224 pages, $24.95.*

Called "the ultimate insider's book" to the Dream Team, this coffee-table book, replete with hundreds of professional, full-color photos, was written by Detroit Pistons coach Chuck Daly, with Alex Sachare, a former sportswriter with the Associated Press who edits NBA publications in his capacity as its vice president in charge of editorial.

From the selection of the players through the Tournament of the Americas and, finally, to Barcelona, Spain, where the Olympics was held, this book is the definitive record of, as the book's subtitle put it, "the quest for Olympic gold."

I'VE ONLY TASTED champagne in a locker room three times in a coaching career that began in 1955 at Punxsutawney, Pennsylvania, Area Joint High School. The first two occasions were when the Detroit Pistons won NBA titles in 1989 and 1990. The third time was in Barcelona, when we accomplished our goal and won the Olympic gold medal. We only had a little champagne that night, but it tasted very good.

"Dream Team" is a lot of name to live up to, but, if anything, the 1992 U.S. Olympic men's basketball team exceeded all hopes and expectations. I think we truly gave the world a glimpse—only a glimpse, since we were never seriously challenged— what basketball can be like at its highest level.

Chris Mullin accurately summed up all the elements that had to come together to produce this phenomenon, starting with the decision three years ago to open the Olympics to NBA players. Then he ticked off some more: "How badly we wanted to get back the gold. A number of top players in their prime, and a couple of others at the end of their careers. And everybody willing to throw egos, individual statistics, and all that other stuff out of the window to prepare to be the best team ever."

The one thing I will remember most about this team is the professionalism of the athletes. That's what got us past all the distractions, all the controversies. They wanted to play as a team, put individual statistics aside,

and work toward a common goal. A lot of bonding took place among these 12 athletes during the weeks we were together, and it was great to see and be part of.

Many people have asked me, what was I feeling when that final buzzer sounded?

Relief, mainly. This had been a long process, not just seven weeks but almost a year's worth of thought and preparation. There were high expectations and some trepidation. All the players were major stars on their own teams, and as coaches we had some questions as to what would be needed to bring them together. So I felt a form of relief, mixed with joy and a sense of accomplishment, at having put it all together and won the Olympic title.

We finished the way we had begun—with a prayer. Before our first game together in Portland, Michael Jordan said, "Let's say a prayer. 'Our Father. . . .'" After we beat Croatia in the gold medal game and got back to the locker room, I called everybody together and we said the same prayer. Somehow, it seemed fitting.

Afterward, Magic was asked, "When will there be another Olympic team like this one?" He answered the reporters, "Well, you guys won't be around, and neither will we."

I watched the medal ceremony from the front row of press seats along with my assistant coaches, Lenny Wilkens, Mike Krzyzewski, and P.J. Carlesimo. Only the players get medals and climb up on the victory stand, because the Olympics are supposed to be a celebration of the athletes. At the end of the ceremony, however, Magic Johnson, Charles Barkley, and some of the other guys started waving for us to join them. We declined, because this was their moment, but I was very touched that they wanted to include us in it.

Some of the players had been on that victory stand before—Michael Jordan, Patrick Ewing, and Chris Mullin were on the 1984 team that won in Los Angeles—but most had never won gold medals. For some, this was their first taste of Olympic victory, and that made it even more special.

I thought there was true joy and true sentiment on that winner's stand, and the players' comments in the locker room afterward really confirmed that. Karl Malone said it was "an awesome feeling, to see 12 athletes come together and do something for their country." David Robinson, who was on the 1988 team that lost in the semifinals and came away from Seoul with a bronze medal, said, "Everything surges up inside you when they play the national anthem. It will be my happiest memory." And Magic said, "It was the most awesome feeling I've ever had winning anything, especially when the national anthem was played. Goose bumps just came all over my body. It's definitely the most exciting thing I've ever been through."

Being with this team was like traveling with 12 rock stars, that's all I can compare it to. Our every move caused quite a commotion. I'm sure there are some people in Barcelona who arc happy we're gone, like the owner of the little restaurant next to our hotel who said his regulars couldn't make it down the street because of all the security surrounding us, but there was real adulation everywhere we went.

The Dream Team was very special in terms of talent, but I think it was also special on a personal level to people around the world—to the French fans who came out at midnight to meet us at the Nice airport, to the UC–San Diego students who waited outside their gym for one of our practices to end so they could see us, and to the many fans in Barcelona who staked out our hotel day and night to watch us come and go. And, of course, it was special to the thousands who saw our games in person and the billions who watched us on television worldwide.

Worldwide interest in the sport is what the International Basketball Federation had in mind when it voted in 1989 to let NBA players participate in the Olympics. Yes, we dominated the tournament, to the point where the only competition was for the silver and bronze medals. And surely we reestablished U.S. dominance in the sport. But I believe we did a lot of good. By capturing people's imagination, the Dream Team gave a big boost to the popularity of basketball around the world. We really won't be able to gauge the overall impact for a while. But when you have a team with this magnificent talent on TV in roughly 180 countries, before some three billion people, it's got to improve the way the game is played.

Out there somewhere was a 12-year-old or a 13-year-old, not necessarily in the United States or in Spain but in any country, who perhaps was seeing these players for the first time. Now that youngster has a dream, and will be willing to work to make that dream come true. And maybe someday that child will get to compete in the Olympics and perhaps win a gold medal.

You know, it's one of those situations where the challenge is going to be playing together as a team. When you look at the talent and the teams we're supposed to play against, it's a massacre. It should never be close. We taught them the game of basketball. We've got people who have the ability and the height. We're talking about the greatest players that play the game now and the team is the best team that's ever been put together. Who's going to beat us?

—Michael Jordan, on the Dream Team (from his Playboy interview)

12.

The Third NBA Championship: They're History

by Jack McCallum (1993)

For Jordan, the 1992–93 season proved particularly demanding, especially off court where he was accorded no privacy. As gambling allegations tarnished his image and Jordan defended himself off court, he led the Bulls on court to an unprecedented third consecutive championship—something that hadn't been done in the league since 1966 when the Celtics, led by Bob Cousy, had their historic run.

FORGET FOR a moment that he ever played a high-stakes Nassau. Pretend that he went to visit George Bush two years ago at that beautiful 19th hole on Pennsylvania Avenue. Don't ask him to be as glib, as personable, as irrepressible as his good buddy Charles Barkley. Stop expecting him to live up to the Captain America image created by his commercials. Now, consider this: Is Michael Jeffrey Jordan simply the best basketball player in the history of the planet?

No matter what you think of Jordan as a person, as a role model, as a shoe salesman, or even as a high-stakes gambler, you know the answer to that question: yes. A resounding yes.

That was proved beyond a doubt on Sunday night when the Chicago Bulls concluded their long and arduous drive to a third straight NBA championship by staggering across the finish line in Phoenix with a thrilling 99–98 victory over the surprisingly resilient Suns in Game Six of the playoff finals. In winning an unprecedented third straight finals MVP award, Jordan loomed over the series from start to finish, just as he had in both of the Bulls' previous title runs. Three-peat? Without Jordan the Bulls don't even peat. His performance in Sunday's clincher was typical—a game-high 33 points, eight rebounds and a team-high seven assists in 44 minutes. The most astonishing thing about the victory was that John Paxson, not Jordan, took—and made—the winning shot, a dead-eye three-pointer with 3.9 seconds remaining.

Indeed, as the game drew to its unlikely conclusion, Jordan seemed to be playing, more than ever, as a solo act, a tranquil island in a bubbling sea of confusion and nerves. "I don't know what it was," said Jordan after the game, "but everybody was hyper." Well, maybe it had something to do with the situation. The Bulls, who led the series three to two but were reeling after having lost two of the three previous games, were ahead 87–79 going into the final 12 minutes of Game Six. Then they allowed the Suns to open the period with a 5–0 run, at which point Chicago coach Phil Jackson decided to give Jordan a rest. *Shaky* would not be the word to describe the Bulls' next two possessions—try *tortured*—which resulted in a 24-second violation and a frantic miss as the shot clock was about to blare once again.

And so Jordan, Chicago's one-man M*A*S*H unit, quickly checked back in and instructed his teammates that he would take the shots from now on, thank you very much. Over the next eight minutes he was the only Bull to score, and his rebound and ensuing unimpeded coast-to-coast layup drew Chicago to 98–96 with 38.1 seconds remaining.

The Suns had a shot to regain a four-point edge, but Dan Majerle air-balled a short jumper, and the Bulls got the ball back with 14.1 seconds left. After a timeout, a betting man (which no. 23 most assuredly is) could have gotten 100-to-1 odds that Jordan would take the final shot. The ball was indeed inbounded to Jordan, but he soon passed to Scottie Pippen in the frontcourt. Jordan then cut past Pippen, hoping for a return pass. But Jordan was too closely covered by Phoenix guard Kevin Johnson, so Pippen spun and charged toward the basket, only to find his path blocked by Suns center Mark West. That forced Pippen to dish the ball to Horace Grant along the left baseline. Considering that he had missed his last nine shots, including an uncontested layup, Grant wisely chucked the ball back to Paxson, who was hovering quietly behind the three-point line "just in case they needed me." Paxson took his two pitty-pat steps, released a shot that "I've taken hundreds of thousands of times" and watched. "It seemed like the ball was in the air for about an hour," said Phoenix coach Paul Westphal. Then it dropped through.

The Suns still had those 3.9 seconds in which to try to win the game, but Grant blocked Johnson's driving jumper to preserve the win and put the Bulls in the history books as only the third team to win three straight titles, the Minneapolis Lakers having done it in 1952 through '54 and the Boston Celtics having won eight straight from '59 through '66.

Jordan, his presence of mind extending even beyond the final buzzer, immediately chased down the historic game ball before joining his celebrating teammates.

To a man, the Suns seemed stunned by the final turn of events. It had taken a while, but with two victories, 129–121 in triple overtime in Game Three and 108–98 in Game Five, at Chicago Stadium, Phoenix had established itself as a team of character and heart. Along the way the Suns made the significant discovery that champions have to play tough and tenacious defense, which they did in Game Five and for long stretches in Game Six. Indeed, Phoenix should be the preseason favorite for the 1994 title—as long as Barkley doesn't follow through on his postgame musings concerning his possible retirement.

Sir Charles's departure would be a shame because he has clearly surpassed Jordan as the NBA's premiere "personality." Before the Suns' Game Five win, Barkley (registered in Chicago's Westin Hotel under the name of Quinn Buckner) received a call from Walt Disney chairman Michael Eisner, who asked whether, win or lose, Barkley would deliver the company's famous "I'm going to Disney World" message after the series. (He turned him down.) In contrast to the dread with which the Bulls approached the three-peat task, Barkley continually reminded us that a dominating player can actually have fun on the court.

Though he wouldn't admit it—"I don't want to say any basketball player is better than I am," he said early in the series—Barkley knows in his heart that his bald-headed homeboy, the guy he described as "the one player I'll accept losing to if I have to lose," is clearly the best man between the lines.

Perhaps the most amazing thing about Jordan is the huge gap in sheer ability between him and his contemporaries. True, Barkley won this year's regular-sea-

Cover to the September 1993 issue of *Beckett Basketball Monthly,* depicting Jordan celebrating the Bulls' third NBA championship.

son MVP award, breaking Jordan's bid at a three-peat in that category, too, but it's doubtful that he would have gotten a single vote had the voting occurred after the playoffs. Jordan's postseason run was nothing short of magnificent, especially considering the off-court distractions with which he had to deal. His buzzer-beating shot in Game Four of the Bulls' Eastern Conference semifinal against the Cleveland Cavaliers did not just complete a sweep, it also shook up the franchise. Longtime Cav coach Lenny Wilkens resigned seven days after the series ended, and Mike Fratello was hired last week to pick up the pieces of a team psyche that had been shattered time and time again by Michael Miracle. That's power.

Then came the Eastern finals and the New York Knicks, who were plenty tough. Making things tougher for Jordan were the revelations of his late-night foray to an Atlantic City casino before Game Two and the allegations in Richard Esquinas's book, which cropped up before Game Six. During that series Jordan stopped talking publicly and then ripped off 54 points in Game Four and steady 29- and 25-point performances in Games Five and Six, respectively. Run silent, run deep.

Finally, against Phoenix, Jordan had to overcome a dizzying array of defenders (Johnson, Majerle, and Richard Dumas all guarded him from time to time) as well as the hard reality that his team—dare we use Jordan's favorite description of "supporting cast"?—was disappearing before his very eyes. All you need to know about Jordan's work in the six-game series, during which he averaged 41 points (a finals record), 8.5 rebounds, and 6.3 assists a game, was that he scored his average in Game Five and the Suns were overjoyed with the defensive job they had done on him. That's because he had bopped them for 55 in Game Four, a 111–105 Chicago win.

"I think Michael would like to have been right there in the thick of it with me and Larry," Magic Johnson said before Game Five in Chicago. "See, with us, we didn't have to look for motivation all the time. We knew right where it was—in Boston for me, in L.A. for Larry. But Michael doesn't have the benefit of that."

Indeed, there is no foil for Jordan, not even the shining Sun—for all of Barkley's belligerent brilliance, he was still outscored by Jordan by an average of 14 points per game in the finals. One can only wonder what at all is left for a man who has won seven straight scoring titles while being named to the all-defensive team six straight years. How much better can he get? Which basketball ghosts is he chasing on his way to the Hall of Fame?

There would seem to be four players with whom realistically to compare Jordan: Magic and Bird, both of whom were three-time regular-season MVPs; Bill Russell, the ultimate winner, who led the Celtics to 11 championships in 13 seasons; and Oscar Robertson, whose versatility, leadership, and coldhearted competitiveness during 13 seasons make him closest to Jordan in playing style.

The first two players are picked off by the simple fact that Jordan has guided an average team to three titles, while Magic and Bird made already-good teams great. It's indisputable: Jordan never had an Abdul-Jabbar, a Worthy, a McHale, a Parish. He had a Pippen, an All-Star, to be sure, and turned him into a Dream Teamer.

Comparisons made across the ages are often unfair, but they are most judiciously made by players from the distant era who have seen both generations. And Jordan gets overwhelming support from two such men, Willis Reed and Bob Cousy, perceptive observers then and now.

"There's no question in my mind that Jordan is the best," says former Knicks star Reed, now general manager of the New Jersey Nets. "Bill Russell won all those championships, so you can't take anything away from him. But if you take all the aspects of the game, you have to say Michael is the best. The guy wins scoring titles, and he's one of the best defensive players of all time. That says it all."

Cousy, a centerpiece of Celtic lore, once selected Bird as his all-time best, but not anymore. "As far as I'm concerned, Michael is Nureyev against a bunch of Hulk Hogans," says Cousy. "His talent is that far above everyone else's. Russell was the most productive center I've ever seen, and he complemented the talent we had. But you can say that he wasn't as good a shooter as some other people. Jordan doesn't have *any* area like that."

Robertson? Well, the Big O's feat of averaging a triple double over the course of a season (30.8 points, 12.5 rebounds, and 11.3 assists in 1961–62) will probably never be matched, not even by Jordan. But night in and night out, he did not play Jordan's brand of defense, which on the ball is hard-nosed and off it is a gambling, sneak-into-the-passing-lanes nuisance.

"Oscar was great defensively when he wanted to be," says 68-year-old Bulls assistant Johnny Bach. "But Michael is the Tasmanian devil."

Perhaps the most sincere, and succinct, vote for Jordan comes from the Atlanta Hawks' Dominique Wilkins, who was asked before Game Six to assess Jordan's place in history. Said Wilkins, "Can't nobody have done better."

It's not just the obvious that makes Jordan special. Dave Twardzik, the Charlotte Hornets' vice president of personnel, says that the most incredible thing about Jordan is his stamina—he averaged nearly 40 minutes a game during the regular season, which increased to more than 45 in the championship series. "It was a long time ago when the best players used to play 45 to 48 minutes a game," says Twardzik, "and that was when the game was a lot slower."

Paxson is most impressed by Jordan's steadfastness in accepting responsibility. "Night after night, year after year, he just carries this team," Paxson said before Game Six. "He never avoids it, never shirks it." Incredibly, the Bulls have not lost three games in a row since the beginning of the 1990–91 season, a statistic that is directly attributable to Jordan's competitiveness and drive.

Then, too, Jordan simply adds a distinctive *style*, an elan that only a few players in NBA history could have matched (Connie Hawkins, Earl Monroe, George Gervin, Pete Maravich, and Julius Erving come to mind). Jordan captured our imagination, of course, with his aerial acrobatics—the spectacular dunks, the knifing between defenders, the switching of the ball from one hand to the other in midair. The most distinctive facet of his game these days, however, is his ability to create space for his jump shot. Typically, he puts on the brakes after a full-bore dribble toward the hoop, often literally skidding to a stop, like the Road Runner about to befuddle Wile E. Coyote, then sweeps the ball across his body and heads in another direction before firing away with a nearly unobstructed view of the rim.

"The main thing to remember about Michael," says Bach, "is that God only made the one."

But "the one," as we all know, seems to have grown less and less content over the years. Does it matter that in this series Barkley clearly beat Jordan in the ancillary contests of Mister Congeniality and Mister Popularity, just as Magic had beaten him in the 1991 finals? Sure, it matters. Gone is much of the spontaneous joy that Jordan brought to the game in 1984, when he entered the league with a head of hair, a pair of North Carolina shorts beneath his Bulls uniform, and a boyish appetite for fame and glory. But somewhere amid all the adulation and pressure, a spark went out of Jordan—one that, it seems, will never return.

Not long after Game Six, Jordan sat in a quiet room in the America West Arena, having just completed an interview with ESPN. He held a bottle of champagne and an unlighted cigar. "Okay if I just sit here a minute?" he asked ESPN's Dan Patrick. "It's crazy out there."

And when he finally left the room, it was indeed crazy again, with reporters, fans, photographers, family members, even a man with a monkey clamoring for his time and attention.

"Hey, Michael, just one picture," said the monkey man. Jordan obliged him, glancing at the creature that was clinging to the man's shoulder. "Hey, look, it's Charles," said Jordan.

It was nice to see the world's greatest player, at the moment of his greatest triumph, able to make a joke. Can't nobody have done better.

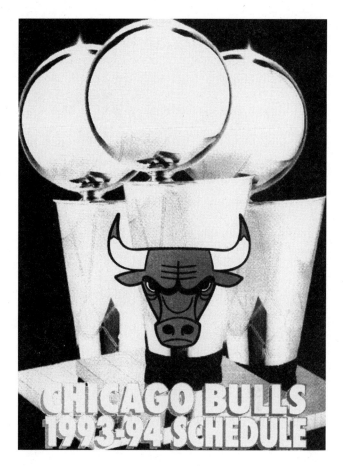

Cover to the Chicago Bulls 1993–94 game schedule.

13.

A Public Statement

by Michael Jordan

In August 1993 Michael Jordan—seemingly blessed with everything that money and fame and good fortune can buy—found himself having to come to grip with what is surely one of life's greatest tragedies: the loss of a loved one.

His father and his "best friend," James Jordan had been brutally murdered in an act of random violence for which there is no protection; he was, simply, in the wrong place at the wrong time.

Just as some in the media—notably Bob Costas of NBC, during the Bulls' playoffs against the Knicks—jumped on the Richard Asquinas book and gave what should have been a minor footnote a page, these same self-styled journalists who should have reported the facts engaged in speculative journalism, raising the possibility that James Jordan's tragic death was somehow linked to his son.

It was not journalism's finest hour.

Though Jordan said that most of the media handled this responsibly, it didn't seem that way to me; all the major news networks and many in the print media—loving a conspiracy theory—raised the specter of Michael Jordan's gambling debts as a possible motive.

The media should hang their heads in shame; instead of responsible journalism, we got tabloid journalism—news laced with the spice of speculation.

When the facts came out, when it became obvious even to the obtuse that this senseless murder had no linkage whatsoever to Michael Jordan, the media quickly dropped that angle.

Meanwhile, as the Jordan family met in Charlotte to gather their composure and find the strength to move on, the media camped outside the house, stalking Jordan with telephoto lenses, since they were not admitted past the iron gate.

Throughout all this, despite the media's attempts to get a comment from Jordan, he kept his silence. Finally, he broke his silence and, through his lawyer-agent David Falk at ProServ, released a terse public statement.

Two months later, the night before Jordan was to announce his retirement, announcements were aired on television and published the next morning, assuming that the death of James Jordan was the principal reason for Michael's Jordan's decision to retire.

Nothing could be further from the truth. The next morning, Jordan laid that notion to rest, stressing—time and again—he was thinking of retiring, and while his father's death gave him pause and caused him to reevaluate the mortality of his own life, it simply wasn't the reason.

Nobody would have blamed Michael Jordan if indeed that was the reason.

His father had seen the success that his son—against all odds—had achieved, culminating in being acclaimed, by general consensus, the best basketball player of our time, backed up by three championship wins. Michael Jordan made his father proud. What more could any father ask?

I AM VERY grateful for the outpouring of sympathy which is comforting the Jordan family during our time of bereavement. The many kind words and thoughtful prayers have lifted our spirits through difficult times.

I also want to express my appreciation to the local, state, and federal law enforcement officers for their efforts. Certainly, there have been lingering concerns about the handling of Dad's body which, in turn, triggered controversy. Fortunately, the investigation has identified the apparent perpetrators of this heinous act, and their forthcoming trials will ultimately establish their culpability and mete out their punishments.

Throughout this painful ordeal, I never wavered from my conviction that Dad's death was a random act of violence. Thus, I was deeply disturbed by the early reports speculating there was a sinister connection to Dad's death. I was outraged when this speculation continued even after the arrests of the alleged murderers.

These totally unsubstantiated reports reflect a complete lack of sensitivity to basic human decency.

When James Jordan was murdered, I lost my dad. I also lost my best friend. I am trying to deal with the overwhelming feelings of loss and grief in a way that would make my dad proud. I simply cannot comprehend how others could intentionally pour salt in my open wound by insinuating that faults and mistakes in my life are in some way connected to my father's death.

As a public figure, I have always respected the media and their role in reporting news to the public. I have always believed that there must be a balance between the responsibility to inform and the obligation to inform responsibly.

During this tragic ordeal, the vast majority of the media reports approached the situation with dignity, sensitivity, and respect for human decency. Unfortunately, a few engaged in baseless speculation and sensationalism. These few should cause us all to pause and examine our consciences and our basic human values.

My dad taught me to carry myself with love and respect for all. The wisdom of his principles will help me rise above any thoughtless insensitivity and unfounded speculation. With the help of God's strength, I will find the inner peace to carry on in Dad's way.

• *In the wake of his father's untimely demise, Michael Jordan tried to carry on as normal a life as possible, but life would never be quite the same again. Jordan, at least, took comfort in the fact that his father saw him become the success that he is; and that his father saw him lead the Bulls to a three-peat. It was the last basketball game James Jordan saw—a memory that the son would come to cherish, taking a tragic situation and, even then, finding a ray of optimism.*

Michael Jordan greets his father, James Jordan, 1991. (Photo by Todd Sumlin, courtesy of the *Wilmington Star-News*.)

Three
Retirement

What if my name wasn't in lights? What if my face wasn't on the TV every other second?
What if there wasn't a crowd around every corner? What if I was just a basketball player?
Can you imagine it? I can.
—*Michael Jordan, Nike ad, 1993*

Everyone knew the day would come—the day when Jordan would, instead of hanging in the air to dunk a basketball, come down to earth and hang up jersey no. 23 for good, but nobody thought it would come this early.

That day came on October 6, 1993, when Jordan held a press conference at the Berto Center in Deerfield, Illinois, where the Bulls hold their training camp and workouts.

Jordan, flanked by his wife Juanita, announced his retirement, effective immediately, before a jam-packed room. Photographers aimed cameras at him with telephoto lenses the size of siege howitzers, and a nest of microphones, like snakes ready to strike, seemed poised for attack.

Jordan's conference drew everyone who was anyone in the Jordan world, all bearing funereal expressions: from the Bulls, his teammates, owner Jerry Reinsdorf, general manager Jerry Krause; from the NBA, commissioner David Stern; from the corporate world, Nike CEO Philip Knight and ProServ's David Falk, whose companies rose as Jordan—a shooting star—shot across basketball heaven, scratching fire in the sky.

Immediately, the speculations began: Would Jordan come out of retirement—and if so, when, and under what circumstances? What chance would the Bulls have to win their fourth consecutive championship title? (Las Vegas bookies, who had favored the Bulls 2–1, now gave 25–1 against. Ironically, in the locker room after the third championship win, Jerry Krause said, "You know, I really think the fourth one is going to be a lot easier," never knowing how dramatically their situation would change later that year.) Who would fill Jordan's oversize shoes? (Scottie Pippen, or newly signed Toni Kukoc?) What would happen to the Bulls franchise? (The NBA commissioner jokingly commented that "We're still planning to open the season on November 5.") And what impact would his departure have on his many commercial endorsements? (Nike and Quaker Oats planned to stand by their man.)

With his retirement, Jordan fundamentally changed the worldview of his colleagues, the franchise, his adopted city Chicago, the commercial world (Nike and Quaker Oats stock fluctuated, falling slightly, reflecting the announcement), and a worldwide audience of billions who had come to expect—at least—another season of Jordan, tongue out, driving through heavy downtown traffic on court to lead the Bulls to the "four-peat," as they had termed it.

It's a whole different ball game now.

Larry Bird, then Magic Johnson . . . now Michael Jordan. Who could have imagined those three retiring so *soon*?

The fans could never get enough of Jordan, but Jordan had had enough of the fame, the star-making machinery that imprisoned him. Jordan, in short, set himself free.

The day after the announcement, the world's media turned their attention to other matters, relegating Jordan to follow-up stories. The world had moved on . . . and now, so has Michael Jordan.

14.

A Whole New Ball Game

ON A COOL Tuesday evening on October 6, 1993, Michael Jordan threw out the ceremonial ball before a crowd of almost 50,000 fans at Comiskey Park in Chicago, on the occasion of the first game of the American League Champion Series, the White Sox against the Toronto Blue Jays. The irony was that few in the crowd realized that this would mark Jordan's last public appearance at a sporting event before his imminent retirement.

Even teammate Scottie Pippen was caught off guard, according to the *Chicago Tribune*:

Pippen was making his way to a private box . . . when reporters asked if he heard Michael Jordan was retiring. Pippen shrugged it off as a rumor, but he felt a little uneasy.

So before Pippen sat down to watch the game, he called Jordan, who was sitting in another luxury box [Bulls owner Jerry Reinsdorf's] at Comiskey.

Jordan told Pippen it was true. Pippen's jaw dropped.

"It was real shocking for me," Pippen said. "It was something that was really hard to swallow. I couldn't even enjoy the game."

That evening, the rest of the world got the word, though not officially. The story broke at 10:32 P.M. eastern time when NBC's Jane Pauley announced Jordan's retirement on "Dateline." Network stations reported that Jordan would be announcing his retirement the next morning at a press conference. The only question was whether the retirement would be immediate, or—as many hoped—it would be postponed a year down the road, after the 1993–94 season with the Bulls favored to win a fourth NBA championship.

Would there be a tenth season with Jordan and the Bulls?

Was it to be or not to be?

It was not to be.

The next morning, at 11:00 A.M. eastern time, Michael Jordan somberly announced to a standing-room-only crowd of several hundred journalists that he was retiring, effective immediately.

Air Jordan, finally, had been grounded. Too much heavy downtown traffic off court, it turned out. Jordan could take it on the court with the best of them, but the years of the world wanting a piece of him, the cumulative effect of endless demands from all comers, finally took its toll. The man whom the media had dubbed a superman finally succumbed to the kryptonite of fame: a prisoner of his own success.

Bone-weary of having to *be* Michael Jordan, of having to live up to his superman myth instead of living as normal a life as possible under the circumstances, Jordan slam-dunked a stunned world with his announcement.

15.

Michael Jordan's Statement

When I walked away from the game, I knew a lot of people, especially the kids, would be disappointed. But if parents are watching this and can touch their kids, let them know that basketball is great to play—it's an enjoyment, it's fun, it's a hobby. But there's a lot to life other than sports.

—*Michael Jordan, at his retirement press conference*

Bulls' owner Jerry Reinsdorf's prefatory remarks to Jordan's statement:

I just have a few words to say, and then we'll hear from Michael.

This is a very bittersweet day. There's a certain sadness because the greatest athlete to ever play a team sport is leaving the game, but it's really for me a very, very happy day because someone I admire and respect is doing exactly what he wants to do, and I'm absolutely convinced he's doing the right thing.

About a year ago, when we were getting ready to begin training camp for the last season, Michael spoke to me about losing a little of his zest for the game, and wondering about how long he would play.

He did play and we won another championship.

Several weeks ago, at the Jordan Foundation dinner, Michael again brought the subject up and said that he was considering not playing. I asked him at the time not to make a hasty decision, to be sure he thought everything through, and when he came to that decision it would be one that he could live with and one that he was absolutely certain of.

We agreed at that time to get together in a couple of weeks. We did, last Sunday, October 3. Michael and Curtis and David Falk and I met in Washington at David's home. Michael reaffirmed his decision. I made absolutely no attempt to talk him out of him of it, because I was convinced it was the right thing for him to do. I only asked him to do

one thing, and that was not to make his decision final until he spoke to Phil Jackson and to Jerry Krause, which he did yesterday morning.

After meeting with Phil and Jerry for an hour, Michael again was convinced he did the right thing. I think all of us who know Michael are convinced that he is doing the right thing.

He's living the American dream—to reach a point in your life when you don't have to do anything you don't want to do, and everything you do want to do.

We respect his decision. We're sorry to see Michael leave, but it's really been an honor and a pleasure for me and to the people of Chicago to have had Michael here for nine years.

I can only imagine what it was like seeing Babe Ruth. This man [Jordan] used to say was the Babe Ruth of basketball. I've now come to believe Babe Ruth was the Michael Jordan of baseball.

Michael?

THANKS, JERRY.

I think everyone knows exactly what the circumstances are right now in terms of my decision not to play NBA basketball. It doesn't mean I'm not going to play basketball somewhere else, but I've talked to all my confidants, my family, my friends, and to the organization, as Jerry [Reinsdorf] has just informed you. I even talked to [NBA commissioner] David Stern as of yesterday and [also] today.

I'm very solid with my decision to not play basketball in the NBA. I've heard a lot of different speculations about my reasons for not playing, but I've always stressed to people that have known me and the media that has followed me that when I lose the sense of motivation and the sense to prove something as a basketball player, it's time for me to move away from the game.

It's not because I don't love the game—I love the game of basketball, and always will. I just feel that at this particular time in my career, I've reached the pinnacle. I've achieved a lot in that short amount of time—if you want to call it short—but I just feel that I don't have anything else to prove to myself.

I met with some of my teammates this morning, and it was very, very emotional because they've meant a lot to me, and we've shared a lot of time together over the last nine years—John Paxson I've been with the last eight years; the other guys I've spent a lot of time with for the last five years. We've achieved a lot; we've gone through a lot of stages, and my success has been as much their success. They've been a part of that, my family's been a part of that, my wife, and my father, who as everyone knows has left us.

The biggest gratification, the biggest positive thing that I can take out of my father not being here with me today is that he saw my last basketball game, and that means a lot. It was something that he, we, my family, and I have talked about for a long period of time.

He advised me, quite frankly, to retire after my first championship, but we had many discussions, and my discussion was that I still had a lot to prove as a player and wanted to win more.

At the end of the year after we won our third championship, we talked once again and I was leaning toward [retirement]. He and my family knew that. It was just a matter of waiting until this time when basketball was near to see if my heart would change.

I went through all the different stages of getting myself prepared for the next year, but the desire was not there. It wasn't like everyone had speculated about: all the different media pressure and all the different pressures that I was feeling. I deal with pressure all the time, and I've always said I would never let [the media] run me out of the game, so don't think that you've done that.

This is my choice. I've always wanted to make it my choice. It's the choice that I've chosen to live with. And certainly it doesn't go without some reservations, because I'm going to miss the game; I'm going to miss the opportunities of winning extra championships and spending more time with teammates for eight months, and going on trips and [doing] some of the things that men do in basketball. I'm going to miss it. I'm also going to miss the psychological warfare that Phil Jackson put us all through in eight months. But at some point in time you have to look at the future.

I think one thing about my father's death is that [it made me realize] it can be gone and be taken away from you at any time. And there's still a lot of things out there for me to achieve. There's a lot of family members and friends that I haven't seen, because I've been very selfish in my career to try to get to this point, and make sure that I achieved all the dreams that I wanted to achieve. Now that I'm here, it's time to be a little bit unselfish in terms of spending more time with my family, my wife, my kids, and just get back to a normal life, as close to it as I can. It's going to be tough, but I'm very happy with my decision, and I'm very glad that I'm in a position to make that choice.

A lot of times you [media] guys do all the pushing, but now I'm taking the lead and doing all the necessary steps to walk away from this game without feeling that I need to.

But I'm glad for all the fans and for the organization and for the support that they have given me and my family and for the league. I think that the league is probably the highest-rated and most-watched professional sport there is. I think that means a lot to all the guys who played in that era, especially myself.

So thank you and hopefully I won't see too many of you [media] guys in the future. You can go somewhere else and get your stories; this is probably the first time I've met this many people without a scandal around.

It's really a great feeling to hear all the thank-yous, and certainly the support of these people here from my corporations and Nike, Gatorade, and all the people I deal with. They have been very supportive of my decision, and I think that means a lot to me as a person and an an endorsee of their products. So thanks.

16.

Questions and Answers Following Jordan's Statement

Did your father's death bring about your decision?

I WOULD HAVE made it even if he had been here. It was a decision that I was contemplating when the season ended, so naturally when my father died it put a different emphasis on life in general, but it didn't alter my decision.

A lot of people doubt this team because of my retirement, but I know this team is prepared to step up and take what they want.

I told all the guys: You still have the faith, the ability to achieve what you want to achieve. You just have to believe in it. You've got to go through all the determination processes that you go through every day to step on that basketball court and feel you have something to prove.

I'm still an avid basketball fan and an avid Chicago Bulls fans. I will come to some of the practices; they haven't banned me from them like you guys, and I'm still looking forward to watching this team be successful.

That was one of the reasons I stepped away from the game, because when I stepped on the court, there wasn't anything else for me to prove. That's one of the reasons you guys have done in my private life, because you can't blame my basketball.

[On whether or not he'd stay in Chicago:]

My home is here. My wife is from Chicago. Her family is here, and my kids have only known Chicago. I've built some great roots here, and I'd like to remain here. So long as you guys stay away from my house, I'll have peace and quiet.

Will you ever un-retire?

I don't know. I think that the word "retire" means you can do anything you want from this day on, so if I desire to come back and play again, maybe that's what I want to do. Maybe that's that challenge that I may need some day down the road. I'm not going to close that door. I don't believe in "never."

Can you ever have a normal life?

I don't think I ever would have a normal life, but I think it could be reduced some because there's going to be other basketball stars; there's going to be other focuses in the game of basketball. I realize [life can never be normal for me], but if it can lessen just a little bit, it's better than what it is now. So I think it will, over a period of time. I don't have any reservations about stepping away from the spotlight.

I was watching George Brett when he was talking about his retirement, and he had one interesting scenario. He said that if you ride a roller coaster for nine years, don't you want to ride something else?

That's what I feel right now. I've been on this roller coaster for nine years, and it's just time for me to ride something else.

What about golf?

Golf is my relaxation. I haven't looked at it as a professional interest right now. My family is my interest right now. Golf is going to be very competitive for me; I think golf will sap up a lot of that competitive attitude that I had for the game of basketball.

What was the toughest decision about retiring?

The toughest decision was leaving my teammates. I really love them a lot, and told them there were a lot of times when different personalities had to clash off the court and even in the locker room, but when we stepped on the basketball court, we had the same focus and the goals in mind. That's something that I'm going to miss, but I had to do it for my own sake.

It was very tough to talk to Phil and to the organization and tell them it was time to move on.

How do you want to be remembered?

First of all, everyone wants to be remembered for the good things.

I just want to be remembered as a guy who enjoyed

the game, played it 110 percent, always had something to prove, and when that challenge was in front of me, I stepped forward and proved it. Loved the game. Totally enjoyed it. Would play the game even if I didn't get paid a dollar. That's how much I love the game.

Are you sorry you're leaving now?

No, because I never wanted to leave the game when my skills started to diminish. Because once that starts to happen, I feel the foot in my back. People pushing me out of the game, saying I don't have the skills that I have.

One thing I try to remember about my game is that I tried to maintain high consistency levels every year. I felt that when the consistency started to diminish, the foot starts pushing. And I didn't want to get to that situation. When I get to a pinnacle and I feel my skills are good and I'm not starting on the downside of the career, I want to walk away from the game.

It's been very fortunate that I'm on top and coming off three championship seasons. I'm coming off a great situation with my team, where the team members believe in themselves. A lot of [my teammates] have stepped up and gained their identities, and their own expectations for themselves.

It's the perfect time for me to walk away.

Will the game find someone to replace you?

It always will—that's just how life is. You're always going to have a better man out there somewhere. It may be one, two, three, four, five, maybe ten or twenty years down the road, but there's always a better man somewhere.

That is not one of my fears, because as long as I was playing the game, I believed in myself as a basketball player and as a person, and hopefully when that person comes along and has the impact as a Magic Johnson, Dr. J, myself, Larry Bird, Charles Barkley, he feels the same way.

But there will be another player.

Do you consider yourself the ambassador of the NBA?

A lot of people have tried to make me an ambassador of the league, but I've never accepted that role. I think a lot of players must carry that label for the NBA, so that when something like this happens, when a player reaches a point in his career when he wants to step away, there's enough players in the spotlight to carry that label. That's where I think NBA basketball is right now. You've got a lot of superstars in this league, and with myself stepping away, there's other players who carry that label.

Dr. J did it many years by himself. He carried that label for a long period of time. I don't think there will ever be a person who will want to carry that responsibility by himself.

I never wanted to do it, I don't think Larry or Magic wanted to do it, and I don't think they did.

I think basketball is here to stay. I think you've got other rising stars who can carry that label, and [the league] will be successful.

[In response to a speculation voiced by a journalist the previous night that the announcement had been timed to overshadow the White Sox game.]

I heard you last night. You took it the wrong way. I don't appreciate what you said. My whole initiative was to do it today, but it leaked out yesterday. And the reason I did it here today is because training camp starts Thursday. I wanted to get it over and done with before then, because I feel the team had to start on its own two feet and should start on the first day of training camp.

It wasn't to overshadow the White Sox. If it was, I wouldn't have went to the game. I'm here to support the White Sox; I'm not here to overshadow anyone. I'm here to say good-bye to the game, at this particular time, so the lives of my teammates and the franchise and the Chicago Bulls moves forward when the season opens.

How could you tell when your motivation had gone?

I'm in touch with my feelings about the game, about my skills to the game. I've always been in tune with what's right for me as a player and a person in these circumstances, and that's what I went with. I went with my feelings and not the circumstances surrounding it.

If I didn't have the desire to step on the basketball court and have something to prove, then I must admit that. I can't step out there and know that I'm out for no reason—it's not worth it to me, and I don't think it's worth it for my teammates. When I step out there on the basketball court, I'm out there for a reason: to prove something and help my teammates to achieve.

Will you attend some games?

I will attend some games, but I won't tell you which ones because I like to surprise the team and certainly eliminate you guys bringing more pressure to that particular game. But I am a fan and I still want to go to some of the games. I will talk to some of the players, but I won't give any coaching—that's Phil's job. But if I can be a friend to any of the players to help them through some trying times with the media, I'm willing to pass my advice to them—not to talk to you.

Do you respect the media?

I've always respected the media, and I will continue to respect *some* of you. You guys have a job, just like I have a job, and I've always respected that. Sometimes you've gotten on my nerves, and sometimes I've omitted it and sometimes I have admitted it. I've always tried to keep a good relationship with you guys. I don't think I have any bitterness toward you guys as I walk away from the game.

I'm not a hating type of person. I don't carry any grudges. When I'm walking away, I'm walking away with a clean slate. I wish you guys well in your careers as reporters, as well as my teammates and their success.

Your contract situation?

A lot of people speculated that I was leaving because I'm not getting paid the astronomical dollars that some of the other players are getting paid. I signed my contract when I signed it. You guys have known that for years. When I put my name on the dotted line, I'm not going to go back and cry about what I'm getting paid. If you deserve a raise, you would get a raise. I will not ask for any compensation because I'm walking away from the game. I didn't walk away from the game because Larry Johnson [Charlotte Hornets] got $84 million for 12 years. That's great for Larry Johnson; he had the leverage and he should do so. If anyone else comes into the league and has that kind of leverage, he should utilize it because your length of [time] prospering in your abilities in playing the game are limited, and you should take advantage of it.

I'm very happy with my financial situation, and I will not sit here and twist Mr. Reinsdorf's arm and ask him for compensation as I walk away from the game. He's been very straightforward with me, as much as I've been straightforward with him.

What was your biggest thrill?

The first title is probably the biggest thrill I had, because coming into the city of Chicago, it wasn't a bright situation and we weren't out on top; we were not even in the middle. But I've seen every stage in getting to the top. And the city has been waiting for a long period of time. All they could say was, "Wait until next year." And it gives me great gratification that during the time that I played the game of basketball in the city of Chicago, they don't have to say that anymore. They've got bragging rights all over the country.

For many years it's been known as a gangster town. Now it can be known as a championship town. And hopefully the White Sox can carry that on, as well as other sports, but that's the fondest memory I can have about the city of Chicago and its sports programs.

[Responding to a question about him and Magic Johnson, and the sense of competition:]

Magic's got a whole different agenda than I do. He still loves the game and wants to play competitively— I don't. I want to play leisurely, and I want to play with smaller companies than he's doing right now. I support Magic Johnson, but I want to do other things than play basketball in an exhibition situation.

Would you play for another NBA team?

No way. My heart has been here. I can't even think of playing for another team. That's not even a train of thought.

Olympic participation in the future?

My Olympic days are over and done with. It was great. I think every athlete in college or in the NBA who never really had an opportunity to represent his country should do that. It's the greatest feeling you can ever go through.

Anybody try to talk you out of retirement?

A lot of people have. And I needed that side of the coin to make a good picture of what my decision was going to be. But once I made a decision, everyone supported it because they understood it from my point of view.

Out of 100 percent, 95 percent supported me; the other 5 percent wanted to see me play. It wasn't selfishness; they felt that I had a gift that would be missed. That's the highest compliment I could take under the circumstances, but I had to make a decision for myself and for what I wanted to achieve.

Will you play basketball again?

No—if so, I would still be playing.

I looked at basketball and talked to Phil, and asked him frankly, "Is there anything for me to prove as a basketball player?" He stopped for a second, and that's all I needed, because if there was, he would have told me real quickly. That's the way I left it. There wasn't anything for me to prove as a player.

When I walked away from the game, I knew a lot of people, especially the kids, would be disappointed. But if parents are watching this and can touch their kids, let them know that basketball is great to play—it's an enjoyment, it's fun, it's a hobby. But there's a lot to life other than sports.

Yet my life goes on and I'm still in love with the game, but at some point in time someone has to make a decision to move forward and away from the game—either your choice or someone else's choice.

I've been fortunate in that I was able to make that choice, instead of one of you guys pushing me out and saying I'm old, and it's time to move on.

I know the kids will be disappointed, but hopefully they'll learn that Michael Jordan was once a basketball player, but now he's a human being, he's a man, he must continue, he has a family, he's got other things he must achieve.

What will you do now?

In retirement, you do whatever comes to mind. Relax. Enjoy the time you've been deprived of for many years. I still have opportunities to get with my companies and do endorsements, and that's what I'll do when that time hits me. But up until that point, I'm going to watch the grass grow, and I gotta go cut it.

I'm capable of relaxing. I've been relaxing for the last couple months, so I am capable of hiding from you guys and doing what I want.

Will you miss the sport?

I'm pretty sure I'll miss the sport. To come back is a different thought—I can't answer that. I'm not making this a "never" issue. I'm saying right now I don't have the mental drive to come out and push myself to play with a certain focus. Five years down the line, if the urge comes back, if the Bulls will have me, if David Stern lets me back in the league, I may come back.

Your special contribution?

My special contribution was the Tongue. You never saw anything like it, and you won't ever see anything maybe not like it again.

It is a magnificent thing, his rise, as articulate a refutation of the forces that hold humankind earthbound as the drawings of Leonardo or the joyous music of Louis Armstrong. His legs start to churn in midair, mocking gravity, and he begins, at his apex, to climb even higher; he begins to fly. Jordan made this move scores of times; television multiplied it a hundredfold. And each time he went up he held out the hope that this time—for the sake of all who believed themselves slaves to gravity—he would never come down. . . . Suspended in air, he reshaped his sweat and sinew into a work of art, a metaphor for the limitlessness of human potential.

—*John Leland, introduction to* Newsweek *Special Issue (October/November 1993)*

17.

Reactions to Jordan's Retirement

As the Chicago Tribune *explained in a piece covering worldwide reaction to Jordan's sudden retirement announcement, "The world press reaction . . . was among the best measures of his magnitude."*

If Jordan were simply just another basketball player retiring, it would have been—at best—a minor mention on sports channels like ESPN and on CNN, some coverage in local media, and the subject of articles for sports magazines. Instead, Jordan, a worldwide phenomenon, made the network and local news nationwide, took the front page story on virtually every newspaper in the country, and outside the United States commanded international attention.

In France, Jordan was worth the first three pages of a sports daily. In Argentina, Jordan's coverage matched that of the return of a national soccer hero. In Kenya, it was the lead story. In China, where according to recent polls he's a favorite, the Beijing Daily *covered Jordan's announcement. In Spain and Germany, Jordan got three pages in the sports section. In Japan, network TV, in lieu of its first scheduled broadcast of an NBA game, aired instead a retrospective on Michael Jordan.*

Sports and the Corporate World

Bob Weiss (L.A. Clippers coach): "The first word that comes to mind is shock. . . . I am disappointed for him as an individual to cut his career short. It is also disappointing as a member of the NBA because Michael has brought so much to the game. It's pretty much the same feeling you had when Magic and Bird retired. These guys are in a class of their own."

Charles Barkley (Phoenix Suns star, 1992–93 MVP): "One thing that was weird about Michael is that whenever we're together, we're in a hotel room because he doesn't ever go out. So I don't ever want to be in that predicament—where I can't go out and do anything. . . . Michael Jordan is the only person in this entire world that I've ever met who is as competitive as I am."

Charles Grantham (NBA Players Association executive director): "He's set a standard by which to play and retire. Michael is a unique talent and person not to be replaced."

David Falk (Jordan's agent/lawyer, ProServ): "Michael is a well-rounded individual. There's a lot more to Michael Jordan than just being a great basketball player. And I think his sense of mortality, after his father's death, made him realize he ought to enjoy some of those things while he's still a young man."

David Stern (NBA commissioner): "Michael Jordan is somebody who we had that when he stepped on the court, there was an air of electricity that was something special. . . . You don't replace somebody like Michael Jordan or Babe Ruth. . . . (But) we'll play the season."

Dean Smith (UNC basketball coach): "A great period in basketball history has ended with Michael's retirement. What a tremendous nine-year run he's had in the NBA. I personally think it's a good decision, based on all he must go through and to certainly go out on top after three world championships. He seems comfortable with his decision and that's extremely important."

Doug Collins (former Bulls coach): "He's changed how basketball is played."

Gerald Wilkins (Cleveland Cavaliers): "He will stick in the minds of everyone who played the game, watched the game, and enjoyed the game."

Jerome Bureau (editor, *L'Equipe*, sports daily in France): "He was more than the world's greatest player, he was like a mythical hero. He alone made the sport popular throughout the world, and I can't see anybody replacing him."

Jerry Reinsdorf (Bulls owner): "As a sports fan I feel deprived. I wish that I had known I was watching Michael's last game. I think I would have viewed it a little differently. But when you think about it, it's greedy to feel deprived. We've had nine years of the greatest man that ever played. He's an incredible human being, an incredible athlete. But we'll always have the memories. We should feel lucky that he passed through here."

Jerry West (L.A. Lakers general manager): "I think Michael became a victim of his own success."

Joe Montana (quarterback, Kansas City Chiefs): "I'm as shocked as anyone else. I can understand where he was coming from. It gets wearing on you. There are always eyes on him. I understand that. . . . He just hit the wall where it got too overpowering."

John Paxson (teammate): "Michael's not the type of guy to rush into a decision like this. The best part about it is he's happy. We have no right to feel any other way."

Kevin McHale (former Boston Celtic): "They said football would never be the same when Jim Brown retired in his prime. It goes on. I mean, I can guarantee you people . . . in five years people will be saying, 'Michael who?' And that's the way it is in this league. Someone's going to come out—maybe it's Shaquille— someone's going to come out and dominate. The names on the back of the jerseys change; the league just keeps rolling on."

Larry Bird (former Boston Celtics star): "No one was ever better than him. He was a true joy to watch on the court."

Magic Johnson (former L.A. Lakers star): "I think that Michael probably just wants to be left alone now. He is tired of being under the microscope and just needs a little time off to be with his family. He's got so much, it weighed him down, and he just got tired. He probably will come back in one year to show everyone he's still the king. It's a big, big loss. No one else was that type of player and has that kind of flair. Michael is different from the other players. Larry Bird and myself were different. I've always been in awe of his talent on the court, and I'm even more in awe of him as a man off the court."

Mark Eaton (center, Utah Jazz): "I think that given the circumstances surrounding his recent family death

and everything else that's gone on in his life the past year, it's certainly understandable. He has the chance to go out on top. I don't think there's anyone who doubts he's the greatest basketball player of all time. With three straight championships, it will be a very long time before anyone approaches that."

Philip Knight (Nike CEO): "Michael Jordan did not retire from Nike today. Our nine-year creative collaboration has always been more than an endorsement deal. It is a partnership that will continue, and we have already discussed future plans.

"What has set the Air Jordan line apart is Michael's personal input into design and development. Who better than the world's greatest basketball player to collaborate on the development of the world's greatest basketball shoes."

Scottie Pippen (teammate): "It's a tough situation for us and a tough situation for the organization, but life goes on and we realize that. We learned how to walk with Michael. Now is the time for us to walk on our own. . . . He left as the greatest player. If he came back in five years, he would still be the greatest player."

Shaquille O'Neal (Orlando Magic star): "I can remember a time when I was watching him on TV, and then to be on the same court as him was a great feeling. He's great. All the things you see him do on TV, jumping on one side of the lane, ending up on the other side of the lane, it's for real. He's the best in the world and I'm gonna miss him."

Stefan Ostrowski (French basketball player who guarded Jordan during pre-Olympic scrimmages): "He was only thirty, which is very young to leave the game. I guess the NBA schedule is very hard both mentally and physically. We are all very sad to see him go, because kids everywhere would identify with him and try to copy his game."

William D. Smithburg (Chairman and CEO of the Quaker Oats Company, which produces Gatorade, a product Jordan endorses): "Like all fans who have been awed by Michael Jordan's amazing talent on the basketball court, we are sorry to see one of the greatest playing careers in any sport come to an end. We respect Michael's decision; we understand the personal reasons behind it, and we support his determination to retire from basketball at the very top. Michael's unparalleled drive for excellence would allow for nothing less.

"Michael will continue to serve as a spokesperson for Gatorade. His greatness transcends the sport of basketball, and his retirement in no way diminishes his value to Gatorade and Quaker Oats.

"We wish Michael and his family all the best, and we look forward to continuing our business relationship and friendship."

Youngsters Are Understanding of Basketball Hero's Decision

by Lisa Leff and Debbi Wilgoren

Role models operate on more than one level. Parents and teachers are the guiding lights for everyday reality. Star athletes and other celebrities—the Muhammad Alis and Babe Ruths, the Jordans and Larry Birds—are the models in idle fantasy. They represent an impossible dream, perhaps, but something to grow on.
—David Gelman, "When a Role Model Quits," Newsweek *Special Issue (October/November 1993)*

The day after Jordan's retirement announcement, the media—taking one last shot—debated his departure, pro and con. Because Jordan transcended the sport he played in, becoming one of the most recognizable celebrities in our time, he has an international appeal; he belongs not only to the United States, but to the international community, whose media made it clear that with Jordan's retirement, they felt as if they had lost one of their own.

The children, though, will miss Jordan the most. Clearly his largest audience, the kids were the ones that saw in him the pure and the beautiful—a contrast to the many journalists who treated Jordan as a meal ticket, good for another quote, another column, another story, just another public commodity to be traded in print or on the air.

In this piece from the Washington Post, *two reporters went out and covered the retirement from his fans who, literally and figuratively, looked up to him.*

THE WORLD's biggest basketball star found a sympathetic audience in his littlest fans yesterday. Although area children were saddened to hear about their athletic idol's retirement, Michael Jordan's reasons generally made it all right.

Just as the 30-year-old Jordan always had inspired young people to emulate his life on and off the court, his decision to leave the game he loved made it easy to imagine the pain of a son whose beloved father was slain, the weariness of a hero who had nothing left to prove.

"You have to understand," said Kerbi Ware, 10, a fifth grader at Saratoga Elementary School in Fairfax, where Jordan's news was the talk of the schoolyard. "His dad died, and you have to understand."

"I can see it," agreed Christopher Jordan, 15, of Palmer Park, a Chicago Bulls fan ever since the team acquired the dazzling player who shares his last name. "My uncle just passed in '92, and after he died, I didn't want to go to school anymore."

As much as any other public figure, Michael Jordan appealed to children, making his exit from basketball at least as stunning to them as Michael Jackson's recent legal troubles. His popularity was easy to gauge: On the playground at Kenmoor Middle School in Landover, all the seventh graders who were asked said that they owned at least one article of clothing with Jordan's name, face, or soaring silhouette printed on it. Outside a Fairfax school, children took turns singing jingles from his many television commercials.

"His dunks and his free throws," said Darius Porter, 8, a third grader at Matthe Henson Elementary School in Palmer Park, attempting to explain why he always pretends to be Jordan when playing ball with his friends. In other words, youngsters appreciate someone who is simply the best at what he or she does, and does it with style.

Jordan's popularity with children in the Washington area was especially evident at Chicago Bulls–Washington Bullets games, where hundreds of children came dressed in Bulls and Jordan jerseys, pants, and caps, and screamed their approval every time Jordan scored.

"I like the Bulls and I like Michael," said Ebony Malloy, 12, who was watching several boys playing football at Shaw Junior High School in the district. "I like the way he does jump shots. I try to play like him."

Taking a break from his daily pickup game at Shaw, Charles Allen, 16, said he did not try to play like his idol, but rather tried to model Jordan's ability to lead his team, to come from behind and to win.

"I learned from him that anything you can put your mind to, you can do," he said, wearing a faded Bulls T-shirt.

"I think Michael Jordan was a great person because besides being a great player, he also did a lot for children," donating time and money to charitable causes aimed at youths, said Andre Gerald, 12, a Kenmoor student. "I'm with him all the way."

But there were some grumblings of discontent from youngsters who thought Jordan was too young to retire, even at the ripe old age of 30.

"I think it's slum," Christopher Jordan said. "He should have went on with his career until he felt he couldn't play anymore. He is so talented, and he is letting it go to waste."

At Robert E. Lee High School in Springfield, 10th graders Chavaughn Jones and Falecia Yosufy said Jordan was letting down his team as well as himself. "He's young, his team needs him. He could at least go another year," said Chavaughn, 14.

Falecia, 15, said she doubted the retirement would last.

"I think he just needs a break, then I think he'll come back," she said.

Despite the sensation his retirement announcement was causing, managers at several sporting goods stores in Springfield Mall said an expected flurry of Jordan purchases had not materialized by late afternoon.

"Not one person. Not a phone call. Nothing so far," said Cindy Coleman, assistant manager of Herman's World of Sporting Goods. The chain, which has 14 stores in the Washington area, plans to make a special display of Jordan T-shirts, tank tops, autographed basketballs, and high-tech sneakers at the front of each store.

Manager Muhammad Aziz said prices would remain the same: $19.99 for a basketball, $30 to $40 for a T-shirt, and about $130 for top-of-the-line sneakers.

Even if the superstar does stay on the sidelines, youngsters interviewed yesterday said he will remain one of their favorites. Most thought he would continue to be as popular as he is today, noting that his legend would live on through video games based on his basketball prowess.

"People will still like Mike. They'll still be fans of him," said Matthew Banuelos, 11, of Springfield. "He influenced a lot of people to play basketball. He'll still be considered a basketball player."

But Albert Smith, 13, an eighth grader at Kenmoor, made it clear he would not be mourning over his six Michael Jordan trading cards for long.

"I was shocked at first and then again I was like, that's all right, because my team is the Charlotte Hornets. They haven't made it to the championships yet," he said.

Hometown Reactions
by E.L. Rogers (1993)

In this piece that appeared in a special Jordan supplement published on October 7, 1993, in his hometown newspaper, the Wilmington Morning Star *(Wilmington, North Carolina), the reactions were mixed, but as in Chicago—and everywhere else—everyone wished him well.*

MICHAEL JORDAN's face filled the big-screen television at the Philly Deli as lunch customers walked in. Basketball's best player was still explaining why he was leaving the pro game at the height of his career.

"It's so sad," said a woman as she stopped on the way to her seat. "I think I'm going to cry."

For the rest of the world, Mr. Jordan's retirement means the end of a pro basketball era. For Wilmington, it means a hometown hero whom many remember growing up in gyms around the county has quit while at the top of his game.

Mr. Jordan retired Wednesday after nine years with the NBA's Chicago Bulls. His team won championships the last three years and Mr. Jordan has won three MVP awards and seven scoring titles. He has played on two Olympic gold medal teams and he won a national championship in college at North Carolina.

But in recent years, Mr. Jordan had become so famous that he had almost no private life. He was also hounded by allegations of gambling and, worst of all, his father was murdered in July.

He said that he didn't have anything left to prove in basketball, and those watching his press conference agreed. But his decision still came as a surprise.

"I don't blame him," said Danny Naylor, who was watching at Philly Deli. "He's 30 years old, a multimillionaire, and he owns several businesses. I'd go for that, too. There's not a lot more for him to accomplish in that game anymore."

Josephine Woodruff and her husband, John, of Wrightsville Beach, stood and stared several minutes as Mr. Jordan fended off questions during the press conference.

"I feel like he's a fine example, an outstanding athlete and a leader," Mrs. Woodruff said. "I feel he wanted to go out at the height of his career, which I feel he did. I wish him the best."

At Laney High School, where Mr. Jordan played from 1978 through 1981, teachers and coaches were disappointed—not in Mr. Jordan's decision, but because they will not be able to watch him play.

"I really was surprised that Michael gave it up because I thought he would play at least two or three more years," said his former coach, Clifton "Pop" Herring, who was visiting Laney on Wednesday. "I mean, he isn't that old. He's 30."

Fred Lynch, Laney's current head coach, was an assistant when Mr. Jordan was at Laney. He said he had a hard time believing the story at first.

"Michael had talked about retiring before, but I did not take him seriously in the past," Mr. Lynch said. "Even when I heard the announcement that Michael was thinking about retiring, I just thought, 'Oh, it's just another rumor.'

"But then when he held the press conference, I knew it must have been the real thing this time."

Teachers and administrators had mixed reactions at Laney. Some scratched their heads, wondering why the decision came now.

"I was surprised that he retired," math teacher Carolyn Varner said. "I thought he would play for at least maybe three or four more years."

Ms. Varner said she wasn't sure the death of James Jordan didn't have something to do with his son's decision.

"I don't know if I buy into that," she said. "I think his father's death may have had something to do with it, because his father was a big part of his life."

Laney assistant principal Dave Berenson agreed that the elder Jordan's death played a role.

"I simply think Michael moved to a different level of adulthood when he lost his father," he said. "When the older generation passes and then you become that generation, then you start to wonder what you can do to leave your legacy. I think Michael realized that, and now he's looking at what he can do with his life from this moment onward."

Mr. Jordan's former coaches recalled two of his qualities that might indicate a return to basketball. Mr. Herring cited his love of the game.

"When I was working as the school's baseball coach I can remember calling Michael, telling him that we needed to practice and for him to come out from the gym shooting ball," he said. "But it was so hard to get him out of the gym, even though you knew he loved baseball, too."

Mr. Lynch recalled Mr. Jordan's competitive nature, citing pickup games from Mr. Jordan's high school days. A group of teachers would always beat the students, and Mr. Jordan did not like it a bit.

"Man, Michael would get so mad when we would beat them," Mr. Lynch said. "Michael was and still is a sore loser. He just doesn't like to lose because he was just so competitive."

Mr. Lynch said his biggest reaction from students was "Hey, why would Michael want to give up all that money?"

And Mr. Lynch's response?

"I told these students that they just don't understand," he said. "Michael saw the opportunity to spend more time with his family and to be himself. Of course, he'll never have a normal lifestyle because he's Michael Jordan. Even now, he still won't be able to go to a movie or go out to get something to eat without getting so much attention.

"But I think eventually, after six years or so, all of the attention that Michael's getting will wane. Some new stars will come up and will start getting all the attention."

But not everyone believes Mr. Jordan will sit out that long.

"He'll be back. I hate to see him retire, but I think he'll be back," Laney maintenance worker Walter Graham said. "Hey, there's not any more Michael Jordans out there in the NBA right now. He will be back."

Chicago Newspapers' Reactions

When rookie Michael Jordan came to town in 1984, the Bulls' PR department took the opportunity to promote their team as never before. "A Whole New Breed" of Bulls, they called themselves, as their newspaper ads proudly proclaimed, "Here comes Mr. Jordan."

Somewhat embarrassed by all the publicity, Jordan focused on what was important: trying to be part of the team, working toward an NBA championship. It took them seven years, but after that, the Bulls did it a second, and then a third time. The Bulls had finally become—as they had prophetically announced—a whole new breed.

When the running of the Bulls stopped, it was as if the city of Chicago held its collective breath, wondering if what they heard was true, that Jordan was finally leaving the game that helped define the city.

The day of Jordan's retirement press conference, all local programming went live, covering the most newsworthy event in sports—the American League playoffs between the Chicago White Sox and the Toronto Blue Jays took a backseat.

The day after the press conference, the two local papers— rivals on the order of the Bulls against the Knicks—pulled out all the stops to reflect on just how much Jordan meant to the city.

The 20-page "late sports final" of the Chicago Sun-Times *had a full-page color photo of Michael Jordan smiling broadly at the press conference. The legend underneath, which said it all, simply read: "Thanks."*

IN THE CHICAGO Sun-Times, the Jordan coverage included:

- "Is It Retirement, Or Just Vacation?" a column by Jay Mariotti in which he speculated about Jordan's possible return. "You can't convince me we've seen the last of Michael Miracle," he wrote.
- "Jordan Retires As Game's Best" by staff writer Mike Mulligan highlighted the fact that Jordan, unlike some other athletes in the prime of their careers, "left basketball Wednesday the way he always said he would—at the top of his game, on his own terms, in his own time."
- "Jordan Leaves Door Ajar for Comeback" by staff writer J.A. Adande speculated on Jordan's possible return. "Superman might have put his cape in mothballs, but he didn't say he wouldn't wear it again," wrote Adande.
- "Timeout Call Sets Up New Game: Retirement" by staff writer Lacy J. Banks focused on what lay ahead—retirement, Jordan's new challenge.
- "League Probe to Continue" by Chris D. Amico, a small piece on Jordan's gambling allegations, briefly mentioned "unfinished business," which was resolved to commissioner David Stern's satisfaction shortly thereafter.
- "Nothing Hasty About This Decision" by J.A. Adande stated that Jordan's decision wasn't spur-of-the-moment, pointing out that on September 18, at a dinner for the Michael Jordan Foundation, Jordan brought up the subject to Bulls owner Jerry Reinsdorf, who cautioned him, "not to make a hasty decision, to be sure that he thought everything through, and that when he came to that decision, it would be one he could live with and one he was absolutely certain of."
- "Pippen Is The New Main Man: 'Saddened' Sidekick to Step Up" by staff writer Mike Mulligan pointed out that Pippen, though surprised at Jordan's announcement, realized his new role: "It's something I felt would come someday; I was just hoping it wouldn't come until I turned 30. I hope the fans stay behind us and stay supportive. It's going to be a long, tough season for us."
- "Reinsdorf, Teammates Are Happy for Jordan" by staff writer Mike Mulligan focused on the bittersweet memories of those in the Bulls franchise, realizing

that only by retiring could Jordan find peace within himself. As Paxson said, "I'm happy for him. He's able to walk away from the game on his own terms. I feel fortunate to have been his teammate. I can't imagine anyone before him and anybody after him that is such a competitor."

- "NBA Left Without a Leader" by J.A. Adande pointed out that the face of the NBA had changed permanently: "No Magic, no Bird, no Jordan. It's a bit like Hollywood with no Nicholson, no Schwarzenegger, no Cruise. In the last three years, the NBA has lost enough superstars to fill a separate wing of the Hall of Fame."
- "Bulls Will Try to Look Four-ward" by Mike Mulligan points out the obvious, that without Jordan, the prospects of a "Four-peat" look dim indeed: "Nobody really thinks the Bulls can win a fourth straight NBA title without the greatest basketball player in history." But they would give it the old college try, especially with newcomer Toni Kukoc recently on board.
- "Players on the Spot to Fill Roster Spot" by Lacy J. Banks explains how Jordan's absence will open up new positions on the team.
- "Jordan's Absence Will Provide True Lesson in Appreciation" by Lacy J. Banks in his column, "The NBA," points out the obvious: That with Jordan gone, "it's reality-check time. Let's see how his absence will affect . . . how well the Bulls draw at home, where they have had 294 consecutive sellouts, and on the road, where they have led the league four seasons in a row. How many games the Bulls will win. The ratings for televised Bulls games. The league's overall attendance figures, which have grown nine consecutive seasons."
- "Questioning a Legend" reprinted the text of Jordan's retirement statement, with selected quotes from the question-and-answer session that immediately followed. (The story photo showed Jordan, flanked by his professional associates, surrounded by hundreds of journalists as he fielded their questions.)
- "The Best There Ever Was" by Dan Bickley took a retrospective look at his career and life, where "he had escaped the concrete chaos of Brooklyn when he was just a baby" to "a man—not a player—of his determination . . . going out on top after starting at the bottom. And for Michael Jordan, there could be no other way."
- "A Lukewarm Endorsement" by Greg Burns pointed out the pitfalls of retirement on commercial endorsements. As Nike pointed out, "There's still plenty of

air in Air Jordan. It increases our ability to use Michael," said a spokesperson.

- "Nowhere for Bulls, NBA to Go but Down" by Frederick H. Lowe takes the pessimistic—some would say realistic—perspective that "Jordan's sudden departure is expected to slow the bull market for the Bulls and the NBA, financial experts said. . . ."
- "Thanks for the Memories," staff-written, provided the statistics, the 10 top "Kodak" moments by Dan Bickley, and career highlights, point by point.
- "Jordan Feeds Media Dose of Own Medicine" by Dave Hoeskstra pointed out Jordan's thinly veiled pique at the media, summarized by his statement, "Hopefully, I won't see too many of you guys in the future." No love lost.
- "MJ's Legend is World Class" by Chris D' Amico covered the international reaction to Jordan's retirement—a slam-dunk experienced around the sports world.
- "Live Coverage Blankets MJ's Big Announcement" by Dan Cahill, in his column on radio/TV sports, pointed out the scope of the coverage, preempting local channels, supplemented by Fox 32, Sports-Channel, ESPN, ESPN 2, CNN, and CNBC. In addition, "All the major radio stations aired the announcement live and the sports talk shows were filled with commentary on Jordan."
- The special sports supplement concluded with pieces from the trivial to the significant: ticket sellers angry at their devalued Bulls tickets; skyboxes for the new Bulls stadium dropping in value; students reacting to Jordan's announcement; local civic figures responding (the mayor, the governor of Illinois, a senator, and an attorney general), as well as the president of the United States; Jordan's wife Juanita's thoughts on the private life to come, as they build their new 29,000-square-foot home; speculations on Jordan's golf plans—going pro?; Jordan's fundraising efforts on behalf of the Chicago opera; and the revised odds on the Bulls' chances of winning a fourth title.

The *Chicago Tribune* gave it front-page coverage, sharing space with the major national news, "2,000 more GIs planned for Somalia." The cover story on Jordan simply stated the obvious: "So long, Michael; it's been great."

- Sports columnist Bernie Lincicome, in "Jordan's exit leaves a void in city's life," pointed out Jordan's departure created "the huge hole that had just been left in their sport, in their franchise, and in the heart of the town where they still would have to do business."

- In "Gloom in the Cathedral of the Sneaker," Charles M. Madigan covered the reaction at Nike Town, the shoe/clothing apparel emporium where Jordan looms larger than life.
- Columnist Mike Royko, in "Jordan leaves city full-court depressed," recaps a conversation with "Slats Grobnik," in which their talk of Jordan's departure depresses them both, when they realize just how much he meant to the city.
- In "Area's economy could take a hit without Jordan," by Ronald E. Yates and Nancy Ryan, dollar figures show that Jordan added a lot to the city, and that his departure would cost the city plenty in lost revenue. As the economist for the Chicagoland Chamber of Commerce pointed out, Jordan is "the $1 billion man. That's what we estimate his worth is to the Chicagoland economy: $1 billion."
- The lead editorial, "Michael Jordan takes flight," puts Jordan in perspective to the city itself, and other leading Chicago sports figures.
- In "A legend leaves, a thought lingers," columnist Eric Zorn highlighted the fact that Jordan left with an uncommon grace: "It is much more in our tradition for luminaries to linger on the national page until the hook starts to emerge from the wings than it is for them to leave, as Jordan has left, with the crowds still desperate for more."
- "For many, Bulls' no. 23 will always be simply no. 1," by Steve Johnson and Lou Carlozo, compared him to Superman, quoting the character Lois Lane from the storyline, "World Without a Superman," "Damn it! Somebody's got to do something! We owe the man more than this!"
- In the business section, columnist George Lazarus explained that Jordan's retirement doesn't mean he's leaving the commercial scene. As the piece's title pointed out, "Michael the endorser 'won't disappear.'" In another piece, by J. Linn Allen, the linkage between Nike and Jordan was highlighted.

In the sports section, where Jordan ruled, the coverage went into detail on Jordan's life and career:

- Melissa Isaacson wrote about Jordan's timing—leaving at the top of his game, in "Jordan says goodbye to NBA on his terms."
- Sam Smith, the paper's pro basketball writer who in 1992 published the controversial book *The Jordan Rules*, highlighted the shift of burden and responsibility for carrying the team from Jordan to Pippen, in "Changes not certain, but Pippen burden is." Columnist Berni Lincicome took Jordan to task for

taking the media to task at the press conference, in "Jordan's caustic farewell far from his finest hour." Smith also pointed out that there were no regrets, no reason for tears in Jordan's departure, in "Instead of tearful farewell, there's just relief for Jordan."

- Terry Armour wrote about the aftershock to come, in "After shock, Bulls must learn to adjust."
- Ed Sherman, in "Scrutiny too much for Jordan?" speculated about whether or not the intense media coverage over the years took its toll on the superstar. Sherman also wrote a piece discussing the devaluation of Bulls ticket values in "Bulls may not be a hot ticket anymore."

- Steve Nidetz, in "TV digs in for life after Jordan," pointed out the possible ratings impact Jordan's absence will create for Bulls games.
- And, finally, saying it all, saying everything that needed to be said, Jordan's statement was reprinted in full.

The back page of the sports section excerpted Jordan's comments from the question-and-answer session that followed the announcement itself, and had another piece by Sam Smith, "Bulls' NBA heirs apparent line up," and another piece by Melissa Isaacson, "His 'perfect' place to depart is on top."

18.

Life after the NBA

I'm quite sure they don't know just how different our lives are, and how it impacts our wives and children. I don't know how much longer I'll play, so I thought this was the perfect time in my career to give people an inside look at my life.

—*Michael Jordan, on his fans, talking about his book,* Rare Air: Michael on Michael

JORDAN, CITING Julius Erving, knew that one day he would have to retire his jersey, and planned to do so with dignity, as he told *Playboy*:

> Julius Erving is doing exactly what I want to do. Do you ever see Julius? Do you ever hear from Julius? But I know Julius is doing something he wants to do, and he's kind of taken a step back from public life. That's exactly what I want to do. When his time was up and he walked away from the game, he walked away proud, respected. Exactly what I want to do. When I feel that I've reached my peak and I can feel my skills diminishing, or if other players that I used to dominate have caught up with me and are on the same level, I want to step away.

It's never been the money, Jordan insists, as he told *Playboy*. The commercial endorsements from Nike alone have made him a wealthy man. More important, as Jordan said in an interview, ". . . If I don't love the game, no check is going to keep me playing."

What, then, will life be like for Jordan now that he's retired? My guess is that his life will continue just as it has, with the exception that playing professional basketball will be behind him permanently. He'll have the time to spend with his family—time that, as a professional basketball player, he couldn't always give, as he necessarily focused on the preseason, the regular season, and the postseason. He'll devote more time to charitable causes, especially his own foundation, which was specifically set up to help children. He'll no doubt find a lot more time to play golf—his favorite pastime—and improve his game. He'll probably be more active with his basketball camp at Elmhurst College. And he'll likely be involved in business ventures, since they present the kind of challenges that would keep his mind occupied and focused on new goals.

Dispelling rumors on "The Oprah Winfrey Show" that aired October 29, 1993, Jordan told Winfrey that, no, he wasn't going to play pro ball, pro golf, play basketball in a league overseas, or buy a basketball team with Nike—all rumors that originated outside of him; Jordan also made it a point to say that he wouldn't be coming back to the game, at least for the moment. (My private opinion is that Jordan won't be playing NBA ball again; that is behind him, and Jordan's not the kind of person who goes back to the past.)

All of his life, Jordan has had to prove himself—first, to himself, then to the coaches and teammates, then to the media, and then to the world at large. In many ways, he was the little engine that could—an engine that grew big enough, and strong enough, to carry the whole train. The skinny kid who got cut from the high school varsity basketball team rebounded with a vengeance: To Jordan, respect is everything; and you don't get it unless you are the *best*—a point not lost on Jordan, who early in his career, despite his individual excellence, was not considered to be in the same league as his contemporaries like Larry Bird and Magic Johnson because, unlike them, he had not led his team to an NBA championship.

These days, Jordan doesn't have to prove anything to anyone. By any benchmark in professional basketball, Jordan is—indisputably—the best player in the world. (Many will argue that he's the best, period, as *Sports Illustrated* contended in its special Michael Jordan issue published in December 1991, when it named him Sportsman of the Year.)

While all of these professional accomplishments do

not go unnoticed by Jordan himself, he is perhaps most proud of one thing: He challenged *himself* and became the best; and out of that comes self-respect, earned only through years of discipline, dedication, hard work, and focus that literally put him above the rim in terms of playing basketball.

In a league of his own, Jordan stands alone. And these days, *everyone* respects *Mr.* Michael Jordan. He's made it the old-fashioned way: He *earned* it.

Now that Jordan has played his last game, his record stands, a high-water mark for the next superstar to come along and break, if he can. Whether or not that happens is moot, and ultimately not important. What's important, though, is that all over the world, there will be kids lacing up their sneakers, determined to be like Mike, to simply be the best. And among them, there may be someone with the grit to say, "I can do it—I *can,*" and starting from a backyard basketball court, learning how to dribble, shoot, pass, defend, and dunk, begin the long road that might lead to the NBA and the attendant fame. Jordan's legacy is what will be left behind, inspiring and teaching and molding kids today, some of whom will surely go on to play professional sports, but most of whom will go on to assume their adult roles in life outside of professional sports. Even then, the lessons won't be lost; they apply in life, too.

That, I think, is the best thing Jordan has given us—to remind us that, always, you must have the capacity to imagine, to dream, to reach beyond your grasp.

And that, I think, is Michael Jordan's most glorious slam-dunk of *all* time.

• *In a story published on November 8, 1993, in* USA Today, *David DuPree wrote: "Michael Jordan returned to Chicago Stadium [November 6] to receive his NBA championship ring and help his former teammates hoist their third banner.*

"Jordan thanked the sellout crowd for their support and 'for the opportunity to represent you guys for nine years.' In a tearful farewell to tumultuous roars, Jordan pledged his support to the Bulls. 'Deep in my heart, I will always be a Chicago Bulls fan and support them to the fullest,' he said."

On February 7, 1994, Jordan signed a contract with the White Sox to play baseball. Jordan currently plays for the Class AA Birmingham Barons. Questioned by the media about his decision, Jordan commented: "Retirement is a state of life where you get to choose whatever you want to do. I decided to try to play baseball."

We will miss him—here and all around America, in every small town backyard and paved city lots where kids play one-on-one and dream of being like Mike. . . . I want to wish Michael and his family the very best. I know that the past several months have been difficult ones and I hope that he can enjoy the peace of mind that he richly deserves.

—President Clinton, October 1993

Michael Jordan gives his putt the eagle eye. (Photo courtesy of the *Durham Herald-Sun*.)

Nike's Jumpman logo appropriately positioned against the background of the sky—"Air" Jordan. This work is on display at the superstore Nike Town in Chicago, Illinois.

Tar Heel Michael Jordan takes to the air for another two-pointer.
(Photo by Tony Tomsic, courtesy of *Sports Illustrated*.)

Michael Jordan outlined by the city of Chicago.
(Photo by Buck Miller, courtesy of *Sports Illustrated*.)

Jordan on court, in profile.
(Photo by Brian Drake, courtesy of *Sports Illustrated*.)

Rising to the challenge, Michael Jordan goes up for another two-pointer as the defenders watch in vain. (Photo by Manny Millan, courtesy of *Sports Illustrated*.)

"Air" Jordan in flight, slamming another jam. (Photo
by John McDonough, courtesy of *Sports Illustrated*.)

Michael Jordan jams another one home during the 1993 NBA Playoffs against
the Phoenix Suns. (Photo by Manny Millan, courtesy of *Sports Illustrated*.)

At the 1993 All-Star Game, Michael Jordan drives past Dan Majerle
(Phoenix Suns) playing for the West. (Photo by Manny Millan, courtesy of
Sports Illustrated.)

Michael Jordan guards Magic Johnson of the L.A. Lakers.
(Photo by John McDonough, courtesy of *Sports Illustrated*.)

In a charity baseball game in Chicago, Illinois, Michael Jordan—wearing an Upper Deck arm patch—shows that he's equally at home on a baseball diamond as he is on the basketball court. (Photo by Chuck Solomon, courtesy of *Sports Illustrated*.)

A model of "Air" Jordan in flight, ready to jam the basketball through Bugs Bunny's arms and the net. This model is on exhibit at the superstore Nike Town in Chicago, Illinois.

Bugs Bunny's oversize "Hare" Jordan basketball shoe, complete with stitched symbol of Bugs on the side, dwarfs the normal-sized "Air" Jordan basketball shoe with Jumpman logo. The shoes are on display at the superstore Nike Town in Chicago, Illinois.

One of 200 cels used in the production of "Dream Team Barcelona," a Nike ad that ran during the 1992 summer Olympics. Distributed by Name That Toon, this particular cel, valued at $7,000+, is one of the few offered signed by Michael Jordan, Charles Barkley, Scottie Pippin, David Robinson, John Stockton, and Chris Mullin—all Nike endorsers. (Photo courtesy of Craig Wolfe of Name That Toon.)

One of many framed pieces of art by children on display at Michael Jordan's The Restaurant in Chicago, Illinois. Not signed, the art shows the "1991 NBA Champions," with Michael Jordan in the front, surrounded by the Incredi-Bulls.

A jubilant Michael Jordan holds up two fingers to signify the Bulls' second consecutive NBA championship, while holding the trophy. (Photo by Manny Millan, courtesy of *Sports Illustrated*.)

The Bulls' three championship trophies on display at the team's corporate office in Chicago, Illinois.

A display case at Michael Jordan's The Restaurant in Chicago, Illinois, showcasing three basketballs: the McDonald's All American High School Basketball Game, an NBA Spalding ball signed by Magic Johnson, and an NBA Spalding ball signed by Michael Jordan.

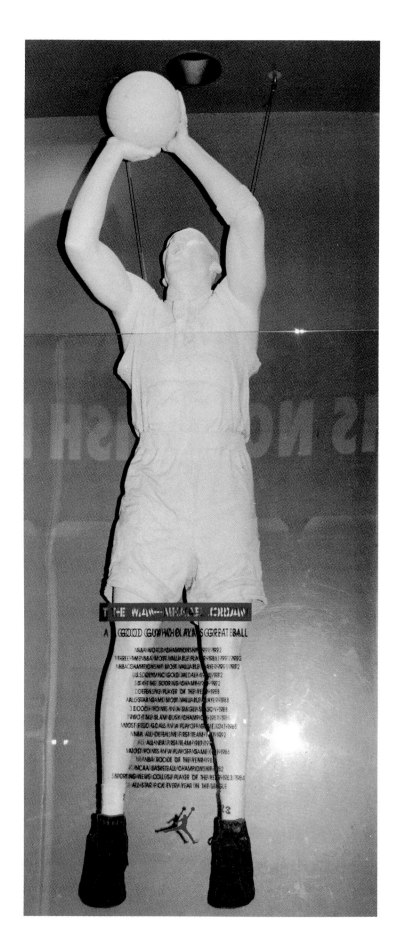

"The Man—Michael Jordan, A Good Guy Who Plays Great Basketball." Statue in the lobby of the superstore Nike Town in Chicago; Jordan's awards are silkscreened on the front of the display case.

A display case highlighting Jordan's NBA All-Star jersey (1990), All-Star shorts (1990), and a pair of autographed Air Jordan basketball shoes.

Four
Jordan and Basketball

The one constant in Michael Jordan's life can be summed up in four simple words: "I love the game," he said, time and again, and it showed.

It showed when he played in junior high and high school, and when he took on his brother in their backyard in Wilmington.

It showed when he spent his senior year preparing for collegiate ball, knowing that, finally, here was an arena where he could rise to the challenge and make a name for himself.

It showed when he moved to Chicago and, through seven long years, carried the Bulls on his back until he brought them to three consecutive championships.

It showed in all the pickup games he played, the All-Star games, the two Olympic Games. Here, clearly, was a guy who was getting paid to do something he'd otherwise do for free.

How much richer we are having seen him perform on and above ground.

In this section, we take a closer look at Jordan in his element—on court, and having a ball.

For anyone wanting a few pointers from Jordan, here's some advice from someone who clearly knows what he is talking about . . . and it shows.

Michael Jordan on the move on court in a 1986 game against San Antonio. (Photo by Robert A. Reeder, courtesy of the *Chicago Sun-Times*.)

19.

How to Be Like Mike: A Jordan Alphabet

A is for

- attitude, essential to developing a professional mind-set;
- air, which is where MJ spent a lot of his time; and
- All-Star, which accurately describes MJ.

B is for

- basketball, for which MJ was paid;
- baseball, MJ's current passion; and
- Bulls, for which MJ played.

C is for

- competition, which MJ thrives on;
- charity, which shows MJ's heart;
- Chicago, which has adopted him as its own;
- championship, as in three-peat; and
- collectibles, mostly cards, with MJ in flight.

D is for

- drive,
- dedication,
- desire, all essential to success;
- dunk, which is MJ's trademark;
- Dean Smith, his college basketball coach; and
- dreams, which MJ believes in—and so should you.

E is for

- energy, necessary to fuel the jumping, floating, spinning, unbelievable slam-dunking machine known as MJ.

F is for

- fans, of which MJ has plenty;
- fantastic, which accurately describes his on-court moves;
- focus, necessary to block out all distractions and concentrate on the task at hand—like winning basketball games;
- football, which MJ played as a kid; and

- foundation, as in The Michael Jordan Foundation, which was set up to help needy kids.

G is for

- golf, which MJ loves to play in his free time;
- geography, which MJ majored in in college;
- goals, which MJ made on court; and
- goals, which MJ sets in life.

H is for

- "Hare," as in the "crazy wabbit" who showed him a thing or two on the court, and on Mars.

I is for

- intense, which is how Jordan played basketball.

J is for

- Jordan, of course; and
- jump shots, which MJ took frequently.

K is for

- killer instinct, which MJ exhibited on the court.

L is for

- Laney High School, where MJ learned a lot, on and off court.

M is for

- Most Valuable Player, which MJ won three times.

N is for

- Nike, which has helped make him a household name;
- NBA, the league in which he played;
- NCAA championship, which he won for UNC with a jumper; and
- North Carolina, which he calls heaven.

O is for

- overdrive, as in maximum, which is how MJ played every game; and

- Olympic, as in gold medals, of which he's won two for playing in the L.A. and Barcelona Summer Games.

P is for

- ProServ, the company that helps him manage his professional affairs.

Q is for

- quizzical, the expression NBA defenders had on their faces after he slam-dunked on 'em.

R is for

- role model, of which MJ is a pretty good example, no matter what the media says; and
- retirement, which came too soon for his fans, but probably not soon enough for him.

S is for

- showtime—game time, in other words.

T is for

- talent, which MJ is blessed with an abundance of; and
- Tar Heels, as in UNC, for which he played.

U is for

- unstoppa-Bull, which describes MJ when he's slicing through defenders and headed to the net.

V is for

- visualization, which MJ used to prepare himself, imagining all the possibilities, before game time.

W is for

- work, preferably hard, for which there is no substitute; and
- Wilmington, the small coastal town in North Carolina where MJ grew up.

X is for

- X-ample, of which MJ is one; and
- X-citing, which MJ is on court.

Y is for

- youth, which MJ is apparently blessed with an abundance of.

Z is for

- zest, which MJ exhibits toward life.

In a 1988 Bulls–New Jersey Nets game, three defenders build a seemingly impenetrable wall to contain Michael Jordan. (Photo by Bob Black, courtesy of the *Chicago Sun-Times*.)

20.

How to Guard Michael Jordan

by Jeff Weinstock

In the wake of the Bulls' "three-peat," the question of who could effectively guard Jordan—a favorite topic among sportswriters—assumed a new importance. In the piece that follows, published in Sport *(June 1993), Jeff Weinstock shares his views on who—if anyone—could effectively guard Jordan.*

Four months after this piece appeared, Jordan retired, making the point moot. Still, just as fans gather to debate questions like who are the greatest players of all time, they will endlessly argue who could guard Jordan.

CAN *ANYONE* here guard this guy?

Nine years, seven scoring titles, and three championships into Michael Jordan's pro career, this is still the million-dollar question. Although several matters await answer now that the NBA's postseason is in session— How long can Barkley sit on his temper? Can Seattle go the distance? Who will cast the first stone, Pat Riley or Phil Jackson?—the Jordan factor must be attended to first.

Now, it may seem an outdated issue, as the blossoming of Scottie Pippen and Horace Grant and deemphasizing of Jordan came in lockstep with the Bulls' two titles. Perhaps only M.J. himself, who still stings with his "my supporting cast" references to his teammates, considers Chicago a one-man show. But any club with designs on beating Chicago . . . will have to solve Jordan, whose presence overwhelms all other concerns.

It is nearly universally accepted that Chicago's competition in the Eastern Conference will come from the New York Knicks and the Cleveland Cavaliers. Should form hold, the luckless task of shadowing Jordan would then fall to five men: John Starks, Doc Rivers, and Rolando Blackman of the Knicks, and Gerald Wilkins and Craig Ehlo of the Cavaliers.

More than he has any other club, Jordan has tormented Cleveland. Since 1986–87, the season Brad Daugherty and Mark Price joined the Cavs, Jordan has averaged 36 points a game and shot 55 percent from the field against Cleveland, including his biggest night as a pro, a 69-point binge in 1990. In three postseason series against the Cavs, Jordan has been toxic, averaging 38.4 points a game and knocking them out of the playoffs all three times.

Ehlo, whose hustle and effort can't totally compensate for his slow feet, has been routinely punished by Jordan and says it never gets any easier. "There's not much you can learn. He gets better each year himself."

But after last season's six-game loss to Chicago in the Eastern Conference finals, Cleveland went out to get Ehlo some help and signed Wilkins away from the Knicks. Wilkins, who clung to Jordan like a garlic scent in last year's bruising Bulls-Knicks quarterfinal series, knows his role. "[Cavalier management] knew what went on in the playoffs," he says. "They needed another big guard to help get over the hump against this guy. Easier said than done."

Wilkins's biggest asset is that he's one of the few shooting guards who can match up with Jordan physically. Jordan's acrobatics tend to obscure how big he has become after working with weights in recent seasons. He's been listed at 198 since he entered the NBA, but the lean-limbed, first-year Jordan looks like an adolescent next to the 1993 Jordan, who could crack walnuts with his biceps. But Wilkins, an athletic six-foot-seven, can approximate Jordan's size and speed as well as any guard in the league.

"The number one thing I do that most guards don't do is match foot speed for foot speed. . . . I stay with him all night long," says Wilkins. "My main focus is defense when I go against him. When you have guys like Clyde Drexler, Reggie Miller, they're scorers. Their main focus is to score, not defend. You're never going to outscore him. I'm more committed to coming out and defending him."

"Air" Jordan attempts an unbelieva-Bull shot in a game against the Miami Heat in Chapel Hill in 1989. (Photo courtesy of the Durham Herald Co., Inc.)

It used to be conventional wisdom that you gave Jordan the outside shot, which, if not weak, was at least less reliable than a dunk. But now that his game has expanded to the point where he shoots 40 percent from three-point range and has possibly the most accurate medium-range jumper in the league, he is nearly as devastating on the perimeter as he is on the drive. Wilkins, though, believes that Jordan's jump shot still determines the course of the game.

"If I get him taking a lot of jump shots [early] and he gets to missing," says Wilkins, "then he wants to go to the hole. Then that's when he more so is playing into my hands, because I know that I can stay in front of him. And if he's trying to go to the hole and I'm in front of him, then I'm slowing him, I'm cutting down his production. He still may score 25 or 30, but he might have a bad shooting percentage . . . [and] I've cut down his efficiency."

With Wilkins's help, the Knicks got after Jordan as no team had since the Detroit Pistons' genial Bad Boys crew of a few years back. It's no coincidence then that Dick Harter, who coordinated Detroit's defense, now has the same job with New York. With Wilkins and Starks tracking him out high and Charles Oakley, Anthony Mason, and Xavier McDaniel waiting to crunch him when he got into the paint, Jordan was limited to 27.7 points a game, two-plus below his season average, and shot only 43.8 percent from the field.

Starks has been compared by Knicks coach Pat Riley to Michael Cooper, the stringy, junk-talking defensive stopper from Riley's years with the Lakers. A slight six-foot-three, 180 pounds, Stark can be abused by Jordan in the post, but he does share Cooper's lip. His somewhat camera-conscious trash-trading sessions with Jordan become one of the subplots of the Knicks-Bulls stories. But Starks says the dialogue with Jordan wasn't intended as a defensive ploy.

"You can talk all the noise you want, it doesn't matter," says Starks. "He'll still hurt you. What you saw in the playoffs was just the two of us having fun."

Rivers, who chased Jordan for years with Atlanta, warns that trying to bait him verbally can backfire. "I've had games where Michael starts to talk and it took him to another level. It's a delicate point [how far] you want to go."

Wilkins says he doesn't see any sense in inciting Jordan. "I don't do that with him," he says, "because the less he feels you're trying to go at him, the less he's going to think about what he's going to do next. He's almost going to have a little pity for you. If you're provoking him, he's gonna have no pity. And then he's really gonna try to get at you. It's head games."

Of course, the larger dilemma with Jordan is that there is no book on him. He's as strong going right as he is left. He's as likely to go baseline as he is to race to the middle. His only pet move is his post-up shot, a fake-one-way, fade-the-other jumper that he favors down the stretch. Otherwise, he improvises.

"Everybody tries to pinpoint some, but I don't see any tendencies at all," says Ehlo. "I see him just making moves on pure instinct: That's what his game is. . . . His mind is to score. . . . That's just the way he thinks."

Says Blackman, "Anybody who says there is [a tendency] would be [seeing] something different, because if there was, somebody would find a way to shut him down."

Because it is impossible to anticipate what Jordan will do, the defender is always at the disadvantage of having to react to Jordan's first step. Stark says the surest way to get burned by Jordan is to try and cheat, to try to reverse the advantage and force him to react to you.

"If you overextend yourself, if you reach, you're at his mercy," says Starks. "He'll go right by you."

But Wilkins, who trusts he can beat Jordan to the spot, says he takes Jordan's strengths away by steering him to one side. "I don't give him the opportunity to wind up on me," he says. "Most guys will play him from here to there. That's a big mistake, because he has so much change-of-direction. I give him one direction, and that's the way he's gonna have to beat me."

Rather than an itemized list of dos and don'ts, what emerges is the consensus that Jordan must, above all else, not be conceded anything.

Says Blackman, "The important thing is to make Michael work as much as you can, work to get the ball, work to get his shots. Make everything very difficult, and also keep things busy on the offensive end, making him work on both ends. I'm not saying shut him down or stop him, because that's not anything anybody can do, but to keep things on or near an even keel. Slow him down, shut him down, those are not words that you use, because he can do so many different things. . . . What you have to do in order to keep things on an even keel is to make the man work for his shots, every shot that he gets."

"You try to play him as physically as possible," says Rivers, whose good-guy traits don't mesh with the rough-and-tumble Knicks. But he's learning. "Physically put enough pressure on him [to] at least wear him down, make him shoot the ball a foot farther out than where he's used to shooting it from, or where he likes to shoot it from. I think over four quarters that

Ennis Whatley of the Bullets watches Michael Jordan slam two of his 36 points in a 1987 game giving the Bulls a 101–75 victory, clinching a playoff spot. (Photo by Robert A. Reeder, courtesy of the *Chicago Sun-Times*.)

can show some wear. Unfortunately, it shows some wear on the defender, too."

There was a time when a defense, such as Detroit's vaunted Jordan Rules, a shifting, diagramed response to its namesake's every move, could fixate on Jordan. But the emergence of Pippen, sort of a Jordan Lite, and Grant, along with the shot-making of John Paxson and B.J. Armstrong have made obsessing over Jordan troublesome.

"You just don't go into the game thinking about Michael," says Blackman. "You go into the game thinking about what their team does. If you start focusing on just one person, all of a sudden you negate everything else on the basketball floor, and other guys will start hurting you even more. Then it becomes a total breakdown.

"Michael is still going to be a constant there. He's still going to be a constant no matter what you or your team does. The thing about it is to try and make the whole team work. We're not playing Michael, we're not playing five-on-one. We play the Bulls. If you play the Bulls, then you'll be doing a better job."

Granted that Pippen and Grant practicipate heavily in Chicago's success. But late in the game the Bulls turn to Jordan exclusively, and with his torrential fourth-quarter flurries he can ice an opponent by himself. There will doubtlessly come a decisive stretch in this postseason when the Bulls are in a tight spot, and Jordan, right on time, will start raging. . . .

Says Ehlo, who has been spin-cycled by Jordan in more fourth quarters than he'd prefer to remember, "When you're out there against him, you're against the world."

Michael Jordan's Favorite Rim-rattlers

1. Kenny Smith. "Bouncing the ball between his legs and off the backboard with his back to the basket for the two-hand slam."

2. Dee Brown. "The no-look dunk."

3. Terence Stansbury. "The Statue of Liberty 360-degree jam off one leg."

4. Darryl Dawkins. "The break-the-backboard slam."

5. Michael Jordan. "Coming in from the side of the basket, leaning, shoulder-first one-handed hurl jam. It was a complete improvisation, but ever since I've seen everybody else trying to copy it."

—from Sport magazine (February 1992)

21.

The Jordan Rules

Unless you've had the good fortune to attend one of Jordan's basketball camps, chances are that you've wanted a few hints from his Airness on how to play basketball from his lofty perspective.

Here, then, are some tips culled from various pieces published in the last decade.

MICHAEL JORDAN on whether to drive left or right on the court: "I look at the placement of his feet. If his left foot is extended, I go to his left because it's harder for him to move his body over the extended leg." (*USA Today*, July 2, 1992.)

"Basketball is a great game. Everyone can play and have fun, no matter how big or fast or good you are. But if you're going to play, you should try to improve as much as you can. I've been playing ball for a long time. I've learned a lot, and I'd like to share a few tips with my Air Jordan Flight Club members.

"**1. Don't leave your feet on defense.** Like all rules, there are exceptions. But, if you're bouncing around all the time trying to block shots, you're going to get beat. Keep your hands high and your eyes open. You'll force more bad shots, get more rebounds, and be a bigger asset to your team.

"**2. Practice your free throws.** This may be the most important shot in basketball. On the average, for every five points scored, one is a free throw. They're easy, but you have to be prepared. Establish a routine. Do the same thing every time. If you want to dribble the ball seven times, fine, but do it the same way every time. Then take a deep breath, let it all out, and fire. You should be able to make these shots with your eyes closed. Remember, it's just you, the ball and the hoop. You've made free throws before, you should be able to make them again." (*Air Jordan Flight Club #8.*)

On the excitement of basketball: "Many times you'll receive a pass on the court and find that, al-

though you are guarded, you are the closest one to the basket. It's now up to you to make a move with the ball so you can get your shot off. This is where you get to add your personal offensive touch and is what makes the game so exciting to play. Being able to execute more than one of the following individual moves with the ball will greatly help you get free for your shot. Practice them when you're alone, using different fakes and speed variations.

"When you practice these moves, be sure that you turn and face the basket and assume proper basketball

In a game against the Detroit Pistons, Michael Jordan drives against Vinnie Johnson. (Courtesy of the *Chicago Sun-Times*.)

position: your feet are shoulders-width apart and pointed toward the basket; your knees are flexed; your shoulders are facing the basket. Also, hold the ball securely with two hands close to your body. If you are right-handed, keep the ball on your right side; if you are left-handed, keep it on the left side.

"**The Jab Step:** The jab is a common foot fake which, depending on the defensive player's reaction, is used to set up either a drive or a jump shot.

"To perform a jab step, keep the ball in your hands at waist level or near your hips and establish proper basketball position. Take a short, hard step (10 inches or less) toward your defensive man while at the same time faking the dribble by bringing the ball down outside your knee when you make the jab with your foot. Pause slightly to see the reaction of the defensive player.

"Depending on what your defender does after you've moved toward him, you now make the next move quickly. If the defender lunges toward you, then take a longer step with the same foot and simultaneously push the ball out and drive right around his hip. To get this move down in your mind, think of it as a one-two count move with a split-second stop in the middle.

"When you make the jab-step move and your defensive player plays you for it—he backs up and blocks your path—your next offensive possibility would be to take a jump shot. You can do it by first pulling back your lead foot and then going up for the shot, or else by going up for the shot without bringing your lead foot back. Take the shot whichever way feels most comfortable for you.

"It's important when you are going to make a jab step that your first step is not too long. Go out too far and you'll be off balance, unable to successfully make your drive or jump shot. Secondly, remember to keep in a crouched position with your knees bent. This coiled position assures you enough power to make the drive or jump shot." (*From* Hoops: The Official National Basketball Players Association Guide to Playing Basketball.)

Hang Time:
The Art of the Dunk, Jordan-style

You, too, can jam like Jordan. Here are some easy steps to tell you how.

1. Be born with the perfect body for basketball—six-foot-six tall, 195 pounds, long sinewy muscles, 5 percent body fat, and a heart like a lion.

2. Study hard on the court and in school. Even Michael won't be able to fly forever.

3. Lace up your Air Jordan® shoes. Wearing two pairs of socks is critical.

4. Steal the ball from your opponent. Head for the hoop.

5. Apply your muscle power in the vertical plane to overcome the earth's gravitational forces. Duck, so you don't hit the rafters.

6. Spin 360 degrees and jam!

—*from "Dunk Like the Master" in* Air Jordan Flight Club #7

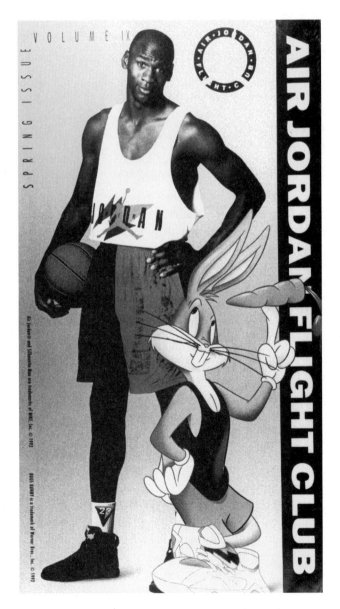

Cover to the *Air Jordan Flight Club* newsletter (spring 1992), featuring "Air" Jordan and "Hare" Jordan.

22.

Jordan's Basketball Camp

Michael's strict rules are about being positive with the kids.

—Al Allen, head coach at Oak Park–River Forest High School, a coach at Jordan's basketball camp

How would you like to spend a week with Michael Jordan next summer?

If you've got four days free in July, are willing to travel to Elmhurst, Illinois, and can afford the reasonable tuition, you can spend a week with him, so long as you're willing to share him with other happy, and starstruck, campers at Jordan's basketball camp. Held annually since 1987—with the exception of 1992 when he played in the Olympics with fellow Dream Teamers—the Michael Jordan Camp offers two camps for boys only, and one for boys and girls.

Imagine, on the first day, hearing Jordan tell you what to expect for the next five days, watching him demonstrate his on-court skills, and then being challenged to go one-on-one against him on court!

As Ed Janka, the director of the camps told journalist Mark Potash, "Jordan's not here every moment. I don't try and disguise that . . . but Michael makes a genuine effort to be here as much as he can. He tries to give as much personal attention to each camper as he can." Still, with 500 attendees, that can get to be a problem because everyone wants Jordan's attention.

Because this is principally a basketball camp, the emphasis is on tuning up your on-court skills. To assist, counselors, coaches, and players—drawn from high schools, colleges, and the NBA—are there to provide the day-to-day workouts.

In addition to the on-court experience, souvenir hunters don't go home empty-handed. As Kristin E. Whitehurst, director of communications at Elmhurst College, points out:

> The camp lasts five days, and Michael is great about being with the campers a lot. In addition to the instruction from Michael and the other coaches, each camper receives a "Michael Jordan" Wilson basketball, a camp T-shirt, a certificate of participation, a player profile card outlining strengths and weaknesses, and a team photograph with Michael. Michael also autographs one item for each camper which the camper gets to select.

For most of the campers when they head home, simply seeing Jordan in person, instead of seeing him on television, is what they remember—and cherish. "The first time I saw Michael, my mouth just dropped. My eyes fell out. I just froze," said Crystal Sciaretti, quoted by journalist Mark Potash in a newspaper story.

Apparently, she's not alone, for other campers had the same reaction: starstruck, then won over by Jordan's off-court charisma. As Ed Janka, camp director, told Potash, "Some kids are kind of bold and some are scared because of who he is, but he's able to handle that. One of the greatest qualities is he's able to make people comfortable."

You can spend the summer doing what all the other kids on your block do: go on a family vacation, play in the Little League, go swimming, goof off—or go to Jordan's basketball camp.

In the fall, when you get back to school, when you exchange stories with classmates of what you did this summer, set up your friends by saying, "I spent a week playing basketball." "Big deal," they'll say. Then pause for effect and add, "Yeah, but with Michael Jordan."

Slam dunk!

For more information

Date: Annually, in July

Location: Elmhurst College

Cost: Inquire via mail or check the camp hotline phone number (below)

Age of attendees: Fifth to twelfth graders

Number of camps held: One coed, two boys only

Camp director: Mr. Ed Janka

Assistant camp director: Mr. Scott Trost (Elmhurst College men's basketball coach)

For more information, call the camp hotline at (708) 617–3710 or write to:

Michael Jordan Basketball Camp
Basketball Office
Elmhurst College
Elmhurst, IL 60126–3296

Michael Jordan drives past a defender at the Jordan Basketball Camp at Elmhurst College. (Photo by Kristin Whitehurst.)

23.

Michael and Me

by Tim Brandhorst

In his foreword to the paperback edition of Hang Time, *Bob Greene shares with his readers a "lovely sketch of an unexpected and pure moment," a firsthand account of a pickup game in Chicago by Tim Brandhorst, a young lawyer who had headed to his health club for a "quick workout before the weekend starts." Nothing unusual about that, you'd say, and you'd be right—but not this time. This time, Tim Brandhorst found himself in a pickup game with another Chicagoan, Michael Jordan.*

What follows is Brandhorst's recollection of that moment, as nice a Christmas gift as any basketball fan could wish for—the stuff of dreams.

THE FIRST thing I do when I get there is start shooting some baskets, just shooting around, waiting to play. There's a couple of teams playing, maybe 10 or 12 guys waiting on the side, the regular after-work crowd on this court.

And Michael Jordan walks in.

Michael wanders over to one end of the court, just standing there, watching. The place starts buzzing. As the players on the court realize who's there, the game picks up, and pretty soon guys are trash-talking and woofing and trying to dunk (this court has some *players* on it). Nobody really bothers Michael, certainly nobody asks him for an autograph or anything like that, and pretty soon he wanders away to go lift some weights. The buzz, the excitement in the air, stays behind.

My team gets called next, and we start playing. Tonight I get lucky. My team includes a former pro and a former college ballplayer. Another guy on my team walks up to me and tells me that I should clear out and let those two guys take over. I don't touch the ball much, which is just as well and the way it often goes on this court. We win, which means we get to stay on the court.

As we're playing the next game, Michael wanders back. He sits down at one end of the court, grabs a ball, and just starts to watch the game. Michael Jordan is watching me play basketball! Another guy and I agree that we have never played under pressure like this. Halfway through the game, when we're at the other hoop, he strolls out on the court and starts launching rainbow three-pointers, like he's trying to hit the ceiling with his shots, every one of which swishes. My team wins again, so again we get to stay out on the court and play the next team.

Michael hasn't stopped commenting on our game since he came back to the court. He has a low voice, and tends to repeat himself, especially when he gets a laugh or a reaction. He walks under the basket and says, None of you can do this. He then does a flat-footed, no-step, three-sixty slam. There are a couple of guys there who are taller than him, and they immediately step up and insist they can—and, of course, not being Michael, they can't.

Michael then says, Gimme four.

It takes me a split second to fully comprehend those two words and everything they imply. Gimme four. Gimme four players. Wait a minute—GIMME FOUR? You don't mean—

And I started playing against Michael Jordan. I *said,* I start playing against *Michael Jordan.*

At first, he stays outside, passes to the other guys on his team, swishes a couple long shots. Which makes sense—of course the guy isn't going to jeopardize everything and take the chance of breaking an ankle or blowing out his knee in a pickup game. I realize this as we're playing, and try to stay as far away from him as possible—I can just picture him coming down on my foot and twisting his ankle, having it be me, a gravity-bound, no-talent, small-town *lawyer*, for heaven's sakes, who ends Michael's career.

Except, Michael can't just take it easy. He continues to talk trash, mostly to the ex-pro on my team who's trying to guard him. And before long, he's driving the lane, he's going inside for rebounds, he's blocking shots. He's playing like he has to prove to us that he's the best player out there. And, well, maybe that's how he got that good, by always feeling like he has to prove it. Or, from watching him, maybe that's the way he has his fun—he looked and sounded like he could not have enjoyed himself more out there. Or maybe it has something to do with the playground ethic of walking the walk to back up your talk, of the only important thing, the thing you judge others by and are judged on yourself, being what you do on the court, what you produce, how you perform—not what you've done in the past, not reputation, not history, not anything but what can you do *now*.

Word travels through the rest of the health club that Michael is not only in the building, but that he is actually playing, and people start to ring the basketball court. There's a running track overhead, and people line that as well. A couple hundred people are now watching. I'm having fun, just watching Michael, not really in the flow of the game because there's so much else to think about.

Someone on my team takes a long shot from the right side, and suddenly the long rebound is in my hands. I'm about eight feet from the hoop on the left baseline. Somewhat stunned I look for an open man to pass to.

Oooh, take your shot, that's your shot, take your shot, ooh comes from everyone on the court, including Michael, and from everyone crowded around the court.

I throw up a shot.

Swish.

It doesn't matter that Michael was on the other side of the lane. It doesn't matter that, if he had wanted to, Michael could have walked over and swatted my shot away. Hey, he chose not to. It doesn't matter that the shot was a heave, a brick, a throw that just happened to go in. And it doesn't matter that his team whipped mine.

What *matters* is that I *scored on Michael Jordan*.

So you see, Christmas came early for me this year. The best Christmas present I could ever get. One I'll never forget. . . .

P.S.—As we were walking off the court I came up from behind him and patted him on the butt. Good game, I said. He didn't even acknowledge me. *As it should be.*

• *Greene elaborated: "'As it should be.' Meaning: Let the moment be. It happened—don't step on it or overanalyze it or try to extend it. Brandhorst and the other men in the health club basketball court that day were privileged to see a Jordan that the rest of the world seldom does. Jordan as a person—Jordan as a man in the act of being himself."*

Five
A Look Back

The day after Jordan retired, newspapers rushed tributes into print to mark the changing of a guard—no. 23 would no longer take to the hardcourt and then to the air. Everyone, it seemed, tried to make sense of Jordan's surprise announcement; speculations about him sitting out for one season and returning for the 1994–95 season were rampant.

Within a week after Jordan's announcement, a special issue of *Newsweek*, coverdated October/November 1993, was published; a $3.95, 64-page one-shot, this issue was simply titled "The Greatest Ever." Even without the cover photo of Jordan smiling, a basketball under his right arm, you knew who *Newsweek* was talking about.

In time, other organizations assembled tribute issues, geared toward the Jordan collector:

- *A Tribute to Michael Jordan* (Trading Cards Presents, $3.95), a "limited collector's edition #1."
- Similarly, *Michael! A Career Tribute* (Basketball Superstars, $4.95), was marketed as a "collector's edition."
- *A Tribute to Michael Jordan* (Publications International, $4.95), marketed as a "commemorative edition," written by Bob Sakamoto, whose previous credits include *Michael "Air" Jordan*, a biography published by Publications International.
- *Michael! A Career Tribute* (*Hollywood Collectibles Magazine*, $4.95).
- *Michael Jordan: A Final Tribute* (Pro Basketball Illustrated, $3.95).

By far the best single tribute issue on Jordan is *Beckett Tribute: Michael Jordan* (Statabase, Inc., $3.95), from the publishers of the authoritative *Beckett Basketball Monthly*.

For an overview on Jordan and the Bulls, *Sports Illustrated Presents: The Chicago Bulls, Three Seasons to Savor* ($4.95) is required reading. (Ironically, the *Chicago Tribune* published its own magazine tribute, *The Chicago Bulls: Three-peat!*, but this $6.99 publication appears to have been rushed into production, lacking the depth and the photo excellence of the *Sports Illustrated* tribute.)

In this section we, too, look back at Jordan's remarkable career, beginning with a piece from someone who is uniquely qualified to comment on basketball and Jordan—Magic Johnson.

24.

Magic Johnson on Michael Jordan

During the 1990–91 playoffs against the Lakers on their home court, the capacity crowd took to its feet when the moment they had waited for arrived: Magic Johnson and Michael Jordan one-on-one; for that brief moment, as the crowd roared, the rest of the team took backseat as two of the best players—two of the most competitive—met on the court during a critical game.

On court, these two temporarily put their friendship aside to do battle with an intensity that gives professional sports its magic appeal; off court, these same rivals can be the best of friends. Nothing illustrates this better than the camaraderie exhibited by the members of the Dream Team during the 1992 Olympics in Barcelona.

For the cover of Newsweek *(June 6, 1992), we see a portrait of Larry Bird, Michael Jordan, and Magic Johnson in their USA Basketball uniforms, smiling broadly for the camera; what the camera didn't record was that, during the shoot, all three were kidding around, having fun; at one point, Magic hugged Michael.*

It looked as if they were having a grand time—knowing, perhaps, that this would be the last time they would ever play together; how fitting that, for these games, they played not for themselves or for their respective teams but for their country. How good it must have felt!

In this excerpt from Magic Johnson's biography, My Life, *cowritten with William Novak, Magic talks about Michael Jordan with his characteristic candor. Magic also talks about the one-on-one game he and Michael were intending to play, raising the question: What happens when an irresistible force meets an immovable object? Perhaps it's best left to speculation, but I can't help but wonder if, one day, away from the cameras and the crowds, they play a little friendly game between themselves, perhaps in Magic's indoor court at his home. . . . Most likely, though, they'll leave the outcome unanswered, since it would probably come down to whoever takes the last shot, as Magic said.*

THERE'S A LOT of bad blood between the Pistons and the Bulls, and especially between Isiah and Michael Jor-

dan. As far as I know, the problem between them started at the 1985 All-Star Game in Indianapolis. Jordan had a bad game, getting only nine shots. Some people, including Michael himself, were convinced that Isiah had kept the ball away from him to teach him a lesson. It's possible. The previous day, in the slam-dunk contest, Michael had shown up in a Nike sweat suit and gold chains instead of his uniform. Some guys thought he was bragging about his many endorsements.

Michael was mad at Isiah, and at me, too. According to one article, Isiah and I had conspired to deny Michael the ball. But that's ridicuous. I wasn't even on Michael's team. I was playing for the West. We were *supposed* to deny him the ball. But I was also a friend of Isiah's. And back then, Isiah and I had the same agent. Maybe that gave people ideas.

For a year or two, everyplace I went I was asked about Michael. It was a little like my early years with Bird, when we didn't know each other and the press made us out to be enemies. Finally, before a game between our two teams, we [Magic and Michael] sat down and talked. "The media would love for us to be fighting each other," I told him. "But I don't want that to happen. And I think it would be a shame if we left this game without knowing each other."

Since then, I've come to know him well. He's one of the first people I talked to when I got the news about HIV. And I believe I helped persuade him to play on the 1992 Olympic team. At first he was reluctant, but could you possibly imagine an American basketball team without Michael Jordan? It's crazy.

I've read stories that say I'm jealous of all his endorsements. Fortunately, I'm not the jealous type. And when you're making the kind of money I'm making, you have no business being jealous of anybody. If you are, you've got the wrong priorities.

But I certainly would have enjoyed being in Michael's position. ProServ did a tremendous job for him, and I take my hat off to them. Earlier on, I had tried to talk

The Lakers' Earvin "Magic" Johnson vs. the Bulls' Michael Jordan in a 1987 game. (Photo courtesy of the *Chicago Sun-Times*.)

Converse into doing for me what Nike did later for Michael. No, they said, a Magic Johnson shoe would never sell. Why not? I asked. Because nobody would buy a shoe with a player's name on it.

Oh, really?

Eventually, Converse did put out a Magic Johnson shoe. But by then it was a few years too late.

Michael Jordan might be the most popular athlete ever. But I wonder if people realize how tough a burden that must be. Everybody wants a piece of him, and people expect him to represent the game of basketball. For years, Dr. J was the ambassador. When he stepped down, I knew it was my turn. And now Michael knows that he's the man.

Larry Bird and I were two of the smartest players you'll ever see. But Michael can do things on the court that we could barely imagine. He's just incredible. Even if he had a bad game and goes 1 for 10, which is rare, that one shot might be the most amazing move you've ever seen. In terms of the excitement he creates, Michael Jordan is the greatest player who ever laced up a pair of sneakers.

There aren't many guys I'd pay to watch, but he's at the top of my list. Everybody knows about his offensive abilities, and there's not much I can add to that except to say that the players enjoy watching him just as much as the fans do. But Michael is even better than most fans realize. In addition to everything he can do with the ball, he's also a great defensive player.

And I've got to admire the way he's adjusted his own game to make his team a winner. For a while, the Bulls consisted of Michael and 11 other guys. He was great to watch, but Chicago wasn't winning. Michael always wanted to win, and he realized that the Bulls could never win a title unless he became less dominating. A lot of players *say* they want to win, but they find it impossible to see beyond their own stats. They're into the "I" syndrome instead of the "we." Michael understood that one player can't win in the NBA, no matter how great he is; five guys can always shut down one. But if that one guy is a *team* player, and he has a partner like Scottie Pippen to work with, that's another story.

A few years back, the idea came up for a one-on-one match between Michael Jordan and me. It would be shown on pay TV, and a lot of the money would be given to charity. But not all of it. Michael and I both play in a sport where each team has a salary cap, and we thought it would be fun if for just one night, we could make as much as the market would allow. Both of us were excited about it, and our agents, Lon Rosen and David Falk, started discussing how it might work.

But the NBA has a clause in its collective bargaining agreement that says any sporting event involving a player has to be approved by both the league and the player's team. My contract has a "love of the game clause," which would have allowed me to participate in the one-on-one. Michael's contract was a little more limiting, and there would have been problems.

Then Lon came up with an interesting twist: Michael and I would both retire from basketball, play our game, and then come back again. We kicked it around for a while, but we decided against it. The last thing we wanted was a fight with the NBA.

Then the players' association came out against the whole idea of Michael and me playing each other. The head of the player's association was Isiah Thomas. Michael's response was that this was personal on Isiah's part, and that if Isiah was playing, nobody would be interested.

In the end, we decided not to go ahead. But I still think it would have been an amazing event. We would have staged it shortly after the playoffs. The format would be two fifteen-minute halves, using the half-court. It would have been a huge moneymaker, not only for ourselves, but for several good causes.

When our match was still under discussion, *USA Today* listed Michael as an 8–5 favorite. That suited me fine, because I enjoy being the underdog; it always makes me work harder.

We still talk about it. Whenever I see him, he says, "I could have beat you."

"No way," I reply. "I would have won."

"You can't stop me."

"Maybe not, but you can't stop me, either."

Maybe we're both right. If that's true, the last guy with the ball would win.

Michael Jordan and Magic Johnson at a 1991 press conference at the Hotel Nikko in Chicago, Illinois. (Photo by Ellen Domke, courtesy of the *Chicago Sun-Times.*)

25.

Shooting Star Retires at the Top of His Game

by Scott Whisnant (1993)

No matter the source—books, videotapes, magazine and newspaper pieces, even Jordan himself—an essential part of the Jordan myth, the story of how Jordan got cut from the varsity team, has gone unquestioned. When Jordan retired, and the Wilmington Star-News *published a special supplement on Jordan, managing editor John Meyer told me that he wanted to set the record straight: Jordan was* not *cut from the varsity team; Meyer's source is Clifton "Pop" Herring, who ought to know. Herring was the basketball coach at Laney High School at that time. It's a heckuva story, as everyone agrees, but the problem is it just ain't so.*

Here's what really *happened, and what happened afterward in Jordan's stellar career.*

As CLIFTON "Pop" Herring watched basketball tryouts for the 1978–79 Laney High School basketball season, he noticed a skinny sophomore trying to make the varsity team.

The kid wasn't bad, but he stood less than six feet tall. Mr. Herring had a place for him—the same place most five-foot-eleven sophomores go.

Mike Jordan was headed for the junior varsity.

"He wasn't really that outstanding that day," Mr. Herring said, hours after Mr. Jordan had announced his retirement from professional basketball as possibly the greatest player in the sport's history.

"He had a weakness with his left hand," Mr. Herring said. "I told him to improve with the left hand and work on shooting off the dribble."

Mr. Jordan improved quite a bit.

By the time he left Laney High School, he had given the new high school an enduring athletic legacy, packing gyms everywhere Laney played. But his teams never made it to the state playoffs.

Mr. Jordan took care of that at the next level. As a college freshman at North Carolina in 1982, he hit the jump shot that gave the school its first national cham-

pionship in 25 years and its first under Coach Dean Smith. Before he left Carolina, Mr. Jordan was a consensus national player of the year.

In the NBA, Mr. Jordan took his game even higher, leading the league in scoring seven times and taking the Chicago Bulls to three consecutive championships, the last one in June 1993, before retiring, saying he had nothing left to prove on the basketball court.

By the time Mr. Jordan made his announcement in Chicago, he was one of the most recognized people in the world, his fame spreading to nations where basketball is not especially popular.

Those who watched him play in New Hanover county schools still can't quite grasp that Mr. Jordan got to be that good.

"The thing about Michael is that he wasn't six-nine or seven-two in seventh grade," said Kenneth McLaurin, who was Mr. Jordan's principal at Laney. "He was not a freaky sort of kid you looked at five or seven years ahead of time and knew what was coming."

When Mike Jordan was 12, he might have been a better baseball player. He was the state's Dixie Youth Player of the Year, and he continued with baseball into his high school years. Mike also played football then, but quit after playing on Laney's junior varsity team.

But even though he had more success with baseball, basketball was still Mike Jordan's favorite.

Larry Boylan coached Mr. Jordan's eighth grade team at Trask Junior High. Mike, as he was known then, was about five-two, Mr. Boylan said, so he put him at point guard.

"He was a very good point guard, but he was very small," Mr. Boylan said. "A lot of his shots got slapped away. We only won about three games."

Mr. Boylan had his point guard passing the ball to teammates most of the year, but young Mike became frustrated as the losses piled up.

"I got tired of it and stopped coaching and said, 'Go ahead and shoot,'" Mr. Boylan said. "That's probably when we won the three games we did."

As a ninth grader, Mike Jordan played for a better-than-average team under Fred Lynch, now Laney's head basketball coach. Then he went out for the varsity team as a sophomore and suffered the most celebrated "cut" in basketball history.

Legend has it that Mr. Jordan scanned the player roster after tryouts, only to be crushed when his name wasn't on it. But Mr. Herring said there was never a chance of Mr. Jordan's playing with the varsity team.

"We had talented players that year and most of them were coming back," Mr. Herring said. One of them was Leroy Smith, who went on to play college basketball at UNC-Charlotte.

Mr. Jordan had some great JV games, scoring more than 40 points in some, Mr. Herring said. His team won about three games, but Mr. Jordan got to play most of every one.

"Mike playing JV wasn't bad for him," Mr. Herring said. "He had an outstanding coach in Sam Avery. He taught him to post up inside and use his right and left hand effectively."

But no one could teach Mr. Jordan to do what he did between his sophomore and junior years. Mr. Jordan showed up for practice the next year standing six-foot-three. Now he had a forward's body with point guard skills—and a work ethic matched by no one.

"He'd get upset when I'd stop practice before he wanted it to stop," Mr. Herring said. "He said, 'Coach, we need a little bit more.'"

In his first varsity game, Mr. Jordan scored 35 points, a performance that rated only this mention in the next day's *Morning Star*, in the next-to-last paragraph: "Mike Jordan had 35 points to spark the Bucs."

The team finished about 15–7 and wasn't a factor in either the tournament or the regular-season race, Mr. Herring said. But by the end of the year, Mike Jordan was a factor.

"He was good as a junior, but the last five or six games, it seemed like he blossomed," said Jim Hebron, then the coach at New Hanover High School and now an assistant coach at Georgia Tech.

By then, Mike Jordan had become Michael Jordan, and every college wanted him. But only one was ever really in the running, Mr. Herring said, and that was North Carolina.

"He wanted to go there, but I was a little bit skeptical," he said. "I was a little skeptical because of the situation of him playing as a freshman."

Dean Smith came to watch Mr. Jordan play—Mr. Herring can still point to the door the Tar Heel coach walked through—and Mr. Jordan signed with Carolina early in the season, saying he wanted to put his recruiting behind him.

The day Michael signed, Mr. Herring predicted, "I think in one of his four years at Carolina, Dean Smith will win a national title."

Mr. Herring laughs about that bold assertion now, even though it apparently worked. Just before the next basketball season began, Mr. Smith announced that Mr. Jordan was indeed starting for the Tar Heels, and they won the championship that year.

"I was blowing smoke," Mr. Herring said of his prediction. "I wanted him to play as a freshman."

Laney High School coach Clifton "Pop" Herring horses around with 17-year-old Michael Jordan in November 1980, shortly after his star player announced plans to play for North Carolina. (Photo by Wayne Upchurch, courtesy of the *Wilmington Morning Star.*)

Senior year

Early in Mr. Jordan's senior season, his reputation started growing. Mr. Hebron remembers the *Star-News*/New Hanover tournament that December in Brogden Hall.

"It was an afternoon game and he made a move on the baseline," said Mr. Hebron, who was sitting with Southern Wayne coach Marshall Hamilton. "Marshall immediately said, 'That's a pro move.' It was 15 years ago and I remember it like it was yesterday."

Laney would go on to meet Mr. Hebron's New Hanover team in the tournament final. The Wildcats at that time had Kenny Gattison, now with the NBA's Charlotte Hornets, and Clyde Simmons, now playing pro football with the Philadelphia Eagles.

Mr. Jordan put on the type of show that later made him famous around the world.

He scored nine points in the first three quarters and Laney trailed, 38–29. Then he scored his team's last 15 points, including a jumper with two seconds left to give Laney a 51–49 win.

"He's a great, great player and is capable of doing this to anybody," Mr. Hebron said then.

The Boston Celtics would find this out in 1986 when Mr. Jordan scored 49 points in a playoff game and followed it with 63 the next. The Cleveland Cavaliers would discover the same in 1989, when Mr. Jordan's shot at the buzzer knocked the favored Cavaliers out of the playoffs.

Portland found out in 1992 when Mr. Jordan scored 35 points in the first half of the game of the championship series. The Trail Blazers never quite recovered.

But the Christmas tournament was just the start of Laney's season. There was the game against Eastern Wayne when Mr. Jordan was approaching the school record of 42 points. Mr. Herring let him play long enough to score 44—still a school record—before benching him most of the fourth quarter.

Mr. McLaurin remembers Laney winning at Goldsboro and after the game, a small kid ran onto the court, pretending he was shooting layups and jump shots—all with his tongue hanging out.

The Jordan moves were already attracting imitators.

Mr. Jordan scored on jump shots, but Mr. Herring said his star got most of his points on the fast break. In the open court, no one could stop him. Mr. Hebron remembered that when Laney needed a basket, Mr. Herring would spread out his players on the floor and give the ball to Michael to go one-on-one against a hapless defender.

Reggie Johnson, one of Mr. Jordan's teammates at Laney, remembered how competitive Michael was then—the same trait his college and pro teammates often cite. Mr. Johnson remembered a game against Eastern Wayne during Mr. Jordan's senior year.

"A fan from Eastern Wayne walked up to Mike before the game while we were doing warm-ups," he said. "The Eastern Wayne fan asked Mike for his autograph. Mike gave it to him, but then the fan tore it up right in front of Mike's face.

"Mike ended up having between 27 and 30 points that game. And he got like five dunks, which you didn't hear of any player getting dunks in a game back then. And Mike's dunks in that game were a lot harder than they usually were. After the game, the fan walked up to Mike again, but Mike didn't even recognize him."

None of the success seemed to change the way Michael acted in high school. Mr. Herring said his star was always coachable and got along with his teammates. Mr. McLaurin said Mr. Jordan was also a good student.

"I remember him being a kid in high school," he said. "He was always playing and teasing and joking. He was a great athlete, but that didn't throw him in the big-head category."

The five-year-old school suddenly had a basketball team superior to crosstown rival New Hanover, which had one of the great traditions in the state. Mr. McLaurin said he often closed the gym for Laney home games an hour early because no one else could get inside. A road game at Pender High School was moved to Wallace so more people could watch.

Upset ends prep career

The Bucs were considered to have a good shot at a state championship. They carried a 19–3 record into the conference tournament semifinals at home against New Hanover, the league's fifth-place team that had already lost to Laney three times that year.

New Hanover jumped out to a 14-point halftime lead, but Laney, led by Mr. Jordan, rallied to take a 52–46 lead with 45 seconds left. But New Hanover scored twice to cut the lead to two with 33 seconds left, then fouled Mr. Jordan.

He missed both shots. New Hanover tied the game, then Mr. Jordan missed a shot and fouled out of the game. Ronald Jones made the free throws and New Hanover won the game.

Michael Jordan's high school career was over.

"I thought I would never clear the gym," Mr.

McLaurin said. "There were people there well after one A.M. You would've thought you were in a morgue."

Mr. Jordan cried along with the entire Laney team. But a few days later, Mr. Herring got an idea of where his star senior wanted to take his career.

"He took his whole uniform and took it in front of the trophy case," Mr. Herring said. "Then he brought the uniform in the gym and put it on the door and looked at me.

"He wanted his jersey to be retired."

Three years later, after a national college championship, an Olympic gold medal and the beginning of a pro career, Laney retired his no. 23. Someone stole that jersey not long ago.

The same number was retired after his three-year career at Carolina, and the Bulls have already promised that no one else will wear the number in Chicago.

"I couldn't tell in high school Mike was going to turn out to be this good," Mr. Johnson said. "Don't get me wrong. We knew he was good. But we didn't know he was going to turn out to be this good."

Laney High School Highlights

- School-record 44 points in one game.
- Led Laney to a 19–4 record as a senior.
- Scored last 15 points to lead Laney past New Hanover 51–49 in *Star-News*/New Hanover Tournament.

—from "Highlights of Michael Jordan's basketball career," Wilmington Morning Star, October 7, 1993

26.

The Unlikeliest Homeboy

by Curry Kirkpatrick

All there was to play on was black dirt and tree roots. That's probably why Mike can handle the ball so well, learning to dribble on dirt. It builds up the legs pretty good, too. You ever tried jumping off dirt to dunk?

We were out playing sandlot football, and I was known as a person who was hard to tackle. But that little sucker attempted to tackle me, and I dragged him probably twenty or thirty yards, and he never let go until he got me off my feet. That's the kind of kid he's always been.

—Wayne Loftin, former North Carolina neighbor, from Newsweek Special Issue (October/November 1993)

A hologram—a three-dimensional image—on the cover of the December 21, 1991, issue of Sports Illustrated celebrates its Sportsman of the Year; above his red jacket emblazoned with an NBA logo, Michael Jordan's face changes as the cover is shifted.

One of the pieces written to celebrate Jordan—a retrospective, down-home look at Jordan from his North Carolina days—proves the old adage that you can take the boy out of the country, but you can't take the country out of the boy.

Though Jordan would find his future in Chicago, he never forgot his roots. North Carolina, as he reminds everyone, is holy ground—a point reinforced when, on a road game in Charlotte, he told his deplaning teammates to be sure and wipe their feet because they were now in God's country.

God's country, where a skinny kid named Michael Jordan grew up in a home environment that reinforced the values that hard work pays off, that a fundamental respect for others is essential, and that sports builds character.

Baseball, football, track, and basketball—all were Michael Jordan's playing fields where he would cover himself in glory.

It all began here, in North Carolina—a homeboy who, as they say, had done good.

BECAUSE THE apple doesn't fall far from the tree, isn't it possible that Michael Jordan is not some sort of glorious phenomenon but rather a simple, shining fragment of nature, grounded in family and friends and roots from which he has never strayed? In a word, yes. If the term homeboy wasn't invented for him, surely it should have been.

Only those who have been vacationing in Baghdad for a decade do not know about the Carolina-blue shorts Jordan wears beneath his Bulls uniform to commemorate his undergraduate bliss in Chapel Hill; the "love of the game" clause in his contract, which enables him to join pickup games back on the Hill or in his hometown of Wilmington, N.C., or on the rings of Saturn or anywhere else he wishes; his friendliness and open-faced approachability. "Mike will come out to the park and play," says his high school teammate Leroy Smith, now a rep in Los Angeles for a sporting goods manufacturer.

Smith is not speaking in strictly basketball terms. Jordan always played, talked, schmoozed, kidded around, associated, connected with people. "Sometimes I can't believe I actually was on the same team with this guy," says Smith. "But, you know, we all were—or with somebody like him. I see him now, and he's still just . . . Mike."

Mike? Gatorade didn't originate the tag after all. But if this sounds like another commercial endorsement, that's because sifting through early Jordana elicits nothing but homilies about truth, fairness, and the politically correct American Way. Through the years,

Jordan has been compared with a veritable rainbow coalition of heroes, from Peter Pan to Bill Cosby. Rick Brewer, the sports information director at North Carolina, changed Jordan's name to Michael when he was a freshman only because Brewer thought it sounded better. In maturity, however, Jordan was basically a combo of Richie and the Fonz from the late, lamented TV sapcom "Happy Days"; if that show had featured a true minority character, he would have been like Mike.

Now, having most of his hair and become both a proud father and, in his dotage, one of those tedious, 19th-hole chattering golfers, Jordan hangs on to his own earlier, slap-happy days as if they were sparkling good-luck crystals. Which they may be.

As far back as his days at Trask Junior High and Laney High in the coastal town of Wilmington, Jordan wore his hair so close-cropped that the older guys would give him noogies and call him Bald Head. His dad, James, who worked his way up at the General Electric plant from mechanic to dispatcher to foreman to the coat-and-tie supervisor of three departments, also found time to build a dirt basketball court and two plywood goals out in the backyard. And Jordan's beloved golf? His college roommate, Buzz Peterson (now an assistant coach at North Carolina State), and fellow Tar Heel Davis Love III (now a veteran on the PGA Tour) introduced him to the links as a kind of therapy following the Tar Heels' 1984 NCAA tournament upset loss to Indiana, still the most devastating defeat in Jordan's (and Coach Dean Smith's) career.

Memories. Crystals. Jordan ravages the NBA wearing the left-arm brace he donned in college to honor Peterson, who suffered a leg injury against Virginia in 1983 that ended his season. Jordan travels the world checking into hotels under an alias borrowed from the six-foot-eight fellow who beat him out for the last spot on the Laney team in '78, when Jordan was a callow sophomore, the aforementioned Leroy Smith. Jordan shares sports trivia and pool cues, business deals and advancing baldness with Adolph Shiver of Charlotte, who was recently introduced on "Oprah" as "Michael's best friend" and who introduced himself to Jordan on a junior high playground in '76 by talking trash with a toothpick in his mouth. When Jordan is feeling especially blue—most recently over the ordeal of Magic Johnson—he still picks up the car phone and calls David Bridgers, a short, slight Anyman who wears a baseball cap and lives in a trailer in Wilmington with his wife and baby daughter and who manages Hill's Grocery now that the local Kroger, where he used to work, has shut down.

In chronological order, relationshipwise, that's Bridgers to Shiver to Smith to Peterson; white to black to black to white. Is it any wonder that Jordan would later become known in marketing circles as sports' first multiracial-societal crossover? Something like that.

Jordan and Bridgers have been cheering each other up since they were in the third grade, playing baseball and riding bicycles together through the woods around Weavers Acres in North Wilmington. Jordan claimed "family time" was responsible for his snubbing President Bush in October 1991 at the Rose Garden ceremony honoring the NBA champion Bulls; in reality, he was playing golf with a passel of old buddies, including Shiver and Bridgers. "Mike told me last summer to lose my Fu Manchu mustache before Hilton Head," says the five-foot-nine Bridgers. "I said sure—so long as he got rid of his earring. So I shave and show up, and there he is, that ear rock glittering away. Then he has the nerve to smile and say: 'And it's staying. But David, you sure look good.' Mike? That mug is some shyster."

Jordan's mother, the former Deloris Peoples, met James Jordan (whom she calls Ray) in 1956 after a high school basketball game in Wallace, N.C., some 40 miles north of Wilmington, when she and her cousin caught a ride home with him. She was sitting in the backseat when James almost went past her house. "Oh, I didn't realize I had somebody else in here," he said. "You're pretty cute."

"You're pretty fresh," she said.

"Could be. But someday I'll marry you," he said.

She was all of 15, but someday came surely enough a few years later after Deloris, homesick at Tuskegee (Ala.) Institute, returned to the Wilmington area and to James, then on leave from the Air Force. The Jordans had "two sets of children" (Deloris's term): James Ronald, now 35, an army sergeant working in communications at Fort Monmouth, N.J., and Deloris Chasten, 34, a homemaker in Philadelphia, compose the first set; Larry, 29, Michael, 28, and Roslyn, 27, the second.

The Jordan parents, along with Larry and Roslyn, now work for companies associated with their famous son/sib and live in Charlotte, N.C. Oddly enough, Mike was born at the Cumberland County Hospital in Brooklyn, N.Y., while his father was in Air Force training. Upon returning to North Carolina, the Jordans moved from tiny Wallace to Wilmington, where James build a large, split-level tan brick and clapboard house on Gordon Road with 12 acres of fields out back and the St. Paul's Missionary Baptist Church across the street. The mostly black Weavers Acres neighborhood lies about halfway between downtown and the beach, three miles away, where the Jordans used to buy fresh shellfish or just sit at night on a dock and listen to the ocean.

Jordan takes his sense of humor from his dad, who used to do work around the house with his tongue hanging out (sound familiar?), his sense of business from his mom, and his work ethic from both. "The Jordans are from the old school, where education and teachers and administrators meant something to parents," says Laney High principal Kenneth McLaurin. Young Mike got in trouble in school only once, when he skipped class to go across the street for some junk food at the minimart. Suspended, Mike was made to accompany his mother to her job at the United Carolina Bank, where he studied all day. "The first year I had him, he was scared to death," recalls Janice Hardy, who taught Jordan algebra and trigonometry at Laney. "I liked that. The next year he wound up in the front row. He'd laugh at my jokes and muss my hair. I must have been a pretty good teacher—he's worth, what, a *trillion* a couple of times over?"

Jordan's legacy in education and finance seems to have been grasped only partly by his six-year-old nephew, Corey Peoples, who, when editorializing upon some recent problems in school, announced, "I don't have to do no work; I got the richest uncle in the world." Jordan's response was to promise Corey $20 for every "A" he earned—a bribe, perhaps, but one with a worthy message. Maybe this is what Mike meant when he told NBC's Maria Shriver last August that "even my mistakes have been perfect."

But, as even his mother allows, Michael hasn't always been perfect. "Way back when I came crying home from Tuskegee, my mother should have put me right back on the train," she says. "I wanted to correct that error with our kids. Mike wasn't the easiest to bring up. We had to be stern. But if I'd had to pick one of the children who would turn out this way, yes, he would have been the one."

In fact, Michael was the laziest of the Jordan offspring. "Never knew him to hold a job—or want to," says Larry, only semilaughing. Larry is the storied Jordan brother whom Mike credits with motivating him to much of his success in basketball, the five-foot-seven brother who teased Mike about his big ears and then fought him and dunked on him and beat him all the time in the backyard until Mike couldn't take it anymore and decided to grow nearly a foot taller.

"We grew up one-on-one," says Larry, who played in the six-foot-four-and-under World Basketball League two years ago. "But the last time we competed, he just looked down at my feet, and he said, 'Remember whose name is on your shoes.'"

While the eldest Jordan brother, who's known as Ron, drove a school bus and worked at Shoney's before leaving for his life in the military, and while Larry is mechanically oriented, quiet, and thrives on privacy, Mike seemed allergic to toil anywhere but on athletic fronts. He bribed his brothers and sisters to get out of doing errands. He was the ultimate jock, the social animal. "He could never be in his room by himself," says his mother. "He always had to go out, spend the night with a friend, go camping." Jordan quit his only high school job, at a Wilmington hotel, posthaste. "Mom!" he explained. "What if my friends saw me? The boss had me out on the sidewalk, sweeping!"

In high school Mike's friends ranged across the board, from ballplayers to members of the student government to debaters to guys in the band (in which he once played the trumpet).

"Laney seemed like a family back then," says Leroy Smith. "It had about a 60–40 white-to-black ratio, but it was really cool. No tension or anything. It was a new school. For there to be no real 'sides'—that was unusual. Mike being Mike, he was unusual too. We were all searching for an identity. But Mike . . . it was like he'd already found his."

Pre–high school, Jordan's close friend Bridgers, the son of a taxi driver, had moved to Wilmington from South Dakota. But after his parents were divorced, James Jordan became a surrogate dad to this white kid from another planet who shared with Mike a passion for baseball. The two alternated pitching and playing centerfield on a Little League team that made the district playoffs and fell one game short of making the Little League World Series (Jordan pitched a two-hitter but lost 1–0 in the last game). "Before every pitch, I'd look at Mike in center, and he'd give me thumbs-up," says Bridgers. "With him on the mound, I'd do the same."

While riding bikes one summer afternoon, they jumped into a neighborhood swimming pool. The owners weren't home, but Bridgers knew the babysitter. What he didn't know was that the owners would return right away.

"They saw Mike and threw us out," Bridgers says. "The rest of the bike ride he was very quiet. I asked him if he knew why they threw us out. He said yes. I asked if it bothered him. He said no. Then he just smiled. I'll never forget it. He said, 'I got cooled off enough. How about you?' Mike taught me a lot about dealing with prejudice.

"I got called nigger lover and white trash, but he showed me how to ignore it. Once when I was visiting Mike up at a party in Chapel Hill, a fight broke out along racial lines. He got me out of there quick. Mike always said, 'Don't worry about race unless somebody slaps you in the face.' He's so positive. Every time I see him, it's a natural high."

Jordan's gravest burden may have come in high school when he was compelled to handle a "situation" in which his two best friends nearly came to blows over remarks Shiver made to Bridgers's girlfriend. Bridgers had gone for a stick, but Jordan stopped him from using it and went after Shiver himself. "Mike didn't exactly mediate," says a man who remembers the day. "He threw Adolph up against the wall and threatened to kill his butt if that happened again. It was the only time we'd ever seen him lose his cool."

Somehow Shiver and Bridgers both still take part in Jordan's golf outings, coexisting peacefully, perhaps out of respect for their mutual pal. But, oh, those games.

Ordinarily, though, the young Jordan was reluctant to confront emotionally charged situations. While he was away at college, a high school friend named Cythia Canty died of kidney failure. Jordan went to Wilmington to pay his respects, but he didn't go to the funeral. Likewise, when his grandmother Rosabell Jordan died, he couldn't bear to attend the ceremony. Last Christmas an interviewer asked Jordan what gift he would cherish most. He said one more visit with Rosabell. Says Deloris, "Mike carries a lot inside him. I read that, and I knew."

There weren't always easy times on the basketball court either. The Laney Buccaneers won 19 games in Jordan's senior season, but they were eliminated by New Hanover in the conference tournament when Jordan fouled out against the Wildcats, a team that featured Kenny Gattison (currently of the Charlotte Hornets) and Clyde Simmons (of the NFL Philadelphia Eagles).

Still to come, though, would be Jordan doing the following: nailing the basket that won the NCAA championship for the Tar Heels, receiving two college Player of the Year awards, leading the 1984 U.S. Olympic team to the gold medal, winning five scoring titles in the pros, and ultimately carrying the Bulls to the NBA championship. Oh, yes, and appearing on the front of the Wheaties box, which Deloris says is what makes her the most proud. "How many moms can walk in the grocery store and see their son all over the cereal counter?" she asks.

There were five Jordans in the class of 1981 at Laney High, four girls—one of them Roslyn, who was able to skip a grade so she could accompany her brother to Chapel Hill—and Michael Jeffrey, whose credits in the yearbook, *The Spinnaker*, read in part: "Homeroom Rep 10, Spanish Club 11 . . . New Hanover Hearing Board 12 . . . Pep Club 10." *The Spinnaker* sailed into prescient waters with its parting message to the school's basketball stars, Jordan and Smith: "Laney only hopes that you . . . expand your talents to make others as proud of you as Laney has been. Always remember Laney as your world."

Little could *The Spinnaker* staff have known that soon enough those two alums would turn out to be the same man—at least in some hotels on some road trips. Or that jug-eared Michael Jeffrey Jordan, all by himself, would pull off one more flying, spinning, double reverse and turn the entire world into just another little piece of Laney.

27.

Alone on the Mountaintop

by Jack McCallum

When Sports Illustrated *selected Michael Jordan in 1991 as its "Sportsman of the Year," it seemed fitting that one of the tribute pieces was written by Jack McCallum, who has covered Jordan and the Bulls for years.*

In this piece, published in the December 23, 1991, issue of Sports Illustrated, *McCallum takes a look at Jordan at the height of his career—one that ended prematurely, 22 months later.*

AT THE relatively tender age of 28, he stands alone on the mountaintop, unquestionably the most famous athlete on the planet and one of its most famous citizens of any kind. We've heard it so often that it's now a cliché, though nonetheless accurate: He *transcends* sports. He keeps a championship ring on his dresser at home and will be making room for another if his team (18–3 at week's end) plays the next six months of the season the way it has played the first two. A two-time MVP, he was probably the best player in the world even before Magic Johnson's retirement, but now the subject isn't even worth debating.

He will earn about $25 million in 1992, only $3.8 million of it from his day job—the rest, an astonishing $21.2 million, from a flood of endorsements. His name and his face are on sneakers, sandwiches, soft drinks, and cereal boxes, to mention just a few items. He has a lovely and loving wife, two adorable sons, and a relationship with his parents that is so good, the sappiest sitcom wouldn't touch it. He is bothered somewhat by tendinitis and a bone spur in his left knee but is otherwise in outstanding health. He has trouble off the tee from time to time, but his handicap is still in single figures and any number of professional tutors are at his beck and call.

And, so, despite a few aesthetic drawbacks—near baldness, skinny legs, overly long basketball trunks, and the continuing tendency to stick out his tongue—we honor Michael Jeffrey Jordan as our Sportsman of the Year for 1991.

It is a virtual certainty that since the award originated in 1954, no athlete has been as popular on a worldwide scale as Jordan is now and, for that matter, has been for the last several years. He has surpassed every standard by which we gauge the fame of an athlete and, with few exceptions, has handled the adulation with a preternatural grace and ease that have cut across lines of race, age, and gender.

"He has a level of popularity and a value as a commercial spokesman that is almost beyond comprehension," says Nova Lanktree, director of the Burns Sports Center in Chicago, an organization that has been lining up athletes for commercials and tracking their popularity for more than two decades. "It is a singular phenomenon. It never happened before and may not ever happen again."

Although it is the singularity of Jordan that is so often celebrated—no one dunks, smiles, or sells sneakers the way he does—it is no coincidence that he is being honored by *Sports Illustrated* only after his *team,* the Chicago Bulls, won a championship. Jordan's seven-year NBA career has been, curiously, both a rocket to stardom and a struggle for vindication. To many NBA observers, the Bulls had to win it all before Jordan could conclusively prove that he was more than a high-flying sideshow or a long loud ring of the cash register. They did. And so he did.

Superstars should be judged, first and foremost, for their consistency, their ability to produce over the long haul, as Jordan most assuredly has (he has averaged between 22.7 and 37.1 points in each of his eight seasons). But the most unforgettable of the breed also offer a collection of moments, rare and incandescent, and Jordan has given us a wide assortment of those: writhing and twisting his way through the Celtics to score 49 and 63 points at Boston Garden in the 1986 playoffs; exploding for 40 points to win the MVP award at his "home" All-Star game at Chicago Stadium in '88; dribbling the length of the floor, pulling up and hitting a 14-foot jump shot to send Game Three of last year's finals, which the Bulls went on to win, into overtime.

Is Jordan the greatest ever? A definite answer is impossible, of course, as it has been whenever the question has been applied to Wilt Chamberlain, Oscar Robertson, Larry Bird, or Magic. But a case can certainly be made. Of that distinguished quartet, only Chamberlain could begin to match Jordan's pure athleticism, but put that aside for a moment and consider his basketball skills and the way he plays the game.

Jordan is now a better shooter than Bird, not from long range, certainly, but from 20 feet in. "I don't do much shooting in the summer anymore, so I don't completely understand it myself," says Jordan. "But it's a fact. Everything about it—my mechanics, when to take the shot, the release—feels better and smoother."

He is not a better passer than the Magic of the 1980s, but were the Bulls, like the Lakers, a fast-break team and were Jordan, like Magic, a point guard, he very well might be. And in half-court situations, when called upon to give up the ball under pressure and find the open man at the last conceivable second, he is without peer.

Jordan never put up rebounding numbers from the backcourt like those of Robertson, who averaged 7.5 per game over 14 seasons. But the Big O played in an era when, at six-foot-five, he was often among the bigger players on the floor, while Jordan, in the era of the seven-footer, is no worse than the second-best rebounding guard in today's game (behind the Portland Trail Blazers' Clyde Drexler). Jordan and Robertson are similar in a way, dynamic, demanding, and fearless leaders who command nothing less than total respect on the floor. But Robertson, though a superb athlete, was subject to the laws of gravity (as Jordan is not) and was never nearly as exciting.

Can Jordan dominate a game in the manner of Chamberlain—he of the 100-point game and the 50.4-point scoring average (in 1961–62)? Not when today's double-teaming and trapping can take the ball out of one man's hands for long stretches of the game. But by dint of nonstop effort, a *rage* to play that Wilt never possessed, Jordan comes close. "Every single game, Jordan plays every single play like it's his last," says Los Angeles Clippers guard Doc Rivers. Then, too, Wilt never provided the level of anticipation that Jordan does merely by touching the ball. Out comes the

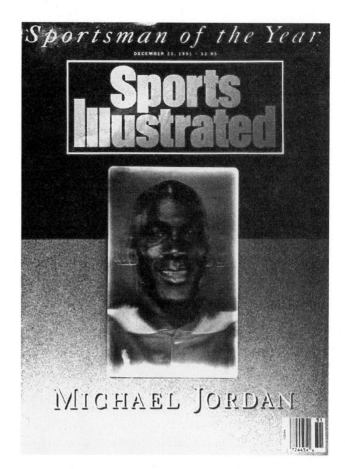

Jordan is immortalized in a hologram for the cover of the December 23, 1991, issue of *Sports Illustrated,* honoring him as Sportsman of the Year.

tongue, from side to side goes the head, and down goes the ball in a hard dribble. *What's going to happen? What will he do now?* Julius Erving came close to inspiring that same edge-of-the-seat drama, but the Doctor never had Jordan's offensive repertoire, lacking mainly the pull-up jumper that makes the contemporary Jordan more unstoppable than ever.

It might be hard to fathom because he has been a household name for so long, but Jordan is now at the absolute peak of his career and could be the league's MVP for another three or four years. His contract (as presently structured, anyway) extends to the end of the 1995–96 season, after which he says he'll retire. Maybe. So, barring injury, look for, at a minimum, another 12,000 points, 1,800 rebounds, 1,000 steals, and five million tongue-waggings from the wondrous athletic machine that is Air Jordan.

"Michael—he's the best," says San Antonio Spurs coach Larry Brown. "I grew up with Connie Hawkins. I saw Julius at his peak. No one went through the ACC like David Thompson. I love Magic and Larry. But Michael, as far as what I've seen . . ." Brown stops and shakes his head. "I'd pay money to see him play. I'd pay money to see him *practice.*"

There are times when his teammates would no doubt pay money so that Jordan would *not* practice. His almost psychotic competitiveness in even the most casual practice situation has caused some strain over the years, much of which has been chronicled in *The Jordan Rules,* the best-seller written by the *Chicago Tribune*'s Sam Smith. But, ultimately, what hath it wrought? A much grittier Chicago team, that's certain. The Bulls had won 17 of their last 18 games through Sunday.

Jordan is, as usual, playing superbly. Never mind the scoring, a category in which he has led the NBA for the last five seasons and in which he is leading again, with a 29.5 average, or the shooting percentage (.531, second in the league among guards). He and forwards Scottie Pippen and Horace Grant have become like a Bermuda Triangle on defense, swallowing up offenses with their court-covering capabilities, and that is why Chicago is clearly the best team in the NBA. Jordan's detractors would theorize that he has now stepped back and given players like Pippen and Grant the chance to breathe and make a name for themselves. But in point of fact, Jordan's own will to succeed, as thorny as it may sometimes be, has inspired his teammates to reach their potential.

"I look forward to playing now, more than ever," Jordan said recently, relaxing in his hotel suite in Berkeley, Calif., before a game against the Golden State Warriors. "It's the only place I can get relief from what's happening off the court. It's always been that way to a certain extent, but it's even more so now. Basketball is my escape, my refuge. It seems that everything else is so . . . so busy and complicated."

Busy he's used to. Complicated, maybe not. For perhaps the first time in his life, Jordan is sensing a backlash against his fame, a subtle dissatisfaction with the whole *idea* of Michael Jordan. He has heard it in all the talk about *The Jordan Rules,* he has read it in letters to the editor, read it between the lines. "Signs are starting to show that people are tired of hearing about Michael Jordan's positive image and Michael Jordan's positive influence," said Mr. Positive Image and Positive Influence. "Five, six, seven years at the pinnacle of success, and it's got to start turning around. I've always tried to project everything positive. People say you need role models in the world, and people were asking for them, and I never thought a role model should be negative. If you wanted negativity, then you wouldn't have asked for Michael Jordan. You might've asked for Mike Tyson or somebody else.

"In retrospect, maybe I was wrong. Maybe I should've shown some negativity, so people had a sense of me as a human being. I could have been more honest, I guess, about some of the mistakes I made. Like what? Well, I did hit [teammate] Will Perdue in the face. That was a mistake, and I could've talked about it [as Smith did in *The Jordan Rules*]. I've made some bad endorsements, like Time Jordan [a watch deal Jordan signed with a Canadian company, Excelsior, that never got ticking]. But what do you know when you're 21 and 22 going through all this? You mature as you go through it all, but you're not mature when it starts."

There are not many 28-year-old multimillionaires who are forced into such introspection about their images, and in all likelihood, a more cautious, less childlike Jordan will evolve out of his self-examination. David Burns, president of Burns Sports Service, says he doesn't see any backlash against Jordan: "He's as wildly popular as ever and still worth every dollar any advertiser wants to pay him." But Jordan feels it is better to hear the whistle in the distance than to get run over by the train, and as a remedy for overkill, he's talking about reducing his off-the-court commitments, taking a step back, becoming a more private person.

"I don't need my name in lights to keep going," says Jordan. "I know people think I do, but I don't. If you told me in college that within a year my face would be all over the world and millions of people would know my name, I'd have said you were crazy. I certainly didn't turn it down when it came my way, but I didn't ask for it, either."

He sure got it, though, and now any conversation about him tends to sound like a global marketing report. Remember the cynical bumper sticker that came along in the Acquisitive Eighties? *The one with the most toys in the end wins.* Well, Jordan has the most toys. Game's over. He's won. So, let's just enjoy the world's best basketball player at the height of his powers.

The game, after all, is what made Jordan what he is today, and fortunately, the game is still what he lives and breathes for. Already this season he has talked trash with the Warriors' Tim Hardaway; shot (and made) a free throw with his eyes closed to have some fun with Denver Nugget rookie Dikembe Mutombo; and driven to distraction his hated rivals, the Pistons, with his usual dazzling all-around game. He may talk about stepping out of the spotlight, but it's not going to happen for a while, not so long as there's an acrobatic slam-dunk left in his Air Jordans and a competitive muscle twitching in his body. The view from the mountaintop is breathtaking, and there's no place that Michael Jordan would rather be. Look up and revel in him, for his equal will not soon be along.

Michael Jordan signs autographs for fans at charity golf event. (Photo courtesy of the *Durham Herald-Sun.*)

28.

Statistics

Michael Jeffrey Jordan

Born: February 17, 1963
Birthplace: Brooklyn, New York
Height: 6'6"
Weight: 198 lbs.
Drafted: First round (third overall) Chicago, 1984
Pro experience: nine years (retired October 1993)
College: University of North Carolina
High school: Emsley A. Laney (Wilmington, NC)
Wife: Juanita
Children: Jeffrey, Marcus, and Jazman
Resides: Chicago, Illinois

College Statistics (University of North Carolina)

Year	G	FGM	FGA	Pct.	FTM	FTA	Pct.	Reb.	Pts.	Avg.
81–82	34	191	358	.534	78	108	.722	149	460	13.5
82–83	36	282	527	.535	123	167	.737	197	721	20.0
83–84	31	247	448	.551	113	145	.779	163	607	19.6
Total	101	720	1333	.540	314	420	.748	509	1788	17.7

1984 Olympic Games (Los Angeles, Calif.)

Year	G	FGM/FGA	Pct.	3PM/3PA	Pct.	FTM/FTA	Pct.	Reb./Avg.	Pts./Avg.	Ast.	Blk.	Stl.
1984	8	60–110	.545	NA	NA	17/25	.680	24/3.0	137/17.1	16	7	12

1992 Olympic Games (Barcelona, Spain)

Year	G	FGM/FGA	Pct.	3PM/3PA	Pct.	FTM/FTA	Pct.	Reb./Avg.	PF	Pts./Avg.	Blk.	Stl.
1992	8	51–113	.451	4/19	.210	13/19	.684	19/2.4	14	119/14.9	4	37

NBA Regular-Season Record

Year	G.	Min.	FGM	FGA	Pct.	FTM	FTA	Pct.	Off. Reb.	Def. Reb.	Tot. Reb.	Ast.	PF	DQ	Stl.	Blk.	TO	Pts.	Avg.
84–85	82	3144	837	1625	.515	630	746	.845	167	367	534	481	285	4	196	69	291	2313	28.2
85–86	18	451	150	328	.457	105	125	.840	23	41	64	53	40	0	37	21	45	408	22.7
86–87	82	3281	1098	2279	.482	833	972	.857	166	264	430	377	237	0	236	125	272	3041	37.1
87–88	82	3311	1069	1998	.535	723	860	.841	139	310	449	485	270	2	259	131	252	2868	35.0
88–89	81	3255	966	1795	.538	674	793	.850	149	503	652	650	247	2	234	65	290	2633	32.5
89–90	82	3197	1034	1964	.526	593	699	.848	143	422	565	519	241	0	227	54	247	2753	33.6
90–91	82	3034	990	1837	.539	571	671	.851	118	374	492	453	229	1	223	83	202	2580	31.5
91–92	80	3102	943	1818	.519	491	590	.832	91	420	511	489	201	1	182	75	200	2404	30.1
92–93	78	3067	992	2003	.495	476	569	.837	135	387	522	428	188	0	221	61	207	2541	32.6
Totals	667	25842	8079	15647	.516	5096	6025	.846	1131	3088	4219	3935	1938	10	1815	684	2006	21541	32.3

NBA Playoff Record

Year	G.	Min.	FGM	FGA	Pct.	FTM	FTA	Pct.	Off. Reb.	Def. Reb.	Tot. Reb.	Ast.	PF	DQ	Stl.	Blk.	TO	Pts.	Avg.
84–85	4	171	34	78	.436	48	58	.828	7	16	23	34	15	0	11	4	15	117	29.3
85–86	3	135	48	95	.505	34	39	.872	5	14	19	17	13	1	7	4	14	131	43.7
86–87	3	128	35	84	.417	35	39	.897	7	14	21	18	11	0	6	7	8	107	35.7
87–88	10	427	138	260	.530	86	99	.869	23	48	71	47	38	1	24	12	39	363	36.3
88–89	17	718	199	390	.510	183	229	.799	26	93	119	130	65	1	42	13	68	591	34.8
89–90	16	674	219	426	.514	133	159	.836	24	91	115	109	54	0	45	14	56	587	36.7
90–91	17	689	197	376	.524	125	148	.845	18	90	108	142	53	0	40	23	43	529	31.1
91–92	22	920	290	581	.499	162	189	.857	37	100	137	127	82	0	44	16	81	759	34.5
92–93	19	783	251	528	.475	136	169	.805	32	96	128	114	58	0	39	17	17	666	35.1
Totals	111	4645	1411	2818	.501	942	1129	.845	179	562	741	738	389	3	258	110	341	3850	34.7

NBA All-Star Game Record

Year	Min.	Reb.	Ast.	Stl.	3-PT	Pts.
1985	22	6	2	3	0	7
1987	28	0	4	2	0	11
1988	29	8	3	4	0	40
1989	33	2	3	5	0	28
1990	29	5	2	5	1	17
1991	36	5	5	2	0	26
1992	31	1	5	2	0	18
1993	36	4	5	4	1	30
Totals	244	31	29	27	2	177

Note: In 1986 Jordan was selected but did not play in the NBA All-Star game because of a foot injury which kept him out for most of the season.

Jordan's Highest Scoring Games

69 points, Cleveland Cavaliers, March 28, 1990

64 points, Orlando Magic, January 16, 1993

63 points, Boston Celtics, April 21, 1986 (playoff game)

61 points, Detroit Pistons, March 4, 1987

61 points, Atlanta Hawks, April 16, 1987

59 points, Detroit Pistons, April 3, 1988

58 points, New Jersey Nets, February 26, 1987

57 points, Washington Bullets, December 23, 1992

56 points, Philadelphia 76ers, March 24, 1987

56 points, Miami Heat, April 29, 1992 (playoff game)

55 points, Cleveland Cavaliers, May 1, 1988 (playoff game)

55 points, Phoenix Suns, June 16, 1993 (playoff game)

54 points, Cleveland Cavaliers, November 3, 1989

54 points, Los Angeles Lakers, November 20, 1992

54 points, New York Knicks, May 31, 1993 (playoff game)

53 points, Portland Trail Blazers, January 8, 1987

53 points, Indiana Pacers, April 12, 1987

53 points, Phoenix Suns, January 21, 1989

52 points, Charlotte Hornets, March 12, 1993

52 points, Cleveland Cavaliers, December 17, 1987

52 points, Portland Trail Blazers, February 26, 1988

52 points, Boston Celtics, November 9, 1988

52 points, Philadelphia 76ers, November 16, 1988

52 points, Denver Nuggets, November 26, 1988

52 points, Orlando Magic, December 20, 1989

51 points, Washington Bullets, March 19, 1992

—*from the* Chicago Sun-Times, *October 7, 1993*

Rookie sensation Michael Jordan launches a jump shot against the desperate defense of San Antonio's Johnny Moore in a 1984 game. (Photo by Robert E. Reeder, courtesy of the *Chicago Sun-Times*.)

29.

Jordan's Top 10 "Kodak" Moments on Court

by Dan Bickley

In the course of a long career—spanning college games, two Olympics, and nine years in the NBA—Jordan gave us, night after night, year after year, repeat performances that we never wanted to see end. To have to pick, then, the high-lights would be tough, but Bickley—in the Chicago Sun-Times *the day after Jordan retired—chose well.*

TRY STANDING in the Louvre and picking out your 10 fa-vorite paintings.

Tough, huh?

Now try scrolling through a library search system that offers 7,192 references about a man named Michael Jordan, and pick out the 10 most memorable things he's done on a basketball court.

Yeah, right.

Alas, it's impossible to measure art. And with Jor-dan, that's exactly what you get every time he puts on a uniform.

"All the things you see him do on TV, jumping on one side of the lane, ending up on the other side of the lane . . . it's for real," Orlando Magic star Shaquille O'Neal said. "I think he scored 64 points on us, so he's the best in the world."

Not that scoring 64 points against the Magic would make anyone the best in the world, but O'Neal's point is well taken. And with that in mind, we'll put a frame around the following images and call them the 10 most memorable acts from a most memorable person.

1. The Beginning: North Carolina coach Dean Smith had a certain feeling about his remarkable fresh-man, so with 25 points to play in the 1982 NCAA championship game and the Tar Heels trailing George-town 62–61, he called a play for Michael Jordan.

Swish.

What else did you expect?

Jordan had taken a pass on the left perimeter, and unleashed a feathery jumper from 16 feet that hit noth-ing but net, eventually giving the Tar Heels their first national title.

"That shot did a lot for his confidence," Smith said.

2. The Showcase: After missing 64 games with a broken foot, Jordan scored a playoff-record 63 points against the Celtics in the Boston Garden in 1986. The Bulls lost the game 135–131 in double overtime and were swept in three games, but Jordan's immense abil-ity became the talk of the NBA.

And it stayed that way for the next seven years.

"I had missed 64 games that year and I was anxious to come back and help us make the playoffs," Jordan said. "I like accepting challenges and proving people wrong. And I was able to do so big-time."

3. The Slam: Jordan scored a perfect "10" when he raced the full length of the floor, took off from the foul line, and converted a slam dunk before a capacity crowd during All-Star festivities at the Stadium in 1988. The dunk enabled Jordan to win his second consecu-tive slam-dunk title, this time defeating the high-flying Dominique Wilkins.

"It was my way of paying tribute to Dr. J," Jordan said. "It was also the only way I could beat Dominique."

4. The Shot, Part I: The Bulls trailed 100–99 in Game Five of a 1989 playoff series against the Cleveland Cavaliers at the Richfield Coliseum when Jordan took an inbounds pass, and drove laterally toward the foul line.

Jordan double-pumped a jump shot in the face of Craig Ehlo that went in as time expired, changing the direction of two franchises.

"Winning that series turned things around for us in a big way," Jordan said. "Some writers even picked us to get swept like we were swept [6–0] during the regular season. But I put my credibility on the line by predict-ing we would win. I had to make good."

5. The Turning Point: The Bulls were trying to win their first NBA championship, but they split the first two games and trailed by 13 points in Game Three at the Forum. But with 3.4 seconds left, Jordan arched a shot over Byron Scott and Vlade Divac that found the bottom of the net, forcing overtime. The Bulls eventually won 104–96, and closed out the series in five games.

"The series could've ended in L.A. if the Lakers won all three games," Jordan said. "But once I made that shot, I knew we'd win the title."

6. The Layup: In Game Two of the 1991 NBA finals against the Lakers, Jordan made a layup that will forever make the rounds on basketball highlight films. He drove the lane as if he were going to dunk with his right hand, then switched to his left in midair and banked in a layup.

We'll let Magic Johnson explain: "He came down the lane, went one way, put it in one hand, floated about five more yards and said, 'Well, I don't know.' Then he changed hands and laid it in off the glass. That's just the kind of power he is. He can do the impossible and unbelievable."

7. The Tears: Jordan had produced 30 points and 10 assists in Game Five of the 1991 finals, leading the Bulls to their first NBA championship. After being named series MVP, Jordan clutched the championship trophy, and wept unashamedly before a national audience.

"I've never been that emotional in public before, but I couldn't help myself," Jordan said. "Winning that championship capped it all for me. It ended seven years of waiting."

8. The Shrug: Game One of the 1992 NBA finals, and even Michael Jordan had a hard time fathoming the talent of Michael Jordan.

He had just nailed the last of his six three-pointers in the first half, establishing an NBA record, and he put his arms out to the side. He looked over at the scorer's table, glanced at Magic Johnson, and shook his head in disbelief.

9. The Shot, Part II: Not as dramatic or as important as the first one in Cleveland, but incredible. In a second-round series against the Cavaliers in 1993, Jordan took an inbounds pass, and had the ball swatted briefly by Gerald Wilkins. Jordan regained possession, then skied a jumper over Wilkins that again eliminated the Cavs.

"There's not much you can do when it's Michael Jordan," Wilkins said. "You just have to appreciate his talent."

10. The Finale: After Jordan missed a shot with 1:29 left, it seemed like the Phoenix Suns would win Game Six at home and force a decisive Game Seven. But after the Suns missed their own attempt at the basket, Jordan pulled down a rebound and cut through traffic for an uncontested layup. It would be the last basket Jordan scored as a member of the Bulls, and moments later, John Paxson nailed a three-pointer to give the Bulls a 99–98 victory.

Jordan finished with 33 points, carted off his third consecutive finals MVP award, and won his third consecutive NBA championship—something Larry Bird or Magic Johnson never accomplished.

"That was my driving force, beating Magic," Jordan said. "It's done."

30.

Career Highlights

Regular-season stats:

- 667 games played
- 3,935 assists
- 5,096 free throws made
- 10 times, fouled out
- 32.3 scoring average
- 21,541 points scored

All-Star stats:

- Made the team every year in the league (played eight times, selected but sat out one time because of a foot injury)
- 22.1 scoring average

Playoff stats:

- 111 postseason games played
- 34.7 scoring average
- most points in a half—35, vs. Portland
- record scoring average—41, vs. Phoenix

Miscellaneous:

- His career scoring average of 32.45 is the highest of any player in NBA/ABA history
- Ranks 15th on the all-time NBA scoring list
- Led the NBA in steals in 1988, 1990, and 1993
- Holds the NBA playoff game record for most points: 63 (vs. Boston, April 20, 1986)
- Times scoring 50 or more points—34
- Times scoring 60 or more points—5
- Free throws made in a quarter—14 (tying NBA record)
- Most points in a single game—69

Season-by-season highlights:

1984–85 season:

- NBA Rookie of the Year.
- Averaged 28.2 points, 6.5 rebounds, 5.9 assists, and 2.4 steals, leading Bulls (38–44) to first playoff berth since 1981.
- Averaged 29.3 points in four playoff games as Bulls lost to Milwaukee 3–1.
- Second-team All-NBA.
- Starter on Eastern Conference All-Star team.
- Scored 16 points in debut, a 109–83 victory over Washington (December 26, 1984).
- Set Bulls rookie single-game scoring record with 49 points against Detroit (February 12, 1985).
- Set Bulls records for points (2,313), field goals (837), free throws (630), free throw attempts (746), and steals (196).
- Bulls average attendance went from 6,365 in 1983–84 to 11,887.

1985–86 season:

- Missed 64 games due to broken foot.
- In 18 games, had career-low averages in scoring (22.7 ppg.), rebounds (3.6 rpg.), steals (2.1 spg.), and shooting percentage (.457), but still scored a play-off record 63 points in a 135–131 double-overtime loss to Boston in the first round of the playoffs.
- Averaged 43.7 points in three playoff games.

1986–87 season:

- All-NBA first team.
- Led the league in scoring (37.1 ppg.) with 3,041 points, the third-highest point total in league history.

- Only player in league history to have more than 200 steals and 100 blocks in the same season.

- NBA Slam Dunk Champion, scoring a perfect 10 when he slammed one home from the free-throw line after a court-length sprint.

- Average attendance up from 11,445 in 1985–86 to 15,871.

1987–88 season:

- Selected NBA Most Valuable Player.

- Selected Defensive Player of the Year.

- Selected All-Star Game Most Valuable Player.

- Selected Slam Dunk Champion.

- Led the league in scoring (35 ppg.) and steals (3.2 spg.) as Bulls (50–32) posted their best record in 13 years and advanced to the Eastern Conference semifinals, where they lost 4–1 to Detroit.

- Averaged 36.3 points in 10 playoff games.

- Scored season-high 50 points in 113–103 victory over Boston.

- Bulls average attendance reached a record 18,061.

1988–89 season:

- All-NBA first team.

- All-Defensive first team.

- *The Sporting News* Player of the Year.

- His 17-footer at the buzzer beat Cleveland 101–100 at Richfield Coliseum in the decisive fifth game of the Bulls' first-round playoff.

- Led the league in scoring (32.5 ppg.).

- Averaged 34.8 points in 17 playoff games, leading Bulls to Eastern Conference finals, their first conference championship series berth in 14 years (Bulls lost the series 4–2 to Detroit).

1990–91 season:

- Selected NBA Most Valuable Player for the second time and the NBA Finals MVP in leading Bulls to their first NBA title.

- Led the league in scoring (31.5 ppg.) as Bulls (61–21) had their best record in team history, then went 15–2 in the playoffs.

- Averaged 31.1 points in the playoffs.

- His 12-foot jumper with 3.4 seconds left in regulation capped a comeback from 13 points down and sent Game Three of the NBA Finals against Los Angeles into overtime, with Bulls winning 104–96 for a 2–1 edge.

- All-Defensive first team.

- Average attendance reached 18,452.

1991–92 season:

- Named NBA MVP for the second straight season, the third time in his career, and became the only player in NBA history to be selected regular-season MVP and MVP of the NBA finals in consecutive seasons.

- Named to the All-NBA first team and All-Defensive first team.

- Captured his sixth straight scoring title with a 30.1 ppg. average.

- Ranked sixth in the league in steals with a 2.28 average.

- Led his team with a .832 free throw percentage.

- Scored his season-high 51 points at Washington on March 19.

- Played in 80 of the 82 games, starting all 80 games.

- Led the team in scoring in 68 games.

- Scored 30 or more points in 44 games.

- Scored his season-low of 12 points against Atlanta, April 13.

- Played his 20,000th career minute on November 20 at Golden State.

- Two triple-doubles (23 for career)—December 6 vs. Charlotte and February 21 at Atlanta.

- NBA Player of the Month for March.

- Named a starter on the Eastern Conference All-Star team for the eighth straight year, and was the leading vote-getter for the sixth straight year.

- Led the East All-Stars with 18 points, 5 assists, 1 rebound, and 2 steals.

- Ranked second on the Bulls in assists, third in rebounds, and third in blocks.

- Named MVP of the 1992 NBA finals after averaging

35.8 ppg., 6.5 apg., 4.8 rpg., and shooting 53 percent from the field vs. Portland.

- Scored 56 points in a playoff game in Miami, his 1992 playoff high and the second highest point total ever in an NBA playoff game. His 56 points in that game made him the only player ever to score 50 or more points in five playoff games. Wilt Chamberlain scored 50 or more in four playoff games.

- His 135 points in the Miami series broke his own NBA record for most points in a three-game playoff series (he had 131 in the 1986 Boston series).

- His 53 field goals made in the Miami series breaks Wilt Chamberlain's mark in 1960 for most field goals made in a three-game series.

- His 15 consecutive points in the first quarter of Game Two vs. New York set a new Bulls playoff record.

- Led the team in scoring in all 22 playoff games.

- Best series was vs. Miami, when he averaged 45.0 ppg., 9.7 rpg., 6.7 apg., 3.0 spg., and shot 61 percent from the field and 91 percent from the free-throw line.

- Scored 20 or more points in his last 55 straight play-off games dating back to April 28, 1989.

1992–93 season:

- Averaged 35.1 points in the playoffs (41.0 ppg. in the NBA finals) to lead Bulls to third consecutive NBA title and won third consecutive NBA finals MVP award. Scored 55 points in Game Four of the NBA finals.

- All-NBA first team for the seventh consecutive season.

- Runner-up to Phoenix forward Charles Barkley in MVP voting.

- Won seventh straight league scoring title (32.6 ppg.), tying the league record set by Wilt Chamberlain (1960–66).

- Average of 41 points-per-game in the NBA finals is the highest ever, breaking Rick Barry's 1967 record of 40.8 ppg.

- Joined Rick Barry (1967) and Elgin Baylor (1962) as the only players to score at least 30 points in each game of a finals series.

- Scored 40 or more points in four consecutive finals games (Games Two through Five), making him the only player to score more than 40 points in more than two straight games.

- His 41 points in Game Five of the finals broke a tie and moved him past John Havlicek into fourth place on the career playoff scoring list. Current all-time leaders: Kareem Abdul-Jabbar—5,762; Jerry West—4,457. Larry Bird—3,897; Michael Jordan—3,850; John Havlicek—3,776.

- Set record for total points in an NBA finals with 246 and for the most field goals with 101.

- First player to be named NBA finals MVP three consecutive years, joining Magic Johnson as the only three-time finals MVP.

"Air" Jordan prepares to go vertical in a game against the Miami Heat in Chapel Hill in 1989. (Photo courtesy of the Durham Herald Co., Inc.)

Two-story Jordan photo on display at Nike Town (Chicago, Ill.).

Six
Holding Court

At the 1991 Bulls Tip-Off Luncheon at the Marriot Hotel in Chicago, Michael Jordan, mobbed by autograph seekers, signed everything from shoes to Wheaties boxes. (Photo by Rich Hein, courtesy of the *Chicago Sun-Times.*)

In the course of Jordan's career, much has been said and written about him—self-observations from interviews, comments from his contemporaries, family, and friends. In this section, a representative sampling provides rare insights of Jordan throughout the years.

Michael Jordan on His Life

On a possible career in golf: "I'm still learning the game. I've never had the opportunity to play year-round, since I don't play during the basketball season.

So I don't practice enough. But when I get to the point where I can shoot consistently in the low 70s, I'd like to turn pro. I'm not saying I'm going to win. I'm gonna try, but I just like to make it out there, to be competing with these guys on the Tour. It's not for the money. I should already be financially secure. But it's a challenge, right? They said Bo [Jackson] couldn't play two sports."

On advice to young people: "Learn to know right from wrong. Stay away from drugs and alcohol. Respect your parents and get the best education you can."

On autographs, after nearly being crushed by five thousand fans at a signing in Houston, Texas: "The autograph stuff drives me crazy. . . . I almost got killed getting out of there. I haven't done any autograph sessions since."

On being a role model: "I try to be a role model for black kids, white kids, yellow kids, green kids. That is what I felt was good about my personality. Don't knock me off the pedestal that you wanted me to get onto."

On being an underdog in golf, at the Western Amateur, 1991: "When my [basketball] career first started, I was an underdog. Everyone didn't feel I could perform well at North Carolina and didn't in the pros. It's a great feeling being an underdog because, hopefully, the expectations are a little bit lower than if you were the favorite."

On being named *Sports Illustrated* Sportsman of the Year: "It's a privilege for me to be in the same class as the other players who have received it. . . . It has to do with your personality, your community service, and how you're perceived in the public."

On business life off court: "It took getting used to, but now I enjoy all the off-court stuff. It's like being back in school. I'm learning all the time. In college I never realized the opportunities available to a pro athlete. I've been given the chance to meet all kinds of people, to travel and expand my financial capabilities, to get ideas and learn about life, to create a world apart from basketball."

On charity: "Nobody has all the solutions to the world's problems. I want to help everybody, but I can't. It's just a matter of us concerned people doing what we can through good thoughts, good prayers, and good deeds because we can make a difference."

On college academics: "Coach Smith challenged us on the court, but also encouraged us in the classroom."

On criticism that he's not a proper role model for blacks: "I think that kind of criticism is totally unfair. I've been trying to have people view me more as a good person than a good black man. I know I'm black. I was born black and I'll die black. That goes without saying. But because I want every kid to be viewed as a person rather than as a member of a certain race does not mean that I'm not black enough."

On drugs: "I've never done drugs, and I'll never have a reason to do drugs."

On fame: "People say they wish they were Michael Jordan. Okay, do it for a year. Do it for two years. Do it for five years. When you get past the fun part, then go do the part where you get into cities at three A.M. and you have 15 people waiting for autographs when you're tired as hell. Your knees are sore, back's sore, your body's sore, and yet you have to sign 15 autographs at three in the morning."

On finishing up his college education when he was sidelined because of an injury on court: "My body could stand the crutches, but my mind couldn't stand on the sideline."

On focusing on one sport: "In high school I played baseball, football, and track, trying to find the right place for my talents. As I grew, I found the best target was the basketball court."

On getting cut from his high school team: "That was a lesson for me to dig within myself. I had to look at things I was being taught by my parents and try to make something out of my life."

On getting good grades (A's and B's) in high school, after his father lectured him about how his passion for basketball interfered with the academics: "My father talking to me really made me think. I knew he was right and I tried to change. I concentrated more on my schoolwork because I set a goal to excel in the classroom to reach college and I had to work to reach it."

On goals: "I've got a family, a home, all the land, money, automobiles, golf clubs, and luxuries I'll ever need. The only things my life lack are a[n] NBA title ring and privacy."

On golf: "You always wonder, especially in my profession, what it would be like if I had to play against myself in a one-on-one game. Well, golf is that way because you compete against yourself in a mental way. That's the challenge."

On his fame and its advantages, using it as a point of discussion for the *Chicago Tribune* Christmas Fund: When he enters a restaurant and is recognized, "They want to buy me dinner. But I don't need it. The person who needs a free meal can't get it. The rich get richer. If that doesn't show how everything is backwards in society, nothing will. If that doesn't make you want to share whatever you have, nothing will."

On his fans and being out of town on Halloween, missing trick-or-treat: "I had McDonald's cards all printed up with my name on them for free Big Macs for trick-or-treaters. I really wanted to see the kids."

On his fans and on great expectations: "I would say that right now, 55 to 60 percent of my daily activities are toward this image. Before I was married, it was close to 85, 90 percent. Now that I have a family I have to cut back, because I want my kids and my wife and myself to have as normal a family life as possible."

On his fans yelling out his name when he's trying to tee off: "It's hard to swing when they're all the time calling your name, 'Michael, Michael, Jordan, Jordan.'"

On his fear that kids might imitate his tongue habit: "I'm afraid they'll bite them off. [To kids:] For your tongues' sake, kids, don't do it."

On his homeboy roots: "But in Carolina I feel at ease. My real friends keep me straight—they don't praise me or ask favors. I would probably be unreasonable without my friends and family to keep me in balance."

On his idea of a perfect day: "Two rounds on the golf course, then spending time alone with my family."

On his mother: "My mother is my root, my foundation. She planted the seed that I base my life on, and that is the belief that the ability to achieve starts in your mind. As I have said before, I hope I'm successful in passing this on to my children."

On his Nikes: "I love 'em right out of the box. No blisters or anything."

On his older brother Larry: "When you see me play, you see Larry play."

Larry Bird blocks the path to the basket, so Michael Jordan looks for a teammate. (Photo by Robert A. Reeder, courtesy of the *Chicago Sun-Times*.)

On his philosophy of life: "If I lost my talent tomorrow, I'd say I had a great time and move on. I live for today but plan for the future."

On his protruding tongue: "My father used to have his tongue out when he'd be working, doing mechanical stuff, and I just picked it up from him. Coach [Dean] Smith wanted me to stop it when I was back at UNC. But it's not a conscious thing. I can't play with it in."

On overexposure: "I want to back off and start organizing things to get ready when I step away from the spotlight. If I was someone else, I'd be tired of seeing Michael Jordan on TV so much. I'll always have a relationship with Nike and with Wilson, because of their connection with sports. Gatorade, too. But the rest, we'll phase them out. I love the spotlight, but when it is time to retire, I don't want the spotlight on me anymore."

On persistence: "If you can take anything from my being here [Western Amateur Championship, golf], it's that you can always give it a try. You never sit back and say, 'I can't do this. I can't do that.' I'm out here giving it a try. And I'm not going to give up."

On being a role model: "The only people I feel I have to give that type of guidance to are my kids."

On success: "Is there ever really a limit on anything? I think people will always surpass. If it's me, that's fine. In the meantime, I've got the greatest job in America. Could anything be better than getting paid a lot of money to do what you love most?"

On the release of *The Jordan Rules*: "I hope they give it to us. If my name is going to be on it, and I'm helping to sell the book, I hope I don't have to go out and buy it."

On the hardest part of being famous: "There are a lot of good things to say about being liked by a lot of people. But, at the same time, you do sacrifice a lot of your privacy. One of the things I miss is just being able to go out with my kids to an amusement park. It's been so long since I've been to one I've nearly forgotten what it's like."

On the kids murdered because of the Air Jordan shoes: "I thought I'd be helping out others and everything would be positive. I thought people would try to emulate the good things I do, they'd try to achieve, to be better. Nothing bad. I never thought because of my endorsement of a shoe, or any product, that people would harm each other. Everyone likes to be admired, but when it comes to kids actually killing each other, then you have to reevaluate things."

On the outdoor playground in Wilmington, N.C.: "It wasn't Chicago or New York by any means. But you did have to wait a few hours to get 'ups.' Then you had to keep winning to stay on the court."

On the White House rebuff: "It's none of your business. If you want to ask me what I did, I don't have to tell you. I have to live my life the way I want to live it. I might want to know what you did, but I'm not asking you. That's only respect."

On what he thought he'd be when he grew up: "A professional athlete."

On when he visited Union Station, a complex of trendy restaurants and shops: "It was the first time I'd been in a mall in two years. So I wore my disguise. I put on my shades, my high-water pants, an old coat, and pulled my hat down over my head."

On why Jordan granted an interview to 11-year-old Maria Sansone of NBC's "Inside Stuff": "I feel everything she would be looking for is positive. She's not like some of the other reporters who are trying to get you down."

On youthful stamina: "Hey, I'm a young thorough-bred, and young thoroughbreds don't need rest."

Michael Jordan on Basketball

On air flight: "I can fly/I can fly/I can fly . . ."

After John Starks of the Knicks scored 13 points on him in the fourth quarter: "It's very demoralizing when you feel you've played tough defense and he still makes the shot."

On an early goal (quoted 1984): "I'd like to play in at least one All-Star game."

On being a temperamental rookie: "I am very conscious of not being a prima donna. I wouldn't want that if I were a veteran, and I try to put myself in our veterans' shoes."

On being the best in the league: "Someone is trying to take something from me, to make a name for himself by outplaying Michael Jordan. I can't let anyone do that."

On creativity in shooting: "I go up for a normal shot, but after that I don't have any plans. I never practice those moves. I don't know how I do them. It's amazing."

On Doctor J (Julius Erving): "Nobody can replace the Doctor. He was the epitome of class and defined the NBA for me. It's a challenge to try and emulate him, but it's not as if I have to go out of my way. Being Michael Jordan means acting the same as I always have."

On goals reached: "I've accomplished everything. Individually, as well as team [goals]. Now it's just a matter of duplicating them. And I don't mind doing that."

On having to prove himself: "Individually, I don't think I have a thing left to prove to anyone. All I'm interested in is winning. I would have to say that I'm pretty easy to build a team around because I can make contributions in all kinds of different ways—scoring, rebounding, passing. The one thing that I see that might make it tough for the other players on the team is the amount of publicity that I receive. Because of that, people have a tendency to overlook the other players."

On his decision to go to UNC: "I was not a gifted athlete as a youngster. I was not heavily recruited out of high school. I wrote to UCLA but never heard from them, and to University of Virginia—I would have loved to have played with Ralph Sampson. But all they sent me in return was a regular application form. I'm glad I wound up where I did. . . ."

On his 57-point game against the Atlanta Hawks: "I guess I make guys feel I'm invading their turf. It's the old playground code and it adds to the fun."

On his biggest thrill in basketball: "Winning back-to-back NBA titles with the Bulls and in Chicago. This is a great town to play for. I love it."

On his choice for "Five Starters": "Guards Magic Johnson and Mitch Richmond, forwards James Worthy and Karl Malone, center Patrick Ewing."

On his creativity when playing above the rim: "I never practice the fancy stuff. If I thought about a move, I'd probably make a turnover. I just look at a situation in the air, adjust, create, and let instinct take over."

On his dad's comment that he would be "more relaxed" after winning an NBA championship: "I've always been relaxed. He felt the pressure more than I did, as a father, and for myself. I think I'm going to be just as relaxed and, I hope, just as enjoyable. I just think the enjoyment that I'm going to get from this whole situation is to see my teammates hopefully prosper and grow and mature to a point where they can enjoy something like this even more."

On his defensive capabilities: "Viewers think I play adequate defense. I think I play good defense. Some people don't think it can happen. You don't find too many who can actually do that, lead the league in scoring and at the same time lead the league in steals and have a sense for the defensive part of the game."

On his final decision to join the U.S. basketball team for the 1992 Olympics: "The Olympic decision will be mine, not one forced on me by what somebody else says or wants. I love my country and I've already helped the Olympic team win one [1984] gold medal. I don't want to prevent another player from having that honor. And I think it's unfair that so many people are trying to pressure me to play. I don't see any public pressure or peer pressure on any other player. Why can't I be free to enjoy my summers with my family like everybody else if I want to?"

On his goal (quoted in 1985): "I'm a winner. My ultimate goal is to help bring a championship to Chicago. I know people laugh and say it will never happen, but it would be a bit foolish to bet against it."

On his matchup against Magic Johnson in the 1991 NBA finals: "It's great for the league, having the two best players going against each other." (Johnson's response: "Sure, it's a little personal. I mean, me going against Michael Jordan in the finals. It's what you live for, right?")

On his motivation to play basketball: "Very few people play because they love the game. Most of them play because they make good money. . . . But if I don't love the game, no check is going to keep me playing."

On his shooting style: "It's me. I can't name any players that I patterned myself after. My style is an extension of my own personality and creativity. I'm a lot of wrist and fingers and I like some arc. But not too much. I can shoot with little trajectory. It depends upon the defense."

On his teammates: "As a leader, I have never been critical or cursed any of my teammates. I've always spoken in terms of 'we.'"

On his vertical leap: "I've never had my vertical leap measured, but sometimes I think about how high I get up. I always spread my legs when I jump high, like on my Rock-a-Baby, and it seems like I've opened a parachute, like, that slowly brings me back to the floor."

On improving his game: "I can never stop working hard. Each day, I feel I have to improve. Hard work, determination—I've got to keep pushing myself."

On Joe Dumars: "One on one, he's the best. He attacks me, on offense as well as defense. A lot of players sit back and wait to see what I'm going to do. Joe attacks me, forces me to react."

On John Paxson (on the 1990–91 NBA finals, foreshadowing Paxson's final shot in the 1992–93 playoffs): "Anybody playing beside me is going to have to knock down those shots that Pax did in the finals. . . . I want Pax around, that's for sure."

On John Starks (after New York won the first game of the 1993 Eastern Conference finals): "He had a better day. I'm not afraid to say when someone gets the best of me, but I know I didn't play the basketball I want to play. I let my team down, and I hope to redeem myself." (Starks's comment: "It's not fear I feel when I guard him, it's respect. You have to have pride and determination to contain him.")

On his hopes for his career (quoted in 1984): "I hope I can say I did my best, achieved a lot, and won a couple of world championships."

On Magic Johnson's retirement: "One thing that really bothers me about Magic retiring is that he didn't get the kind of going-away party he deserves. I think about Dr. J [Julius Erving] and [Kareem] Abdul-Jabbar and the way they left the league and the type of respect fans were able to pay them, and [Magic] won't have that."

On being an NBA ambassador: "You know, I just don't think much about that. I've always said it isn't one person who speaks for the league. When Dr. J was in his prime, he carried the torch all by himself. Now you've got other people to share that: Magic, Isiah Thomas, Larry Bird, David Robinson, myself. These are the people who carry the torch of the NBA, not one person, not one player."

On pacing: "I never try to pace myself. I know a lot of people think I'll wear myself down. Someday maybe I will burn out, physically. But the desire will always burn. I'll go full speed until I give out."

On Patrick Ewing of the Knicks: "I think when he came out of college, Patrick felt a little overwhelmed, a little hesitant about his surroundings. He's an intelligent guy, a great guy, but he's shy, and he didn't want to appear backward or dumb in interviews. He only made himself open to people that he felt comfortable with, and that meant he often didn't sign autographs or smile for the cameras. I think that's changed over the years."

On playing basketball (quoted in 1991): "I look forward to playing now, more than ever. It's the only place I can get relief from what's happening off the court. It's always been that way to a certain extent, but it's even more so now. Basketball is my escape, my refuge. It seems that everything else is so . . . so busy and complicated."

On Shaquille O'Neal: "I'm not afraid to share the spotlight. It'll be lots of fun playing with Shaq."

On taking flight: "I wish I could show you a film of a dunk I had in Milwaukee. It's in slow motion, and it looks like I'm taking off, like somebody put wings on me. I get chills when I see it. I think, when does 'jump' become 'flying'? I don't have the answer yet."

On the Barcelona Olympics: "We weren't worried. When you hire 12 Clint Eastwoods to come over and do a job, you don't tell them which bullets to put in their guns."

On the Barcelona Olympics, before he decided to join the team: "I've been on an Olympic team. If I do that, it would not give me much more feeling than the first time. I'll let some other players have a chance."

On the Bulls' red basketball uniform and UNC's blue uniform: "Red's a hellish color, blue's heaven."

On a Bulls' victory over the New York Knicks being attributed to a father-and-son chat: "I was debating with my father all morning as to how I was going to approach the game in terms of coming out aggressive or coming out passive trying to evaluate how the other guy was going to play. And his advice was like most parents. Be aggressive. Go out and do it and make it happen and they'll take your lead. And that's exactly what happened." (Jordan scored 42 points, giving the Bulls a 110–81 win.)

On the challenge in basketball: "The challenge is to keep winning and get more rings. People don't consider you great until you have three, four, maybe five rings."

On the game in which he scored a career-high 69 points in a 117–113 win over the Cleveland Cavaliers: "This would have to be my greatest game."

On his college coach, Dean Smith: "My college coach . . . was great. I know he gets a lot of criticism for not taking full advantage of my skills, but nothing could be further from the truth. He taught me to play defense and he taught me discipline; without both of those things I could have never attained what I did. . . ."

On the Detroit Pistons: "As soon as I cross half court they'll double me. They just take it out of my hands. When I drive they will send guys at me. They're just more persistent than any other team. That's why they're good at it."

On the difference between winning the NCAA championship and his first NBA championship: "After we won the NCAA championship in my freshman year [at North Carolina in 1982] I felt happy, but not all that emotional. I remember seeing Jimmy Black and a few of the other guys really crying, and I'm thinking, What's going on? This is *supposed* to happen, right? You come to college and you win a championship."

On the early years: ". . . I built up the personality and creativity of my game. What the fans see now is my all-around game, not just a flashin', dunkin', 37-point-a-game Jordan, but a guy who can adjust his game to a team game. I'd rather score 10 points less a game and win 20 more games a year. Because it comes down to this: Winning is everything."

On the game: "The game is my wife. It demands loyalty and responsibility, and it gives me back fulfillment and peace."

On the 1991 L.A.–Chicago NBA playoffs: "You guys [media] made it a mark. I made it a goal, something I wanted to achieve."

On the NBA: "The NBA is an educated playground. It's allowed me to combine all I've learned about fundamentals with my natural skills."

On the offense: "I fight the offense when we lose close games and I haven't given the output I could've given because of the system. On the nights we win, obviously, it's fine. I only want to win. I think the offense can work. But one of the problems is that the offense takes time to perfect, and we still make a lot of mistakes. And it's worse for the second team, which doesn't get as much time to run it. Theoretically, this offense should never be stopped if you have the right guys in the right places. But that doesn't always happen."

On the old Stadium: "I love [the Stadium] because everybody hates it. They think it's old and scraggly and everything. I think it gives us a good edge. The crowd is right there on the floor. I don't think you're going to find another stadium, or build another stadium, like Chicago Stadium, where every seat has a good view and it's right there on the floor. I love it. I know they're talking about a new stadium, but I hope they do it after I'm gone."

On the new Stadium: "I'm not in favor of the new building, and if I had to say now, I'd say I wouldn't be playing in it. I don't know if I'll be around then. We'll have to see."

On the Portland Trail Blazers during the Bulls' second championship playoffs: "A team like Portland still has that hunger. We have to come up with something to motivate us. It's not nearly as easy as we thought it was going to be."

On the Stadium crowds at game time (quoted in 1984): "It gives me a warm feeling. It started with the [Los Angeles] Olympics. Even Duke fans cheered for me then."

On the three-pointer sunk by teammate John Paxson in Game Six of the 1993 NBA finals with less than four seconds on the clock, giving the Bulls a 99–98 victory: "Pax is a heartbreaker. He's had a way of breaking other teams' hearts by hitting that jumper in the clutch ever since he's been here. When I saw him with the ball . . . I knew it was going in."

On UNC-style basketball under Coach Dean Smith and the NBA-style basketball (quoted in 1984): "At Carolina I was in a controlled system, and a lot of the crowd was pleased with my play. So if I just play my natural game, I won't have any problem keeping the crowd pleased. This is the most relaxed time of my career. The games come so quickly that if you have a bad one, you can put the past behind you and get ready for the present."

On watching tapes of his own games: "They motivate me to go back to work, and when I can't sleep, they pass the nights away."

On what he will miss most when he's retired: "The competition, the preseason. I get a kick out of that, coming back for the next year and going through training camp and seeing all the new players."

On winning his first NBA championship title: "I think people will now feel it's okay to put me in the category of players like Magic. Personally, I always felt that in terms of intensity and unselfishness, I played like those types of players [Johnson, Larry Bird, and Julius Erving—all of whom were on teams that won NBA titles]. Some people say that, but many others didn't. And the championship, in the minds of a lot of people, is a sign of, well, greatness. I guess they can say that about me now. It's been a seven-year struggle for me. A struggle for the city and the franchise, too. We started from scratch, we started from the bottom. I vowed when I came to Chicago that we'd make the playoffs. And each year we got closer [to the championship]."

On his 1982 NCAA championship jumper: "That still remains my favorite and most memorable shot because it won the championship."

On shooting: "I believe that shooters are made, not born. I was made. I started with a lot of God-given talent, especially my jumping ability. But I still had to work hard over the years to develop the necessary skills and forms."

On slam-dunking: "I've already done just about everything there is to do in the slam dunk. I guess people now want to see a 360-degree dunk from the top of the key. I'd like to see that myself."

At the public rally at Grant Park in Chicago, after winning the third consecutive NBA title, on shooting for a fourth NBA championship (Jordan alludes to Charles Barkley's comment that it was the destiny of the Suns to win the championship title against the Bulls in the 1992–93 season): "Certainly, destiny tells me I'll be back here for a fourth time."

Perspectives on Michael Jordan

Alexander Wolff (sportswriter): "Move with him, and he'll outjump you. . . . Jump with him, and he'll outhang you. . . . If somehow you counter Jordan's contortions, he'll add a dollop of spin so beguiling that it'll seduce the ball into the basket from almost any angle."

Antonio Diaz-Migeul (Spain's Olympic coach, at the L.A. games): "He's not human. He's a rubber man."

Arthur Ashe on Jordan's appeal: "He has great skin, a great smile, great teeth, and the camera loves him. Plus he's one of the very few athletes who make you go, 'Wow!' And he is a genuinely personable guy. He's a dream. . . .'"

Artis Gilmore (San Antonio Spurs): "The name of the game is to force a player to do the one thing he can't do well, but as far as I can tell, Jordan doesn't have that one thing."

B.J. Armstrong: "If there's one thing being around Michael has taught me, it's that you have to show up prepared to pay the price every day. I realize now that attitude is what makes him so great."

Bob Cousy (former Boston Celtic), assessing Jordan: "As far as I'm concerned, Michael is Nureyev against a bunch of Hulk Hogans. His talent is that far above everyone else's. Russell was the most productive center I've ever seen, and he complemented the talent we had. But you can say that he wasn't as good a shooter as some other people. Jordan doesn't have *any* area like that."

John Bach (Bulls assistant coach): "What he's managed to do is channel this energy. He's more determined, more fixed, more focused. He's well aware he's going to take his blows. But I sense a growing resolve, turning this retaliatory nature into an even more focused sense of what has to be done."

Jerry Reinsdorf (Bulls owner): "There's no question Michael has become a better player than anybody thought. Dean Smith [Jordan's college coach at North Carolina] told me he didn't know Michael was that good."

Joe O'Neil (Bulls ticket manager) after Jordan joined the Bulls and doubled attendance from 6,365 to 12,763 a game: "Without Jordan, we could have *lost* 500 season tickets this year."

Phil Jackson (Bulls then–assistant coach): "Even I get caught up in Michael's show. I try not to, but sometimes I just sit back and enjoy."

Charles Barkley: "Among NBA players, I count very few as friends. . . . The player, though, with whom I share most of my frustrations is Michael Jordan. He and I have been close ever since we met at the Olympic trials in 1984. During the 1987–88 season when the 76ers won only 36 games and failed to reach the playoffs for the first time in 13 years, Michael helped me through what was the most frustrating period of my career. . . . Michael had experienced the same frustration during the first couple years in the league when the Bulls weren't a great team yet. He told me to hang in there and that things would change, but only when the Sixers surrounded me with better teammates. Things were just beginning to change for the Bulls, who finally won the NBA title three years later. I knew Michael was absolutely right about my predicament, but to hear the best player in the league admit that without his teammates he was nothing made my own frustrations easier to accept."

John Bach (Bulls assistant coach who coined the term "Archangel Offense"): "That's where we give the ball to Jordan and say, 'Save us, Michael.'"

Jerry Krause (Bulls general manager) on Jordan and his teammates: "Michael is a great player, probably the greatest player who ever played, but there are difficulties building [a team] around him. Because he's such a great competitor, even in practice, he tends to dominate his own teammates and that can, at times, disrupt practice in the same way that he disrupts opponents during games. Another thing is that his teammates have a tendency to stand around and watch him during games. They sort of have that 'let him do it' attitude. It's hard not to be mesmerized by him."

Scottie Pippen on his on-court relationship with Jordan: "What Michael has brought us, every night, every game, is the spotlight and the pressure that would've been directed elsewhere. All of us . . . had to respond to it, or else we would've died as a team. Eventually, we did respond, and it made us stronger. . . . I'll never be the scorer Michael is. I couldn't put up those numbers even if I tried. And you know what? I hope he leads the

Michael Jordan aggressively pursues a loose ball in a 1987 game. (Photo by Amanda Alcock, courtesy of the *Chicago Sun-Times*.)

league in scoring for the rest of his career. And when it's over, I'll be able to say, 'I helped him do it. And I played with the greatest player ever.'"

Chuck Daly (then-Pistons coach): "You're afraid to go at him offensively because he gets too many steals. But you've got to some time because of the fatigue factor."

Clyde Drexler (Portland Trail Blazers), on Jordan's performance in the playoffs: "Going into the series I thought Michael had 2,000 moves. I was wrong. He has 3,000."

Craig Ehlo (Cleveland Cavaliers): "He can score, or at least take a good shot, any time he wants to. You can double-team him, but that's impossible because someone else will be open."

Danny Ainge (Boston Celtics): "If you had to choose one highlight film to watch, you'd pick Michael Jordan's."

David Falk (ProServ): "Having Michael has brought me my identity, and it would be silly to deny it. I can call up the CEO of any company in the United States, and if they don't know my name, they'll still take my call when they find out I represent Michael Jordan."

David Falk, on Jordan's refusal to appear at the White House: "You wouldn't believe all the requests that Michael gets. He gets asked to do so many charitable and community activities, more than one a day. If he did them it would be a full-time job. Beyond basketball and the community, he has his business obligations, and like all normal human beings, he wants to have enough time for himself."

Davis Love III (a freshman golf star at UNC when Jordan was a sophomore), on Jordan and golf: "Yes, I gave Michael his first set of clubs. . . . I think Michael was more intrigued by golf than interested at first. Maybe he thought it was easier than it is. I remember the basketball team had to run laps at six A.M. every morning, and we didn't. So their guys used to come by and bang on my window to wake me up. After a while, though, Michael decided to try it. He didn't come from a lot of money and had no reason to own clubs, anyway."

Dick Vitale (announcer): "Truly unstoppable one-on-one, Jordan invents moves during the course of the game, throwing a dazzling variety of hitch-and-go wrinkles that befuddle defenses."

Dominique Wilkins (Atlanta Hawks): "No one by himself can carry a team through a season. If Michael has to do this year after year, it will shorten his career."

Doug Collins (former Bulls coach): "Michael is the toughest practice player I've ever seen. He kills people in practice. I tried to tell him to take it easy a few times and he looked at me like, 'What are you talking about?'"

Larry Bird, after Game Two of the first round of the 1986 NBA playoffs in which Jordan scored 63 points in a 135–131 double-overtime loss: "He is God, disguised as Michael Jordan."

Dennis Johnson (Boston Celtics), joking after Jordan's 63-point game: "I wasn't guarding him. No one was guarding him. No one *can* guard him."

George Koehler (limousine driver for Jordan, with a Bulls prediction in 1987): "They're going to be tremendous. Tell people to buy their tickets now. The Bulls will be the hottest ticket in town."

James Jordan, on his son, after winning his first NBA championship: "I was with him when he won the NCAA championship. I was with him when he won the Olympic gold medal. But this is the mountaintop. This is as good as it gets. I've never seen him this emotional. I'm happy for him and the whole team."

James Jordan, on his son ultimately choosing basketball over baseball: "Michael grew six inches during his sophomore year of high school. The baseball team didn't have a pair of pants to fit him, so they sewed different sets of pants together. Michael said it looked so stupid that he refused to wear them and decided to quit playing on the team. Baseball lost a possible Doc Gooden. Michael could throw really hard."

James Jordan: "Michael was probably the laziest kid I had. If he had to get a job in a factory punching a clock, he'd starve to death. He would give every last dime of his allowance to his brothers and sisters and even kids in the neighborhood to do his chores. He was always broke."

Jerry Krause, on criticisms that Jordan is a one-man team, after their win against the Cleveland Cavaliers in the NBA Eastern Conference Playoffs in 1988: "One-man team, huh? No way! No way this is a one-man team!"

John Kerr (former player and head coach, currently a Chicago broadcaster): "I've been around a lot of mega-talented players. I signed Julius Erving to his first contract in Virginia [of the ABA]. I had George Gervin there, too. They were damn good, but they weren't like this kid. Where Julius was smooth going to the basket, like poetry, Michael is vicious. He attacks you. . . . But I honestly believe this kid is the best player who ever walked on a court. He does more things better than anybody."

John Williams (Cleveland Cavaliers): "He's one in a million, one in a billion. I don't think we'll ever see a player like him again."

A Jordan teammate on the financial impact Jordan has had on Nike: "That shoe company should change its name from Nike to Mikey."

Larry Bird: "I have never seen one player turn around a team like that. All the Bulls have become better because of him and pretty soon, this place will be packed every night, not just when the Celtics come to town. They'll pay just to watch Jordan. . . . Never seen anyone like him. Unlike anyone I've ever seen. Phenomenal. One of a kind. He's the best. Ever."

Larry Bird: "There has never been an athlete like him before. On a scale of one to 10, with the rest of the superstars an eight, he's a 10. Everybody understands that. He's great just to watch."

Larry Jordan: "I'm proud of Michael. For me, it was very hard at first, always being perceived as Michael Jordan's brother. You lose your own identity. It's something I've learned to deal with."

Magic Johnson: "When I went to congratulate him after the game, I could see tears in his eyes. You hear so much about him as an individual player, but he's proved everyone wrong with this championship."

Magic Johnson, on himself, Larry Bird, and Jordan: "Everybody always says it's me and Larry [Bird]. Really, it's Michael and everybody else. In Chicago Michael Jordan plays his own game, one-against-the-world. A television announcer called him the 'best player from another planet.' He's so good that it seems he can do almost anything he wants on the court. Michael plays against the *game* every night, rather than a particular opponent. He does his homework on both ends of the floor. He studies the players who defend him, and he breaks down their weaknesses so well that, by the third or fourth time most guys guard him, they're looking at about 50 points on the scoreboard. And he's just as successful on defense. Because he's so strong, he's able to make steals out of plays where someone else might just barely touch the ball or miss it completely."

Matt Doherty (college basketball teammate): "I never saw a guy as talented as Michael work as hard. His work ethic is intense, demanding, all business. He really doesn't need to work on anything. Maybe Coach is just keeping him humble."

Michael Cooper (Los Angeles Lakers): "When people say I do a good job on Michael, or that so-and-so did the job, that's wrong. There's no way I stop him. I need the whole team. As soon as he touches the ball, he electrifies the intensity inside you. The alarm goes off be-cause you don't know what he's going to do. He goes right, left, over you, around and under you. He twists, he turns. And you *know* he's going to get the shot off. You just don't know when and how. That's the most devastating thing psychologically to a defender."

Michael Holton (Phoenix Suns), on a game against his team: "All I saw were the bottom of his shoes."

Mychal Thompson (Los Angeles Lakers), on the Johnson-Jordan matchup in the 1991 NBA finals: "You can't overhype Magic Johnson versus Michael Jordan. Well, you'll try. But, nope, it can't be done. Talent, leadership, winning—Magic and Michael are the ultimate in all of those things. They're it."

Fernando Martin (Spanish Olympic basketball star), on Jordan's performance at the 1984 Olympics: "Michael Jordan? Jump, jump, jump. Very quick. Very fast. Very, very good. Jump, jump, jump."

Phil Jackson: "One thing about Michael, he's extremely competitive. He's not Mr. Nice Guy when it comes to competing. When he gets to this part of the season it's a war to him. For him to keep coming through without injury has been big for us, because he's taken some tremendous blows coming to the basket."

Philip Knight (Nike CEO), on Jordan's commercial appeal: "We were looking for great personalities who cut across racial lines. In my own personal focus group, which is my 17-year-old son and his friends, I guarantee you that Michael Jordan is a better salesman than Larry Bird."

Sam Perkins (Dallas Mavericks), on Jordan's dominance of the game: "Michael plays it down, but he's a one-man team."

Larry Brown (NBA coach): "Michael—he's the best. I grew up with Connie Hawkins. I saw Julius at his peak. No one went through the ACC like David Thompson. I love Magic and Larry. But Michael, as far as what I've seen . . . I'd pay money to see him play. I'd pay money to see him *practice*."

Shaquille O'Neal (Orlando Magic): "Michael Jordan is the best player in the world. That's pretty obvious. . . . I someday want to be like Michael Jordan where I can go into any arena in the country and not hear any boos."

Spike Lee: "Nobody in the world can cover my main man, Michael Jordan. No-o-o-o-body."

The Sporting News: "Jordan is the epitome of the popular athlete. His appeal is so broad that it's not just with blacks or teens or men. It is across the board, to all demographic groups. No matter what an advertiser is looking for, Jordan can relate to that group. That's extraordinary."

Steve Schanwald (vice-president of marketing and broadcasting for the Bulls): "We hope Michael can find a fountain of youth or we can find someone who has perfected cloning. But unless that happens, we have to prepare for a post-Jordan world. It's very sad to think there will come a day when Michael doesn't put on no. 23, but it's a challenge and, in a perverse way, it's enjoyable to meet that challenge."

Eddie Fogler (North Carolina assistant coach) after Jordan hit the jumper that won the Tar Heels the championship: "That kid has no idea of what he's just done. He's part of history but he doesn't know it yet."

Tim Hallam (PR director for the Bulls): "You can't believe the tremendous number of requests he gets, from sick kids, from hospitals, from schools and community centers, and you can't believe how much stuff he does. Stuff nobody knows about."

Wayman Tisdale (Olympic teammate in Los Angeles), on Jordan's on-court skills: "Playing with him was like going to the circus. You'd come to practice and never know what he'd pull off."

Wilt Chamberlain: "Magic, Bird, Barkley, and Jordan are stars because they can play every facet of the game. We are dumbfounded when we see those guys play because we are no longer accustomed to seeing complete athletes. . . ."

I'd have played basketball for nothing. Now that I don't want to play anymore, I'm in no hurry to do anything. I'm 30, I've got a long life left and I intend to live it happily. I left the option open to return—never say never. But I'm gone.
    —Michael Jordan, "Larry King Live," November 1993

Seven
Appendixes

1. Collectibles and Memorabilia

Uniforms and Equipment

If you want a Jordan autograph on sports memorabilia, be prepared to pay big bucks, especially now that Jordan has retired and his next stop is the Basketball Hall of Fame.

Newspaper writer Len Ziehm reported that, at the fifth annual Michael Jordan/McDonald's Charity Golf Classic in Chicago at Cog Hill, the following signed MJ items sold: a basketball jersey—$3,400. A Wheaties box—$800. A pair of Nike Air Jordan basketball shoes—$2,700.

Public auctions generally aren't the best way to get the best price, since bidding fever can easily escalate prices. So what are your other options? Short of seeing Jordan in person and getting an autograph, the best way is to deal with reputable sports memorabilia dealers.

I have no experience with the companies I've listed below; all advertised in trade publications, and I cannot vouch for any of them. Still, if you absolutely must have a signed Jordan item, these dealers offer a wide range of material.

Sebring Sports (437 Fork-Of-River Parkway, Sevierville, TN 37862) offers, in the September 1993 issue of *Tuff Stuff*, a used Jordan jersey worn during a home game ($4,750), as well as a used Jordan jersey worn during a road game ($3,850).

Rock 'n Sports (PO Box 26, Randallstown, MD 21133) offers in the same issue of *Tuff Stuff* the following Jordan memorabilia:

- A basketball signed by all the players on the Bulls
- Practice jerseys signed by all the players on the Bulls
- Michael Jordan autographed basketball shoes, new pair, both signed, $350 (a used pair is $850)

- An issue of *Sports Illustrated* signed by Jordan, $35
- A 12 × 18 inch *Chicago Tribune* newspaper stand cardboard display autographed by Jordan, $30
- An NBA finals program, autographed by Jordan, $50
- Michael Jordan used golf shoes (both signed), $1,000/pair
- A Michael Jordan autographed golf ball, $60
- A basketball signed by Magic Johnson, Larry Bird, Michael Jordan, $250
- A 1992 Olympic basketball jersey signed by Jordan, $350
- A 1992 Olympic basketball jersey signed by Jordan, Magic Johnson, and Larry Bird, $600
- A 1992 Olympic basketball team poster, signed by Jordan, Magic Johnson, and Bird, $275
- A basketball signed by Jordan, $150

Another source is **Sports Alley** (31161 Niguel Road, no. J, Laguna Niguel, CA 92677), which offers autographed photos ($38), an autographed basketball card ($32), and an autographed basketball ($110).

The most reliable source is **Upper Deck Authenticated** (PO Box 182266, Chattanooga, TN 37422–7266; write for free catalog). A collaborative venture between Upper Deck and McNall Sports & Entertainment, UDA has signed exclusive contracts with Magic Johnson, Larry Bird, and Michael Jordan.

What makes this company's offerings unique is their patented, five-step authentication process:

"1. Each and every item, whether it's a jersey, helmet, card or photo, is signed by the athlete in the presence of Upper Deck Authenticated officials. Since every signing is witnessed, we know it's genuine right from the start.

"2. Next, an affadavit of authenticity is signed by

Note: The addresses and prices listed herein are current at press time; however, they are subject to change. Before ordering anything by mail, check with the vendor for availability and the current price.

Also, when writing to anyone, always enclose a self-addressed, stamped envelope (preferably no. 10 size), or you may not get a response.

the athlete and then notarized by a notary public. Now it's official, in writing, and indisputable.

"3. A unique number is then assigned to each piece of signed memorabilia. When we say unique, we mean it—it's your number, and no other item or individual can have it. No confusion there.

"4. This is where paperwork meets product. A tamper-proof UDA hologram with your number is affixed to the item. If an item has this hologram, you can be sure it's the real thing. When you receive your memorabilia, the package will include a Certificate of Authenticity with a matching hologram with your number. This is your proof of authenticity and ownership.

"5. Finally, the item's number is recorded in our secure data bank, so even if you misplace your Certificate you can prove, or find out, that the item is authentic."

Note: the following list of Jordan memorabilia was compiled from their catalog marked "collectors' edition No. 8," which was mailed in April 1994. In cases where UDA indicated a limitation notice, the figure is provided.

- Soccer Card Blowup (#13014). 8.5 x 11-inch color blowup card, "Michael Jordan, Honorary Captain, World Cup USA 94," encased in lucite. An edition of 2,500 copies, $29.95.
- *Rare Air* by Michael Jordan. Unsigned (#12917, edition of 2,500 copies; $99.95), and signed (#12343, edition of 2,500 copies; $499).
- *Sports Illustrated* cover, framed; unsigned, (#13027) $99.95.
- Wilson basketball (#12807); signed, $699.
- First NBA Championship photo [Jordan cradling the trophy in his arms]. Color photo, 16 x 20 inches. Item #12705, signed and framed ($599); #12706, signed but unframed ($499); #12708, unsigned and framed ($149).
- *Sports Illustrated* cover from 1984, "A Star is Born." Color reproduction. Item #12715, signed and framed, $399.95; #12716, unframed and unsigned, $99.95.
- Skylights Card Blowup (#12887). Measures 8.5 x 11 inches, in lucite. A limited edition of 2,500 copies, $29.95.
- Bulls Pin Set (#12721). Three pins packaged in a black plastic box with clear top. (Forthcoming pin sets include career sets from USA Basketball and UNC.) A limited edition of 2,500 sets, $24.95.
- MVP Card Blowup (#13005). 8.5 x 11 inch card encased in lucite, $29.95.

- Mr. June Card Blowup (#12992). 8.5 x 11 inch card encased in lucite; a limited edition of 5,000 cards, $29.95.
- Dream Team Photo. In color, 16 x 20 inches, shows Magic Johnson, Larry Bird, and Michael Jordan. Item #12888, signed and framed, $1,119; #12889, signed but unframed, $1,099.
- Photo by Andrew Bernstein, used to illustrate the videotape box for *Michael Jordan: Come Fly With Me.* In color, 16 x 20 inches. Item #12712, signed and framed, $599; #12711, signed but unframed, $499.
- 4-Card Hologram (#10203), $29.95.
- MVP Hologram. Item #10204, 4-card hologram, $29.95; #10207, 2-card hologram, $19.95.
- *Chicago Tribune* (#12736). A framed copy published the day after Jordan's retirement, headlined "Thanks for the memories." Accompanied by an unframed copy in a pocket on the back. A limited edition of 1,000, $99.95.
- Basketball jerseys (all signed)
  Red Jersey, framed (#12702), $999
  Red Jersey, unframed (#12701), $849
  White Jersey, framed (#12704), $999
  White Jersey, unframed (#12703), $849
- 2-Card Hologram (#10206). Jordan's 1992–93 hologram card, $19.95.
- Retirement C-Card (#12660), "Upper Deck Authenticated Salutes Michael Jordan." A limited edition of 10,000, $39.95.
- Bulls C-Card (#12176), "Three-time champions." A limited edition of 7,500, $39.95.
- Blowup card (#12432), 8.5 x 11 inches, encased in lucite; a limited edition of 10,000, $29.95.
- Blowup hologram card (#12204), 5 x 7 inches, encased in lucite; a limited edition of 7,500, $39.95.
- Baseball (#12988). Signed, $299.

Hammacher Schlemmer (9180 Le Saint Drive, Fairfield, OH 45014-5475) offered in its Christmas 1993 catalog autographed Jordan basketballs, item #54201B, at $1,999. Availability was limited to 24 basketballs, and all have been sold. According to the company, "These genuine leather basketballs were made by Molten for the 1992 Summer Olympic Games in Barcelona. Includes two certificates of authenticity and statistics of Jordan's inestimable career."

The company also carried the signed Jordan book, *Rare Air.*

Because they offer other sports collectibles, you may want to get on their mailing list. Write for a free catalog.

Art

Quality Collectables (71 South Mast St., Goffstown, NH 03045) offers a Jordan lithograph, *After the Game* (1,000 prints, $75); also, a color plate of Jordan (2,500 copies, 10.25 inches), $150. (Note: This company has not responded to any of my letters requesting information. You may want to try an art gallery, which can order the print for you.)

Name That Toon (c/o **Cactus Films,** 1320 Fourth Street, San Rafael, CA 94901), in a special project with Nike, is the publisher and exclusive distributor of 300 cels from the "Dream Team" ad produced by Nike that aired during the Barcelona Olympics. Individually signed, the cels vary in price, starting at $500. (For well-heeled investors, there were four cels signed by Michael Jordan, Charles Barkley, Scottie Pippen, David Robinson, John Stockton, and Chris Mullin—$7,000 each). All cels bear the official Nike gold seal and are accompanied by a certificate of authenticity signed by Phil Knight (founder of Nike) or Mark Parker (Nike's marketing vice president). According to Craig Wolfe of Name That Toon, most of the cels have been sold.

Other projects with Nike are in the works, including a commemorative sculpture of Michael Jordan in flight. According to Wolfe, the edition will be limited to 500 copies (or less), with a plaque signed by the sculptor and Michael Jordan.

Warner Brothers issued a limited-edition cel of "Air" Jordan and "Hare" Jordan, matted and framed, with a limitation notice personalized to the purchaser. This cel is out of print, but a second print is in the works: "Air" Jordan and "Hare" Jordan from the second Nike ad, set on Mars. (This may be carried by Nike Town, as well as the Warner Brothers mail-order catalog. Write to: Warner Bros., Studio Store Catalog, PO Box 60048, Tampa, FL 33660–0048.)

Team Schedules

Available for free, the annual team schedules are minor collectibles but sometimes had a cover photo of Jordan on the front. (For the 1993–94 season, the cover depicts the three championship trophies.) Write to the **Chicago Bulls** (One Magnificent Mile, 980 N. Michigan Ave., Suite 1600, Chicago, IL 60611).

2. Trading Cards

As any printer will tell you, it's easy to print trading cards—so easy, and lucrative enough, that when the country was swept up in Shaquille O'Neal fever, so-called "rookie" cards flooded the market. As the *Orlando Sentinel* explained, "The active, sometimes illicit trade in Shaq cards was made even more intriguing by the nearly 40 cards that were calling themselves Shaq's 'rookie card,' some of them produced by unlicensed maverick printers operating out of their garages."

Card Companies

Currently, the following companies are licensed to publish basketball cards:

Fleer (Executive Plaza, 1120 Route 73, Suite 300, Mt. Laurel, NJ 08054).

NBA Hoops and **SkyBox** (300 N. Duke St., PO Box 3009, Durham, NC 27702-3009).

Topps (254 36th St., Brooklyn, NY 11232).

Upper Deck (5909 Sea Otter Pl., Carlsbad, CA 92008-6221).

Hobby Publications

The card market, like any other collectibles market, is volatile—things can change quickly. Nothing illustrates this more vividly than the often-dramatic differences in price values of cards reflected in annual price guides compared to those in the most current issue of *Beckett Basketball Monthly.*

Currently in its 38th issue, *Beckett Basketball Monthly* is one of several publications published by Statabase, Inc., which also publishes similar publications on other sports (baseball, football, hockey) as well as *Beckett Focus on Future Stars,* and price guides, alphabetical lists, checklists, and an address list.

With news of interest to basketball card collectors, *Beckett Basketball Monthly* ($2.95) can normally be found in most card shops; it is also available by direct subscription (one year, $19.95; two years, $35.95). Send orders to: **Beckett Publications,** PO Box 2131, Marion, OH 43305-2131.

The centerpiece of each issue is the updated "Beckett Basketball Price Guide," generally considered the most authoritative. (Though Beckett cautions that its "price listings are to be used only as a guide" and "do not represent absolute fixed prices," it is the bible for card dealers that, in buying or selling, is commonly used as a pricing tool. Several other publications offer their own price guides, but dealers swear by, and religiously use, *Beckett.*)

Offering both low and high estimates, with markers indicating cards that are rising (or dropping) in value

Cover to *Beckett Basketball Monthly,* December 1993 issue.

from the previous month, Beckett is selective in what it lists:

> Sets listed in the Price Guide typically: (1) have significant market activity on single cards, (2) are widely distributed, (3) have comprehensive player selections, (4) are produced by league-licensed major manufacturers, and (5) focus on players who are active at time of issue.

Covering trading cards in general, *Tuff Stuff* ($3.95, monthly) offers news, ads from sports memorabilia dealers, and its own "Tuff Stuff Price Guide." The criteria for inclusion: "We list cards that are produced by the major manufacturers and that are distributed nationally. The cards in our guide are licensed by the appropriate leagues and players' associations. We will not list any card that has been produced without proper licensing." Available in most card shops, the magazine is also available by subscription, with 12 issues for $24.95. (**Tuff Stuff,** PO Box 1637, Glen Allen, VA 23060–0637.)

Price Guide (Annual)

Dr. James Beckett's *Basketball Card Price Guide and Alphabetical Checklist* (by player) is an essential book for any serious basketball card collector. Listing nearly 100,000 prices for "virtually every basketball card ever produced," along with a useful cross-indexed alphabetical listing by player, this also provides useful background information on card collecting for beginners and experts alike.

As I've said before—and it's a point worth reinforcing—the card market can change suddenly, so it's essential to keep current, which is possible only by reading the most recent issues of *Beckett Basketball Monthly* and *Tuff Stuff.*

Collecting Michael Jordan Cards: A Guide

When it comes to collecting Michael Jordan cards, my advice is simple: be bullish on Michael Jordan, and you can't go wrong—a message not lost on attendees at an annual card show.

Enhancing the value of cards, basketball is enjoying a boom, as Clay Walker of *Tuff Stuff* explained in 1993:

> Something strange is happening in the hobby. As baseball season nears the midseason All-Star break, collectors are still talking about basketball cards. Several months ago, our staff felt basketball card prices would experience a large drop-off following the NBA playoffs. Well, anyone who's been following the prices closely knows that, thanks to Shaquille O'Neal, Jordan, Ewing, Barkley, and company, we were wrong.
>
> This didn't seem possible two years ago. Back then, basketball cards were only slightly more popular than hockey cards. Even the NBA's two flagship licensees, Hoops and Skybox, were haunted by overproduction and were generally considered failures with collectors.
>
> At this time last year, boxes of 1991–92 Hoops and SkyBox were selling in the $8.00 to $15.00 range. This year's boxes are selling in the $50.00 to $75.00 range.
>
> The difference? The Dream Team and O'Neal. The Olympic squad, touted as the greatest basketball team ever assembled, stole the world's spotlight and placed it directly on the NBA. When the Olympics were over, the spotlight was aimed at O'Neal. The NBA's star system couldn't have worked more beautifully.
>
> The collectibles industry rode these two waves to a resurgence in popularity. Basketball cards sold like hotcakes, reminding many of the 1989–90 baseball buying frenzy. Yet most believed, as we did, that this frenzied attention would turn from basketball to baseball.
>
> But as a sport without many heroes and severely lacking in public relations skills, baseball is playing sec-

ond fiddle to basketball. It has become so bad, in fact, that one writer has begun to hail basketball as "the new national pastime."

In our little corner of the world, many collectors are starting to wonder if Shaq can play baseball, too.

Where to Buy

Check out your local card shop or other retail outlet. You can also buy by mail order through dealers. And you can buy at card conventions.

Be *sure* you know what you are buying; keep current on what cards are worth, because if you don't you may overpay! A subscription to *Beckett Basketball Monthly* is an inexpensive way to keep current—essential for self-protection. (While doing research for this book, I checked out several local dealers; one of them, with several locations in shopping malls, had prices that seemed too high. When I asked how they were priced, the dealer said he had priced them according to what he thought they were worth, without regard to any pricing guide. As you might have guessed, I took my business elsewhere; the prices he quoted were considerably higher than current market value. Teaching point: shop around, be informed, and be prepared to bargain down if you are making a sizable purchase; after all, everything's negotiable, especially in this volatile market.)

What Makes a Card Valuable

Condition. Obviously, as with any print collectible, condition is paramount; mint—in perfect condition, regardless of age, as if it had just been pulled out of the pack—is most desirable, since even minor blemishes can devalue a card dramatically.

Scarcity. Here, the mercantile law of supply and demand helps set the price. Obviously, the fewer the cards available, the more valuable they will be. Because of the popularity of basketball cards, print runs today are much higher than a few years ago. For instance, a decade ago, Star printed only 5,000 of the Michael Jordan 1984–85 Star Extended Rookie Card (#101), which now "hovers near the $4,000 mark," according to Grand Sandground, price coordinator for *Beckett Basketball Monthly* (August 1993).

As with other collectibles, the older the item, the less likely copies in any condition—much less cards in mint condition—can be found, since many were traded away, discarded, lost, etc.

Publication date. The older the card, generally the more valuable, simply because it is harder to find.

Player popularity. Every field has its superstars, and these inevitably translate into the most popular cards. Obviously, Jordan is very collectible.

Team popularity. No matter how the Bulls do in the 1993–94 season, they will still benefit from the "halo" effect from Jordan. In the short term, no problem; in the long term, it will depend entirely on the Bulls' performance as a team without Jordan.

Keeping Current

For an overview on the card field, *Tuff Stuff* (monthly, cover price $3.95), is worth your while; for more specific coverage, *Beckett Basketball Monthly* is the most useful periodical, since it updates card value, giving a low and a high price, with indicators to show whether or not a card has risen or fallen in value from the previous month. Its monthly listing is, as they put it, "The hobby's most reliable and relied upon source."

Storage

Cards are fragile and extremely sensitive to heat, sunlight, and humidity. My recommendation: Store them in protectors, away from light, and always in an air-conditioned room.

Michael Jordan's Comprehensive Card Checklist

Compiled by Beckett Publications, published in *Beckett Tribute: Michael Jordan*

1. 1984–85 Wich/Eagle #5M
2. 1984–85 Star Court King #26
3. 1984–85 Star NBA #101
4. 1984–85 Star NBA #195
5. 1984–85 Star NBA #288
6. 1985 Bulls Interlake #1
7. 1985 Star Crunch 'n' Munch #4
8. 1985 Star Gatorade #7
9. 1985 Star Last 11 ROY #1
10. 1985 Star Lite All-Star #4
11. 1985 Star Slam Dunk #5
12. 1985 Star Team Super #CB1
13. 1985–86 Star All-Rookie Team #2
14. 1985–86 Star NBA #117
15. 1986–87 Fleer Sticker #8
16. 1986–87 Fleer #57

17. 1986 Star Best of the Best #9
18. 1986 Star Best of the New/Old #2
19. 1986 Star Court Kings #18
20. 1986 Star Jordan Set
21. 1987–88 Fleer #59
22. 1987–88 Fleer Sticker #2
23. 1987 Bulls/Entenmann's #6
24. 1988 Bulls/Entenmann's #23
25. 1988 Fournier #22
26. 1988 Fournier Sticker #5
27. 1988–89 Fleer #120AS
28. 1988–89 Fleer #17
29. 1988–89 Fleer Sticker #7
30. 1989 NC/Coke #13
31. 1989 NC/Coke #14
32. 1989 NC/Coke #15
33. 1989 NC/Coke #16
34. 1989 NC/Coke #17
35. 1989 NC/Coke #18
36. 1989 NC/Coke #65
37. 1989–90 Bulls/Equal #6
38. 1989–90 Fleer #21
39. 1989–90 Fleer #3AS
40. 1989–90 Hoops #200
41. 1989–90 Hoops #21AS
42. 1990 Action Packed Promo #3
43. 1990 Bulls Equal/Star #1
44. 1990 Collegiate Collection Promo* #C1
45. 1990 McDonald's/Jordan #1–8
46. 1990 NC/200* #3
47. 1990 NC/200* #44
48. 1990 NC/200* #61
49. 1990 NC/200* #89
50. 1990 NC/200* #93
51. 1990 NC/Promos* #NC1
52. 1990–91 Fleer #26
53. 1990–91 Fleer #5AS
54. 1990–91 Hoops #358TC
55. 1990–91 Hoops #382
56. 1990–91 Hoops #5AS
57. 1990–91 Hoops #65
58. 1990–91 Hoops Collect A Book #4
59. 1990–91 Hoops Super #12
60. 1990–91 Panini #91
61. 1990–91 Panini GAS
62. 1990–91 Panini K
63. 1990–91 SkyBox #41
64. 1990–91 SkyBox Prototype #41
65. 1990–91 Arena Hologram* #3
66. 1990–91 Farley-Set
67. 1990–91 Nike Jordan Set
68. 1990–91 Wooden #13
69. 1991–92 Fleer #211AS
70. 1991–92 Fleer #220LL
71. 1991–92 Fleer #29
72. 1991–92 Fleer Pro Vision #2
73. 1991–92 Fleer Tony's Pizza #33
74. 1991–92 Fleer Update #375TL
75. 1991–92 Hoops #253AS
76. 1991–92 Hoops #30
77. 1991–92 Hoops #306M
78. 1991–92 Hoops #317MS
79. 1991–92 Hoops #455SC
80. 1991–92 Hoops #536LL
81. 1991–92 Hoops #542M
82. 1991–92 Hoops #543
83. 1991–92 Hoops #579USA
84. 1991–92 Hoops All-Star MVP #9
85. 1991–92 Hoops/McDonald's #55USA
86. 1991–92 Hoops/McDonald's #6
87. 1991–92 Hoops Prototype #00–004
88. 1991–92 Hoops/Slam Dunk #4
89. 1991–92 Hoops/Super #3
90. 1991–92 Panini #116
91. 1991–92 Panini #190AS
92. 1991–92 Panini #96AS
93. 1991–92 SkyBox #307LL
94. 1991–92 SkyBox #333M
95. 1991–92 SkyBox #334
96. 1991–92 SkyBox #39
97. 1991–92 SkyBox #408GF
98. 1991–92 SkyBox #462TW
99. 1991–92 SkyBox #534US
100. 1991–92 SkyBox #572
101. 1991–92 SkyBox #583
102. 1991–92 SkyBox Canadian #7
103. 1991–92 Upper Deck #22SiS
104. 1991–92 Upper Deck #44
105. 1991–92 Upper Deck #69AS
106. 1991–92 Upper Deck #75TC
107. 1991–92 Upper Deck #8CL
108. 1991–92 Upper Deck Extended #452AS
109. 1991–92 Upper Deck/Award Winner Hologram #1
110. 1991–92 Upper Deck/Award Winner Hologram #4
111. 1992 Bulls/Dairy #3
112. 1992–93 Fleer #238LL
113. 1992–93 Fleer #246AW
114. 1992–93 Fleer #273SD
115. 1992–93 Fleer #32
116. 1992–93 Fleer All Star #6
117. 1992–93 Fleer Bulls Shell #4
118. 1992–93 Fleer Drake #7

*Compiled by Beckett Publications,
published in* Beckett Tribute: Michael Jordan.

119. 1992–93 Fleer Team Leader #4
120. 1992–93 Fleer TotalD #5
121. 1992–93 Hoops #298AS
122. 1992–93 Hoops #30
123. 1992–93 Hoops #320LL
124. 1992–93 Hoops #341
125. 1992–93 Hoops #TR1
126. 1992–93 Hoops 100SS #14
127. 1992–93 Hoops Supreme Court #SC1
128. 1992–93 SkyBox #31
129. 1992–93 SkyBox Oly #USA11
130. 1992–93 SkyBox School Ties #ST16
131. 1992–93 SkyBox USA #105
132. 1992–93 SkyBox USA #37
133. 1992–93 SkyBox USA #38
134. 1992–93 SkyBox USA #39
135. 1992–93 SkyBox USA #40
136. 1992–93 SkyBox USA #41
137. 1992–93 SkyBox USA #42
138. 1992–93 SkyBox USA #43
139. 1992–93 SkyBox USA #44
140. 1992–93 SkyBox USA #45
141. 1992–93 SkyBox MVP #314
142. 1992–93 Stadium Club #1
143. 1992–93 Stadium Club #210 Member's Choice
144. 1992–93 Stadium Club Beam Team #1
145. 1992–93 Topps All-Star #115
146. 1992–93 Topps #141
147. 1992–93 Topps #205
148. 1992–93 Topps Highlight #3
149. 1992–93 Topps Archives #52
150. 1992–93 Topps Beam Team #3M
151. 1992–93 Topps Gold #115 All-Star
152. 1992–93 Topps Gold #141
153. 1992–93 Topps Gold #205
154. 1992–93 Topps Gold Highlight #3
155. 1992–93 Ultra #216JS
156. 1992–93 Ultra #27
157. 1992–93 Ultra All-NBA #4
158. 1992–93 Ultra Award Winner #1
159. 1992–93 Upper Deck Checklist #200
160. 1992–93 Upper Deck #23
161. 1992–93 Upper Deck Checklist #310
162. 1992–93 Upper Deck All-Star #425
163. 1992–93 Upper Deck #453A
164. 1992–93 Upper Deck #453B
165. 1992–93 Upper Deck #488GF
166. 1992–93 Upper Deck Fanimation #506
167. 1992–93 Upper Deck #62
168. 1992–93 Upper Deck MVP #67
169. 1992–93 Upper Deck #90CL
170. 1992–93 Upper Deck #SP2
171. 1992–93 Upper Deck 15,000 Point Club #4
172. 1992–93 Upper Deck All-Division #9
173. 1992–93 Upper Deck All-NBA #1
174. 1992–93 Upper Deck Award Winner Hologram #1
175. 1992–93 Upper Deck Award Winner Hologram #9
176. 1992–93 Upper Deck European #107AR
177. 1992–93 Upper Deck European #178
178. 1992–93 Upper Deck European #181
179. 1992–93 Upper Deck European #38
180. 1992–93 Upper Deck European #4AS
181. 1992–93 Upper Deck Jerry West Selects #1
182. 1992–93 Upper Deck Jerry West Selects #4
183. 1992–93 Upper Deck Jerry West Selects #8
184. 1992–93 Upper Deck Jerry West Selects #9
185. 1992–93 Upper Deck McDonald's #CH4
186. 1992–93 Upper Deck McDonald's #P5
187. 1992–93 Upper Deck McDonald's Hologram
188. 1992–93 Upper Deck MVP Hologram #4
189. 1992–93 Upper Deck Team MVP #1 Checklist
190. 1992–93 Upper Deck Team MVP #5
191. 1993–94 Fleer #224LL
192. 1993–94 Fleer #28
193. 1993–94 Fleer #5AS
194. 1993–94 Hoops #28
195. 1993–94 Hoops #283SL
196. 1993–94 Hoops All-Star #257
197. 1993–94 Hoops Face to Face #11
198. 1993–94 SkyBox #45
199. 1993–94 SkyBox Center Stage #CS2
200. 1993–94 SkyBox Playoff Performance #14
201. 1993–94 Stadium Club #1
202. 1993–94 Stadium Club #169
203. 1993–94 Topps #101AS
204. 1993–94 Topps #23
205. 1993–94 Topps #64
206. 1993–94 Topps Gold #101AS
207. 1993–94 Topps Gold #23
208. 1993–94 Topps Gold #64
209. 1993–94 Ultra #30
210. 1993–94 Ultra All-NBA #2
211. 1993–94 Ultra All-NBA Defensive Team
212. 1993–94 Ultra Scoring King #5
213. 1993–94 Upper Deck #166SL
214. 1993–94 Upper Deck #171SL
215. 1993–94 Upper Deck #180M
216. 1993–94 Upper Deck #187M
217. 1993–94 Upper Deck #193M
218. 1993–94 Upper Deck #198
219. 1993–94 Upper Deck #204M
220. 1993–94 Upper Deck #213

Compiled by Beckett Publications,
published in Beckett Tribute: Michael Jordan.

221. 1993–94 Upper Deck #23
222. 1993–94 Upper Deck #237SM
223. 1993–94 Upper Deck #SP3
224. 1993–94 Upper Deck 3-D Triple Double
     Standout #TD2
225. 1993–94 Upper Deck All-NBA #AN4
226. 1993–94 Upper Deck All-Star Weekend #15

*Compiled by Beckett Publications,
published in* Beckett Tribute: Michael Jordan.

Michael Jordan's Flight Team

In its Series One NBA basketball cards, Upper Deck seeded individual card packs with 20 insert cards, "Michael Jordan's Flight Team." As Upper Deck explains the appeal of the insert set, "They love to fly and it shows. . . . Michael has personally selected each player and offers comments on each member of the flight team's gravity-defying acrobatic skills."

Presumably out of modesty, Jordan does not select himself, though no one would have faulted him for doing so.

Each card noted is prefaced by its official designation, "FT" for "Flight Team."

FT1. Stacey Augmon (Atlanta Hawks)
FT2. Charles Barkley (Phoenix Suns)
FT3. David Benoit (Utah Jazz)
FT4. Dee Brown (Boston Celtics)
FT5. Cedric Ceballos (Phoenix Suns)
FT6. Derrick Coleman (New Jersey Nets)
FT7. Clyde Drexler (Portland Trail Blazers)
FT8. Sean Elliott (San Antonio Spurs)
FT9. La Phonso Ellis (Denver Nuggets)
FT10. Kendall Gill (Charlotte Hornets)
FT11. Larry Johnson (Charlotte Hornets)
FT12. Shawn Kemp (Seattle SuperSonics)
FT13. Karl Malone (Utah Jazz)
FT14. Harold Miner (Miami Heat)
FT15. Alonzo Mourning (Charlotte Hornets)
FT16. Shaquille O'Neal (Orlando Magic)
FT17. Scottie Pippen (Chicago Bulls)
FT18. Clarence Weatherspoon (Philadelphia 76ers)
FT19. Spud Webb (Sacramento Kings)
FT20. Dominique Wilkins (Atlanta Hawks)

3. Nike and Air Jordan

By far Jordan's most extensive commercial endorsement—in terms of advertising exposure and product lines—is his linkage with Nike, which has produced virtually every kind of product imaginable; in fact, you would be hard pressed to name any kind of clothing not emblazoned with the "Jumpman" logo (a silhouette of Jordan jumping in the air, legs and arms outstretched), the number 23 (Jordan's jersey number), or Jordan's name. Baseball-style caps, T-shirts, jackets, pants, socks, and of course the annual Air Jordan basketball shoe makes it possible for a Jordan fan to be completely adorned in Jordaniana.

Because the Nike product line changes constantly, no listing of all the Jordan-related Nike products could be definitive. The best source for the Nike material is through retail outlets like the Nike Town stores and mall stores that specialize in athletic apparel.

While it would be impossible to list every Jordan item ever manufactured, a representative cross section can be seen in the offerings from the Air Jordan Flight Club, which sells "members only" merchandise, as well as selected items available through retail outlets. (Right now, the Flight Club is grounded, and with Jordan's retirement is unlikely to become airborne again. Still, you may want to keep in touch, just in case. After all, Jordan's contract with Nike is long-term, and through traditional outlets, there will be more Jordan apparel from the boys in Beaverton. Contact **Air Jordan Flight Club** at PO Box 2300, Portland, OR 97208-2300.)

Volume 7 (summer 1991)

1. Poster, black-and-white, 24" × 75", "Wings." Shows Jordan with hands outstretched; in his right hand he's palming a basketball, held downward. The quotation is by poet William Blake. $8.

2. Poster, full color, 24" × 24", "Reverse Dunk." Shows Jordan in an indoor court, in a reverse jam recalling the Air Jordan Flight Club logo. $6.

3. Poster, full color, 24" × 36", "Super Jordan." Cartoon of Jordan elevated, ready to slam-dunk. $6.

4. Sport Watch. The face is imprinted with the logo of the Air Jordan Flight Club. $24.95.

5. Classic Watch. The face is imprinted with the logo of the Air Jordan Flight Club. $39.95.

6. Indoor backboard with net, "Ohio Art Jordan Wall Ball." Backboard is a color photo of Jordan, positioned for a free throw. $10.95.

7. Freestanding "Ohio Art Jordan Jammer Indoor/Outdoor Set." Adjustable to seven feet. $39.95.

8. Sunglasses in nylon case. $14.95.

9. Beach towel, 30" × 60" with Flight Club logo. $18.95.

10. Wrist band, 3" wide, terry cloth. $4.

11. Youth cap, 100% nylon, adjustable leather strap. One size for kids ages 5–12. $12.

12. Flight Club cap (termed "Hat"), 100% nylon, adjustable strap. $14.

13. T-shirt, in color, 100% cotton, in medium and large only; "Graduated Jordan Adult T-shirt." Shows Jordan driving in for a basket. $17.

14. T-shirt, 100%, oversize fit, in small, medium, and large. On front, AJFC logo; on back, in color, Jordan driving in to basket. $17.

15. T-shirt, 100%, oversize fit, in medium and large. On one side, AFJC logo (oversize , yellow on black); on the other, a design incorporating the words "Can" and "Can't." (Perhaps a variation of the Nike ad slogan, "Just do it.") $17.

16. T-shirt (jersey style), 100% cotton, oversize fit in small and medium ($17), and size L for kids ($13). Shows Jordan preparing to dunk, with the words "Stuff It" in the background (in yellow letters).

17. Polo shirt, 100% cotton interlock fashion knit collar, with pocket. AJFC logo on left chest; sizes small, medium, large, and extra-large. $26.

18. Sweatshirt, 60% cotton, 40% poly fleece, in medium, large, and extra-large. AJFC logo in center. $36.

19. Crew socks, 80% cotton, 10% stretch nylon, 5% acrylic, with AJFC logo at top. One size only, fits adult shoe sizes 6.5 to 12. $5.50 a pair.

20. Adult T-shirt, 90% cotton/10% polyester, gray; oversize, in small, medium, large, and extra-large. Shows a tight portrait (from the chest up) of Jordan soaring, with the words "Defies the Law of Gravity" in the background. $17.

21. Shorts, 100% cotton, to match #20. In black, with the same design, "Defies the Law of Gravity." $25.

22. Gym bag, 100% nylon, adjustable shoulder straps. In black, with blue AJFC logo on side. $32.

Volume 8 (Fall 1991)

1. Varsity jacket, 70% Melton Wool/30% rayon front and back, 100% cotton sleeves. Red body with black sleeves, with AJFC logo over left breast and centered on the back. $160.

2. Patch sweatshirt, 60% cotton, 40% polyester fleece. Five patches commemorating Jordan's greatest accomplishments. In red, with multicolored patches; small, medium, large, and extra-large. $65.

Jumpman logo for the Nike-sponsored Air Jordan Flight Club.

3. Wool hat, in black, with AJFC logo in blue. Adult sizing (one size fits all). $20.

4. T-shirt, jersey style, "Skyscraper." 100% cotton, in black, with a screen print in yellow and red showing Jordan extending for a basketball. In medium, large, and extra-large. $14.

5. T-shirt, jersey style, 100% cotton. On sleeve, AJFC logo; on front, "League Scoring Champion" with "Jordan from 1986" overprinted. In small, medium, large, and extra-large. $20.

6. Calendar, in color; sixteen-month, square-format calendar with spiral wire binding. Cover shows Jordan in a reverse dunk (see item #2, volume 7). $12.95.

7. [Coffee] Mug, in ceramic black, with gold-colored AJFC logo. $6.95.

8. Key chain, in brass, with AJFC logo. $4.95.

9. Lapel pin, goldtone, with AJFC logo. $2.95.

10. Cross set of ballpoint pen and pencil, with enameled AJFC logo on clip. $49.

11. Plastic photo frame imprinted with "Air Jordan Flight Club" in lower right. $19.95.

12. Director's chair, in black canvas, with white wooden frame. On back, AJFC logo. $49.95.

13. Pen/pencil set, with legend "Air Jordan Flight Club" on pen, pencil, and clip-on case. $9.95.

14. Basketball (indoor and outdoor), synthetic leather in gold, imprinted with Jordan's signature. $34.95.

15. Sports bottle, with cover and capped straw. Shows AJFC logo and legend, "Air Jordan Flight Club." $4.95.

16. Trading cards (a set of six); on front side, poster

images and other shots; and on back, information about Jordan. $6 the set.

Volume 9 (spring 1992)

1. T-shirt (white), "Hare Jordan." From the Nike ad on TV, Jordan on the front and Bugs Bunny on the back. 100% cotton, in small, medium, large, and extra-large. $16.

2. T-shirt, "Truly Untouchable." 100% cotton. On the front, Jordan with the basketball, surrounded by the legend, "Truly Untouchable." A color bar wraps around the back, intersecting with the AJFC logo. In small, medium, large, and extra-large. $19.

3. Shoelace toggles. Red toggles (pair), imprinted with Jordan as jumpman logo, and Nike logo. $1.49.

4. Waistpack. 100% nylon waistpack with woven patch design (jumpman logo). $12.

5. A series of seven "limited-edition graphics" on T-shirts, with Air Jordan shoe designs. AJFC 1984–85 T-shirt, $20; AJFC 1985–86 T-shirt, $20. In small, medium, large, and extra-large.

Sneaker Cathedral: Nike Town, Chicago

NIKE shoes. NIKE clothes. NIKE bags and hats. Posters. Displays. NIKE out the ying yang. No other store sports more cool stuff. A free-form, high-flying, design-inspired assault on the senses. Everything NIKE makes is in this retail laboratory SLASH! museum SLASH! fitness emporium. Part history, part athlete, part village, part cartoon, all NIKE. The past, present, and future of sports and fitness around the world. A store only NIKE could build. NIKE TOWN.

—*from a Nike Town brochure*

If your only exposure to athletic apparel is a tiny retail shop shoehorned into a mall—typically Foot Locker or a sports store—you'll likely find Nike Town in Chicago to be much more than a store; it's simply a universe of sports gear with something for everyone. In fact, it's a virtual museum to the world of Nike.

Naturally, with this particular store in Chicago, Michael Jordan—a larger-than-life figure—is larger than life, with a 28-foot-tall photo on the wall, posi-

tioned behind a real basketball court complete with a suspended backboard and rim. (The temptation to pick up a basketball and shoot is so tempting that Nike makes sure no stray basketballs are nearby.)

Even before you get to the second floor, with its three-story Jordan photo, you encounter Michael Jordan in the form of a statue, encased behind glass, spotlit, with a list of credits superimposed on the glass front (see sidebar).

On the third floor Jordan fans can view glass showcases with Jordan memorabilia like autographed jerseys, basketballs, and (of course) Air Jordan basketball shoes—unfortunately, none offered for sale. Be prepared, though, to break out the wallet because there's plenty to spend your money on: "Here you'll find the complete AIR JORDAN collection, including a ton of stuff Michael Jordan has actually worn during his career! In the center of things you'll find the KIDS pavilion for all your pint-sized superstars. A POSTER GALLERY. T-SHIRTS. Take a break and view some of NIKE'S great media moments in the VIDEO THEATER," states the brochure.

For the investor, the most expensive Jordan collectible for sale is a hand-painted Warner Brothers cel with a printed background; limited to an edition of 250 numbered copies, this $600 print is triple-matted and professionally framed. The cel depicts an indoor basketball court with Michael Jordan, basketball in hand, decked out in Air Jordan gear from top to bottom; to his right, Bugs Bunny, basketball in hand, wearing "Hare" Jordan shoes. (A second cel in this series will be published soon, at $750, using the "Mission to Mars" motif from the second Air Jordan/Hare Jordan ad.)

From the store brochure, here's what's on each floor, written in Nike-prose (written especially to appeal to the MTVers):

1. Enter gawking, in the front door, through the NIKE museum and into the Town Square. Cool, huh? Men's and Women's RUNNING stuff is in the pavilion with the huge spinning globe. Look for Aqua Socks over by the fish tank. There's more: OUTDOOR CROSS-TRAINING, CYCLING, MEN'S FITNESS (look for the memoraBOlia), VOLLEYBALL.

Take the escalator (You can't miss it. It's the biggest, greenest thing in all of NIKE TOWN) up to:

2. B-Ball! FORCE. FLIGHT. And a basketball court with a life-size rim and a bigger-than-life Michael Jordan (28 feet tall!). Two collections of tennis: SUPREME COURT and CHALLENGE COURT. Over in the corner, GOLF. When you see the elegant spiral terrazzo flooring, you'll know you're in the pavilions for WOMEN'S FITNESS—aerobics, walking, cross-training.

Take the escalator (Still big. Still green. On the side by the Golf stuff.) up to:

3. Here you'll find the complete AIR JORDAN collection, including a ton of stuff Michael Jordan has actually worn during his career! In the center of things you'll find the KIDS pavilion for all your pint-sized superstars. A POSTER GALLERY. T-SHIRTS. Take a break and view some of NIKE'S great media moments in the VIDEO THEATER.

4. Sorry, no stops here—strictly inventory. Don't stop until you get to:

5. Friendly, knowledgeable customer service folks ready to help with returns and exchanges. Even more important, the bathrooms. Each has a changing table for the unexpected performances of those littlest athletes.

NIKE TOWN: 669 North Michigan Avenue, Michigan & Erie, Chicago, IL 60611; (312) 642–6363.
NIKE TOWN HOURS:
Monday through Friday, 10:08 TO 8:09:07
Saturday, 9:23 to 5:50
Sunday, 10:00 to 5:33
Why the weird hours?

There are six reasons for the weird hours. We'll tell you five of them. It's up to you to put them in the right spot and then figure out the reason behind the last one. Four come from the uniform numbers of David Robinson, Michael Jordan, Scottie Pippen, and Bo Jackson. Another is Mark Allen's record triathlon time. The last one is . . . ? (Hint: It's the shoe size of a Las Vegas racquet man.)

The Man—Michael Jordan

A Good Guy Who Plays Great Ball

NBA World Championship—1991, 1992, 1993
Three-Time NBA Most Valuable Player—1988, 1991, 1992
NBA Championship Most Valuable Player—1991, 1992, 1993
Olympic Gold Medal—1984, 1992
Six-Time Scoring Champ—1986 to 1993
Defensive Player of the Year—1988
All-Star Game Most Valuable Player—1988
3000+ Points in a Single Season—1988
Two-Time Slam Dunk Champion—1987, 1988
Most Field Goals in a Playoff Game (24)—1988
NBA All-Defensive First Team—1987 to 1993
All NBA First Team—1987 to 1993
Most Points in a Playoff Game (63)—1986
NBA Rookie of the Year—1985
NCAA Basketball Championship—1982
Sporting News College Player of the Year—1983, 1984
All-Star Pick Every Year in the League

—silk-screened on glass in the showcase of Jordan's
statue in the lobby of Nike Town, Chicago

Michael Jordan's/The Restaurant

"It's an exciting day for me. I've always wanted my own restaurant and we've worked hard to develop a place that I think everyone will enjoy."

—*Michael Jordan, on the opening day of his restaurant*

Opening date: April 28, 1993.

Address: 500 North LaSalle, Chicago, IL 60610.

Exterior: 1940s brick facade building with a 25-foot basketball on top.

Interior: Three levels

Sports bar: located on the first floor, it can seat up to 150 people. Eyecatcher: A 6 × 20 foot, $350,000 video wall comprised of 2 × 3 foot projection cubes, allowing three different projections simultaneously. The video wall hangs behind the main bar, which is 35 feet long. Comfort zone: A three-tier "Skybox" seating area, including seats designated by name for principals in Michael Jordan's life.

Main dining room: seats 200 people.

Michael's dining room: on the second floor, with a private entrance from the back of the restaurant.

Meeting and banquet facilities: seats up to 250.

Gift shop: 500 square feet; retail only (*no mail-order or phone-in orders accepted*). Restaurant and bar-themed items exclusively available here; Chicago Bulls and Nike clothing apparel also available.

Chef: Peter W. Heise, formerly with Vern's Rib Garage, Rooney's Original Lobster House, Trattoria No. 10, and Old Carolina Crab House.

Food: American cuisine.

General Manager: David K. Mazzorana, with nearly two decades of restaurant management experience.

Decor: Sports motif. MJ on magazine covers worldwide, oversize trading cards, international basketball team jerseys, *Sports Illustrated* covers with MJ, sports memorabilia. Says Jordan, the decor is supposed to be "sporty, casual, and comfortable."

Artwork/Photos: artwork and fan mail by children worldwide; a portrait (8'6" × 7'6") by Chicago artist Ed Paschke; several murals by Greg Gove; photos by official Bulls team photographer Bill Smith.

Besides basketball, what does Michael Jordan have in common with Phoenix Suns star Dan Majerle? A sports bar.

Detail of shopping bag from the gift store at Michael Jordan's/The Restaurant.

As other sports figures have discovered, investing in a restaurant can simply be good business. And Jordan's own restaurant can offer one thing not found anywhere else—privacy, on his terms, which is otherwise impossible when he chooses to dine out in Chicago, where everyone wants to come by and chat or get an autograph.

The establishment is a combination souvenir shop, sports bar, and restaurant that celebrates sports, Michael Jordan, and fine dining with both an adult and children's menu. (By the way: If you forget the address, don't fret because, according to the cabbie who took me there, "Every cab driver in town knows this place.")

A multilevel restaurant, the first floor features a 500-square-foot retail shop, located to the left as you walk through the lobby. The gift shop offers a wide range of Michael Jordan memorabilia for sale, including Nike gear and Chicago Bulls items.

Gary Silver, who manages the retail store, is in the enviable position of not having to sell his customers on the merchandise; they come in droves, ready to buy, cash or plastic in hand. After all, if you want T-shirts or other apparel with the restaurant logo, you cannot get it anywhere else.

Though the store offers an outstanding selection of merchandise, it lacks two product lines: books on Jordan—except for *Rare Air: Michael on Michael*, Jordan's authorized book—and autographed items. According to Silver, they have been approached on numerous occasions from customers offering to pay premium prices for an authentic Jordan autograph on store merchandise. Even though Silver estimates they could get up to $500 for a signed basketball, the decision was made long ago to simply not offer signed items. Otherwise, they'd have to lock Jordan in the back room and have him sign continuously to meet the demand.

As the restaurant logo is *only* available on merchandise sold exclusively through the store, buy some T-shirts instead; those will one day be collector's items, especially if they change the design or shirts in the future.

As you enter the first floor of the restaurant, a bar runs the length of its right side, with a three-section television screen on the wall behind the bar; on the left side, steps lead up to a counter with stools, each designated by name, honoring friends.

Naturally, sports memorabilia from Jordan's career decorates the restaurant—autographed basketballs, Nike shoes, and jerseys; framed art by children, presumably for the *Chicago Tribune* contest from which one piece was selected for the cover of the children's menu; and framed magazine covers with Michael Jordan on them.

In a corner of the restaurant, a basketball-shaped arch hangs over framed copies of *Sports Illustrated* with Jordan on the cover—22 of them.

The basketball motif is obvious throughout the restaurant. For instance, from the stairwell you can see an oil painting, a portrait of Jordan that spans two floors; and on the second floor, a neon sculpture of a basketball backdrop catches the eye, as a basketball arcs in the net.

But, you wonder, what about the food?

There are two menus. The adults menu offers a full line of traditional American fare. Appropriately, the children's menu features food named after basketball terminology.

As for Jordan sightings: According to hometown journalist Julie Deardorff, Jordan enters through a private back door but exits through the front door, "giving stargazers their big chance." Also, according to store personnel, Jordan keeps in touch with the customers the same way any restaurant owner would, by

Cover art to the children's menu at Michael Jordan's/ The Restaurant. On the back of the menu: "The featured artwork on our cover was created by 11-year-old Matthew Pulchalski of Carol Stream, Illinois. Matthew won the 1993 *Chicago Tribune* KidNews contest to 'draw your idea of what Michael Jordan means to Chicago.'"

mingling with them and asking how they're enjoying their meal.

So how's the food? Greg Boeck of *USA Today* quoted Charles Barkley, who remarked that the food is "very good" but "not as good as Marjerle's." Michael Jordan responded, "Next time he comes in, it won't be free."

Items in the Jordan Souvenir Shop

Pennants
Oversize mugs

Drinking glasses

Coasters

Magnetic restaurant logos

Golf balls

Shot glasses

Restaurant menus

Copies of the *Chicago Tribune* with "Three-peat" cover story

Commemorative coins

"Be Like Mike" cassette single

Coffee mugs

Ties (a wide selection)

Jump pants

Denim dress shirts with matching ties

T-shirts (a wide selection)

Rings

Posters (a wide selection)

Sweatshirts (a wide selection)

Baseball-style caps (wide selection)

Jackets (wide selection)

Pins

Wilson basketballs

Sports bottles (two styles)

and much, much more

---

4. Resources

Books

America's Dream Team: The Quest for Olympic Gold by Coach Chuck Daly with Alex Sachare (Turner Publishing, hardback, $24.95, 224 pages). There are 275 full-color photos and illustrations, and 45,000 words of text.

Published in conjunction with the NBA, this is a coffee-table book celebrating America's "Dream Team," the start-to-finish story written by Coach Chuck Daly with Alex Sachare from the NBA. Recommended, especially for the photos, which are outstanding.

Hang Time: Days and Dreams with Michael Jordan by Bob Greene (Doubleday, hardback, $22.50, 406 pages; St. Martin's, paperback, $5.99, 391 pages, with a new foreword by the author). No photos. Audience: adult.

Jordan has, over the years, had a love-hate relationship with the media; he can't live with them some-

times, but can't live without them. Generally accommodating to the media, Jordan has imposed media silences only when he has found it absolutely necessary. (For instance, during the playoffs against the Knicks when questions arose regarding his presence at a gambling casino in Atlantic City, Jordan—visibly upset that the media would dwell on his personal life during the middle of the playoffs—avoided the press; however, before the playoffs ended in Phoenix, Jordan resumed normal relations with the press.)

What makes this book unusual is that Jordan, over the course of a season, lets his guard down with Bob Greene. The result: a personal, illuminating book on Jordan, on and off court.

My recommendation: Buy this book. Even without any pictures, this book's a treat.

Jordan: The Man, His Words, His Life by Mitchell Krugel (St. Martin's Press, hardback, $22.95, 288 pages). According to the publisher, this is a "first-person account" compiled from interview material.

The Jordan Rules by Sam Smith (Simon & Schuster, hardback, $22, 333 pages; Pocket Books, paperback, $5.99, with a new chapter on the 1992–93 championship drive.) Eight-page black-and-white photo section.

Smith, a *Chicago Tribune* reporter, has the distinction of publishing the most controversial book about Jordan *and* the Bulls. The subject of endless discussion during the playoffs that led to the Bulls' second championship title, *The Jordan Rules*—depending on whom you believe—is either a creditable piece of work from a Chicago journalist who showed an unseen side of Jordan, or a skewed interpretation flawed in the extreme. (When asked if he had read the book, Jordan told an interviewer he hadn't.)

As Sam Smith states about his purpose in writing the book: "This book has been an attempt . . . to open the door to the locker room, take you on the team bus and plane, and let you sit with the players while they talk about their teammates, their coaches, management, and friends."

There is a tendency to gloss over the flaws of someone like Jordan—an approach fundamentally dishonest, to the author as well as the subject. In fact, if a book on Jordan doesn't cover everything—the good, the bad, and the ugly—it will read like an enthusiastic press release from home office. But the question remains: *Is this book accurate in its portrayal, or does it err in its reportage?*

Read the book and come to your own conclusions,

but I feel the truth—as it usually does—lies somewhere in the middle: Jordan is neither a saint nor a sinner; he's human just like anyone else (as he's maintained), and to expect him to be superhuman and supergood is simply unrealistic.

After reading this book, you're convinced that Jordan is far less a hero than he appears to be, and at times is clearly much less—an interpretation that die-hard fans won't want to hear or care to admit, no matter what the facts.

The press, of course, had a field day with this book. Some reactions from newspaper journalists:

"*The Jordan Rules* might become one of the most damaging books ever written about a sports team. It is six feet, three inches shorter than Bill Laimbeer and much thinner than Charles Barkley, but the book ultimately could pose a bigger threat to the Bulls' repeat hopes than injuries, complacency, Detroit, Portland, or any other force." (Excerpt from book review by Jay Mariotti, November 11, 1991.)

"This book does not make Jordan out to be selfish or to be a tyrant. It makes him out to be a mortal.

"Only Jordan knows what it is like to be Jordan, to have so much talent, to be at the mercy of so much competitive fire, to be smothered by so much attention, to be used and misused by so many.

"We'll have to wait for Jordan's book to learn all of that.

"As for this one, nothing in this book diminishes Michael Jordan. It only illuminates him." (Bernie Lincicome, November 20, 1992.)

Michael "Air" Jordan by Bob Sakamoto (Signet, paperback, $3.99, 128 pages). Black-and-white photos throughout, as well as a full-color photo section.

Like Bob Greene, Sakamoto works at the *Chicago Tribune*; unlike Greene, Sakamoto—a sportswriter with a decade of experience, who has also spent four years covering Jordan and the Bulls—is more at home covering on-court activities, but does a creditable job covering off-court activities, too.

The book's eight chapters include: Genesis, From Brooklyn to Wilmington, King of Chapel Hill, Rare Rookie, Offensive Force, Most Valuable Player, Midas Touch, and Champion.

Because it is a general biography, it covers pretty much the same ground as Bill Gutman's biography on Jordan. Recommended.

Michael and Me: Our Gambling Addiction . . . My Cry for Help! by Richard Esquinas, with Dave Distel ($19.95, 209 pages). A thin, expensive, self-published hardback,

this book has no reason for its existence, except to make money for its author.

The subject of controversy during the Knicks-Bulls playoffs in 1993, the book could not be ignored because the media accorded it more air time and print space than it deserved—it deserved none, but got plenty. Jordan finally broke his self-imposed media silence instituted after the media attacked him in print for going to Atlantic City to a casino before a playoff game. Said Jordan:

After much deliberation, I have decided to interrupt my media silence and respond to yesterday's reports. Ordinarily, I would find it inappropriate to publicly respond to unsubstantiated allegations about my private life. But current circumstances are different and they compel a different response from me.

Right now, my total focus and attention is on helping the Chicago Bulls defend our world championship. However, my responsibilities to my family, my team, the NBA, and Bulls fans do not allow me to remain silent and let this sensationalized report undermine the Bulls' mission to win the championship. Therefore, I am issuing the following statement and I will not comment further on the matter.

I have played golf with Richard Esquinas with wagers made between us. Because I did not keep records, I cannot verify how much I won or lost. I can assure you that the level of our wagers was substantially less than the preposterous amounts that have been reported.

It is extremely disappointing to me that an individual whom I caused no harm and who held himself out as my friend would shamelessly exploit my name for selfish gain. It is equally disappointing that my off-the-court activities are receiving more attention in the midst of the NBA championship than my on-court activities.

I want to publicly apologize to my family, my teammates, Jerry Reinsdorf, the NBA, and Bulls fans for the distraction this story has caused. I also want to thank those members of the media who had the courage and independence to report this incident and the coverage it received for what it is: an embarrassment for all of us.

Michael Jordan by Chip Lovitt (Scholastic, paperback, $3.25, 166 pages). Eight-page full-color photo section.

The author of several books for children, including sports biographies on Magic Johnson and Ivan Ledyl, Lovitt offers a biography written especially for children. Interesting and informative, this book had many tidbits of information that I had not encountered in other, similar books. (This book is also the most recent general biography available on Jordan.)

Michael Jordan by Mitchell Krugel (SMP, paperback, $4.50, 185 pages). Eight-page black-and-white photo section.

Krugel, who has written *Magic and the Bird: Magic Johnson and Larry Bird*, offers another biography of Jordan.

While there is a good deal of factual information on Jordan, the book is marred by Krugel's overly enthusiastic writing. For instance, the book starts out, "As he moved to his right and drove the baseline, Michael Jordan prepared for a takeoff the Wright brothers and NASA never dreamed possible."

It's too bad, in a way, because Krugel knows his subject but perhaps felt he had to "write down" to make the book appeal to teenagers.

Michael Jordan by Jack Clary (Smithmark, hardback, $9.95, 64 pages). Full color photos, oversize (9.5 × 13 inches). Shrink-wrapped, with a color poster of Jordan folded and laid in.

Though there is text, the main emphasis of this book is the photo selection. Published as a "markdown" book, this is a difficult book to find in bookstores because of its "remaindered" status.

Michael Jordan: A Biography by Bill Gutman (Pocket Books, paperback, $2.99, 140 pages). Black-and-white photos.

A well-done biography. Gutman—author of several sports books, including a biography on Bo Jackson—offers a straightforward, factual telling of the Jordan story.

Gutman has done his homework, once again. Recommended.

Rare Air: Michael on Michael by Michael Jordan, edited by Mark Vancil, photographs by Walter Iooss, Jr. (Collins Publishers San Francisco), 112 pages. One hundred photographs in full color; a coffee-table book (11 × 13 inches). Jordan's text: approximately 10,000 words.

Published in three editions:
- trade paperback, $24.95 (first printing, 200,000)
- trade hardback, with dust jacket, $50 (first printing, 50,000)
- limited edition of 2,500 copies, signed ($499); and 2,500 copies, unsigned ($99.95), from Upper Deck Authenticated.

Because this is the *only* authorized book on Jordan, it offers what other books—for the most part—cannot: Jordan on Jordan. If you want to know what Jordan thinks, instead of what he thinks as interpreted through others, this book will be indispensable reading. It is, simply, a photo-illustrated look into Jordan's world with him as your guide.

Not surprisingly, Jordan's talk of retirement seemed to foreshadow his actual announcement in October 1993, but according to Jordan, in an interview on "The Oprah Winfrey Show," he had pretty much made up his mind to retire after winning the third championship, and wanted to spend a summer to see if he was comfortable with that decision. He was, and in the last paragraph of the book, Jordan made it obvious: "I know there will be pressure on me to stay. But that will be my opportunity to tell people why I played the game. It's never been for money and it's never been for cheers. If you don't believe me, then just watch. And take a good look, because one minute I'll be there and the next minute I'll be gone."

A photo-autobiography, this book is unique. As sportswriter Mark Vancil explained:

I think part of the reason Michael wanted to do *Rare Air* is that he perceives much of the glory of the past years as truly the good old days of his career. I also think that he wanted to do a "photographic autobiography" at this point rather than a traditional words-only autobiography because he wants the curious to see what it's like to be Michael Jordan on a minute-to-minute basis. And believe me, as much as I admire him both as an athlete and as a person, after having seen the incredible demands on his time and his basic existence up close, I'm not sure I'd want to be Michael Jordan for a day let alone a whole career. In *Rare Air*, the reader will get to see why.

Walter Iooss, whose credits include having shot over 200 covers for *Sports Illustrated*, has been with the magazine for a quarter century. Says Iooss, "I wanted to create a book that would be Jordan's personal photo album, something he could look at after his career had ended, to show his children, or even his grandchildren, what his life was like at 30 years of age, when he was the most famous and gifted athlete of his generation." (Because the photos aren't captioned, a special section in the back of the book gives Iooss's perspective on each shot.)

According to the publisher, the book is indeed "rare air," with Michael, finally, speaking about himself:

. . . Jordan writes candidly about growing up in North Carolina and what it meant to play on the U.S. Dream Team at the Barcelona Olympics; he shares his inner thoughts about his home life, marriage, and what he wants for his children. Readers learn how he prepares his mind and body for each game, the pregame ritual he always performs, and the mental discipline required to achieve apparently effortless mastery on the basketball court. And he explains why he could simply walk away from the sport he's dominated for years.

Said Jordan, "I decided to do this book now because I want people to see how my life really is on and off the basketball court. I'm sure there are fans who think they know what it's like being a professional athlete. But I'm quite sure they don't know just how different our lives are and how it impacts our wives and children. . . . I thought this was the perfect time in my career to give people an inside look at my life."

Michael Jordan by Devra Newberger (Scholastic Inc., saddle-stitched pamphlet, approximately 3 × 4.5 inches, $1.25, 44 pages). Black-and-white photos.

This is properly a souvenir, not a book. One in their "Sports Shots" series, this is the "Collector's Book 1."

A brief overview—a short magazine article, really—this pamphlet consists of four chapters (Growing Up, High School, College Days, The Pros) and a short section on career highlights.

Taking to the Air: The Rise of Michael Jordan by Jim Naughton (Warner Books, $18.95, 264 pages). Eight-page black-and-white photo section.

This is an essential book in any Jordan library. Naughton knows his subject and, to his credit, managed to get the cooperation of Jordan, his family, and his professional associates, on and off court.

This book does an excellent job covering Jordan's commercial endorsements. Highly recommended.

One-shot Publications

To celebrate the three-peat (a word coined by coach Pat Riley), two magazine-format retrospectives were published:

• The souvenir issue of *The Chicago Bulls Three-peat!* (Tribune Publishing, from the staff of the *Chicago Tribune*, $6.99, 64 pages, full color). Comparisons between this and the *Sports Illustrated* publication (see below) are inevitable, so here's what you need to know: In terms of text and in photos, this appears to have been rushed into print. The text, while adequate, doesn't have the scope and detail that the *SI* pieces have; worse, the photos seem grainy and blurred, as if they printed from color photos and not color transparencies—essential for good print reproduction.

• By far the collectible to get is the "Special Collector's Edition" of *Sports Illustrated Presents: The Chicago Bulls, Three Seasons to Savor* ($4.95, 120 pages, with advertising). An outstanding retrospective with top-quality photographs, this magazine was distributed only in the Chicago area; elsewhere, it was available by mail order from *Sports Illustrated*. Sold in a package with the

official 1993 NBA World Champion video, "Three-Peat: The Chicago Bulls' Historic Third Championship Season," the magazine and videotape give a thorough look at the unstoppa-Bulls.

Tribute Publications

To date there have been six different tribute issues published on Michael Jordan. All are in magazine format with full-color photos. None was authorized by Jordan.

A Tribute to Michael Jordan by Bob Sakamoto (Publications International, Ltd., 1993, $4.95, 64 pages). Sakamoto, a sportswriter, had previously published a biography, *Michael "Air" Jordan*. Unlike the other publications, this one is ad-free, and is printed on glossy stock with heavy covers, and is a recommended buy.

A Tribute to Michael Jordan: The World's Greatest Athlete (L.F.P. Inc., 1993, $3.95, 78 pages). A compilation of articles covering his career.

Beckett Tribute: Michael Jordan (Beckett Publications, 1993, $3.95, 80 pages). Part of an ongoing series (the next tribute issue will highlight Shaquille O'Neal), the collectibility of this issue is enhanced by the fact that there exists only one printing. Because of the limited printing, I asked a Beckett spokesman for the print run figure, but was told that was proprietary information. Beckett—the publishers of *Beckett Basketball*—provides a compilation of articles covering Jordan's career, a comprehensive checklist of Jordan cards to date, and an article on Jordan card collecting. Printed on glossy stock with heavy covers, this is a recommended buy.

Michael Jordan: 1985 to 1993, A Final Tribute (The Sterling/Macfadden Partnership, 1993, $3.95, 96 pages). This tribute issue is, in fact, being sold as the "Winter 94" issue of *Pro Basketball Illustrated*. Printed on newsprint, this tribute issue offers several oversize pinups, including a centerfold pullout.

Michael! A Career Tribute (Hollywood Collectibles Magazine, 1993, $4.95, no pagination) is principally a compilation of statistics on Jordan. Oddly, this publication is also referred to by its publisher as *Michael Jordan: The Official Record and Stat Book, A Career Tribute*, and in its colophon, *Michael Jordan Career Record and Photo Album*. Printed on newsprint. The main value here is in the statistics, not the text.

Newsweek (October/November 1993, $3.95, 64 pages). Published within a week after Jordan's retirement announcement, this special issue on Jordan is more a souvenir of Jordan's retirement than an overview of his career. Interestingly, considering how quickly this went to press, *Newsweek* was able to get farewell ads from major corporations. McDonald's had the inside front cover, with an ad that had the headline, "Nothing but net." The word "net" is crossed out so that the line reads, "Nothing but the best." Likewise, Gatorade ran an ad with Jordan drinking Gatorade, with the words: "To Mike. And to those who dream to be like Mike. Cheers." Amway had the inside back cover position, with elementary-school students from Grand Rapids, Mich., holding a banner that read, "Good luck Michael!" Beneath the photo, Amway added, "Believing in a dream inspires excellence. Our thanks for all the lives you've touched."

Videotapes

Videotape offers the best format for showcasing athletic prowess. This is especially true with basketball, a fast-paced game that—if your VCR is so equipped—can slow down the action so you can see what is happening. (In *Magic's Touch*, as Magic Johnson points out, "Fans always tell me they have trouble trying to watch a basketball game. They see the ball, so they know someone scores, but they can't catch the quick moves or see the strategies develop until it's too late. . . .")

In addition to tapes specific to Jordan, there are numerous tapes—often offered by *Sports Illustrated* as a subscription builder—on the NBA's most prominent players, which typically includes Jordan.

Michael Jordan: Come Fly with Me (1989, CBS Fox, $19.98, 40 minutes).

The tape begins with Jordan on an indoor court, alone. He is shooting the basketball, and never misses. In a monologue, Jordan credits his game to "hard work and determination . . . I've got to keep pushing myself."

Developing that theme, we are given a biographical look at Jordan, his evolution from a Little League baseball player, through his days as a Buccaneer (no. 23) at Laney High School in Wilmington, North Carolina, where he played for the junior varsity and, later, the varsity team, which he led to their first championship.

The college years are chronicled, highlighted by what Jordan has termed, over the years, "The Shot," which brought him to nationwide prominence—a jump shot that, with 17 seconds on the clock, won UNC the 1982 NCAA championship.

Though current only through 1989, the video provides an excellent overview of Jordan's career, with excellent footage of Jordan's on-court moves that, simply, have to be seen in slow-motion on your VCR to appreciate.

Michael Jordan's Playground (1991, CBS Fox, $19.98, 40 minutes).

Unlike the first Jordan video, with its emphasis on biography, the second (as the liner notes put it) "conveys Michael's own insights about how hard work and dedication will help you reach your goals."

This video story begins as Jordan, on a playground court, basketball in hand, states simply, "This is where it all begins." Far from the cheering crowds in the NCAA and far from the lofty height of the NBA, Jordan began his basketball career like everyone else: at the bottom, with adversity steeling his will along the way.

This is the story of Walt, an aspiring high school student at Eastside High, who was cut from the basketball team. "For those of you guys who didn't make it, I'd like to tell you something: Michael Jordan got cut from his high school team, and he came back a better ball player," says the coach after the tryouts.

It's a year later on the eve of the tryouts, and Walt is practicing on an outdoor court by himself. Discouraged, his coach's words still ringing in his ears, Walt seems resigned to failure—there's always a good excuse.

Michael Jordan walks on the court and asks, "You don't mind if I shoot with you, do you?"

Jordan pumps up Walt's motivation. The next day, Walt is aggressive and makes all the right moves, impressing the coach—a sharp contrast to last year's tryouts.

The storyline draws from a real-life incident that was pivotal in Jordan's realization early on that you can either accept defeat or rise to the challenge and overcome it.

The real-life incident happened when Jordan, then a sophomore in high school, allegedly got cut from the basketball team. (In retrospect, people ask incredulously, "How could they cut Michael Jordan?" As his high school coach Fred Lynch pointed out years later, "He was still growing. . . ." Lynch wanted a player with more height, and picked Leroy Smith instead.)

Fired up with determination, Jordan went back the next year for tryouts and made it—the point of this video story.

The video also shows highlights of his career, as well as Jordan's observations about himself, the game, and his philosophy.

Wrote Lynn Voedisch (*Chicago Sun Tribune*, February 12, 1991): "*Playground* is not aimed just at the sports-freak market. I don't know a slam dunk from a free throw, but I loved watching Jordan amaze fans and baffle foes on this tape. One particularly effective series of slow-motion shots follows an athlete's statement that Jordan is so graceful, he looks like a dancer. Jordan's physical style is beautiful, even to viewers more used to arabesques than tip-ins. . . . *Michael Jordan's Play-*

ground is about a man who clearly has a zest for achievement and approaches life with a positive outlook. In this era of war and recession, you can't go wrong with that."

A companion tape, *The Making of Michael Jordan's Playground* (1991, CBS Fox, $9.98, 23 minutes), takes you behind the scenes on the shooting of the video, with outtakes and a glimpse at "a side of him few get to see—dancing around, clowning with the crew." (Recommended only for completists.)

Michael Jordan: Air Time (1993, CBS Fox, $19.98, 40 minutes).

In this video we are brought up to date on Jordan's activities since 1981. With an overview of his career to set the stage, the video focuses on the back-to-back NBA championships won by the Bulls, led by Jordan.

For Jordan, the second championship season marked a time when, off the court, the media hammered away at him: for not going to the White House with his teammates after winning a second NBA championship, and for initially declining a spot on what would be termed the "Dream Team" for the Olympics. Additional distractions took the form of gambling allegations—unfortunately, true—and a portrait of a fractious Jordan in *The Jordan Rules*.

Coverage of Jordan as a member of the Dream Team concludes the video, along with footage of Jordan as a family man, Jordan as a celebrity figure in Michael Jackson's music video "Jam," and the famous Nike ad with Bugs Bunny, "Air Jordan and Hare Jordan."

Michael Jordan: On and Off the Court (*Sports Illustrated*, 1993, 50 minutes). Not available in stores or through the *Sports Illustrated* mail-order company that sells other Jordan videotapes, this is available only if you place a new subscription (54 issues, $75.06).

The Bulls on Videotape

Learning to Fly: 1991 Bulls' Championship (1991, CBS Fox, $19.98, 50 minutes).

A video retrospective on the Bulls' first championship quest, which put an end to the questions regarding Jordan's ability to lead the team to an NBA championship.

UntouchaBulls: The Chicago Bulls' Second Championship Season (1992, CBS Fox, $19.98, approx. 50 minutes).

A video retrospective on the Bulls' second champi-

onship quest, culminating in a victory against the Portland Trail Blazers.

Three-Peat: The Chicago Bulls' Historic Third Championship Season (1993, CBS Fox, $19.98, 50 minutes).

As the copy on the box says: "Relive the Chicago Bulls' dramatic charge to a historic third consecutive NBA Championship, with this unique, behind-the-scenes look at their 1992–93 NBA season.

"Join the Bulls on the court, in the huddle, and in the locker room as they become only the third team in history to win three straight NBA finals.

"From their spectacular regular season, to their memorable playoff march through Atlanta, Cleveland, New York, and all the way to Phoenix for their championship matchup with Charles Barkley and the Suns, you'll follow this remarkable team every step of the way.

"More than just a highlight tape, this personal profile will provide an intimate look at Michael Jordan, Scottie Pippen, Horace Grant, rising star B.J. Armstrong, and coaching great Phil Jackson as they face the toughest challenges that the league has to offer on their incredible journey into the NBA record books."

Addresses

Air Jordan Flight Club, PO Box 2300, Portland, OR 97208. (Parent organization: Nike, One Bowerman Drive, Beaverton, OR 97005.

Chicago Bulls, 900 North Michigan Avenue, Suite 1600, Chicago, IL 60611-4501.

Michael Jordan Basketball Camp, Basketball Office, Elmhurst College, Elmhurst, IL 60126-3296; camp hotline: (708) 617-3710.

Michael Jordan Foundation, 111 East Chestnut Street, Suite 52K, Chicago, IL 60611.

Michael Jordan's/The Restaurant, 500 North LaSalle, Chicago, IL 60610.

Nike Towns

- Nike Town, 669 North Michigan Avenue, Chicago, IL 60611; phone: (312) 642-6363.
- Nike Town, 930 Sixth Avenue, Portland, OR 97204; phone: (503) 221-6453.
- Nike Town, Orange County, Triangle Square, 1875-B Newport Blvd, Costa Mesa, CA 92627; phone: (714) 642-6363.
- Nike Town, Phipps Plaza, 3500 Peachtree Road NE, Atlanta, GA 30326; phone: (404) 841-6444.

Michael Jordan talks to kids at a basketball camp in North Carolina. (Photo courtesy of the *Wilmington Star-News.*)

The commemorative issue of *Newsweek,* published within a week after Jordan's retirement announcement on October 6, 1993.

Sports Illustrated published in 1993 a special collector's edition celebrating the "three-peat" NBA victory, *The Chicago Bulls: Three Seasons to Savor.*

His legs bestrid the ocean;
his reared arm crested the world . . .
but when he meant to quail
and shake the orb, he was,
as rattling thunder.
—*playwright* **William Shakespeare**

Copyright Extensions Page

"UNC's Jordan 100 Percent Again" by John Roth originally appeared in the *Durham Sun* (March 1982) and is reprinted with permission.

"Jordan Lives up to Coach's Prophecy" by John Roth originally appeared in the *Durham Sun* (March 22, 1982) and is reprinted with permission.

"Dean Smith Gets First NCAA title," staff written, originally appeared in the *Durham Sun* (March 30, 1982) and is reprinted with permission.

"UNC Beats Georgetown by One Point to Take Title" by Keith Drum originally appeared in the *Durham Sun* (March 1982) and is reprinted with permission.

"Jordan's Pregame Warm-up" by Bob Greene: From *Hang Time* by Bob Greene. Copyright © 1992 by John Deadline Enterprises, Inc. Used by permission of Doubleday, a division of Bantam Doubleday Dell Publishing Group, Inc.

"An Interview with Michael Jordan": Copyright © 1990 by John Edgar Wideman, first printed in *Esquire* magazine November 1990. Reprinted with the permission of Wylie, Aitken & Stone, Inc.

"On Chicago's West Side, Poverty Surrounds the Bulls" by Michael Abramowitz and David Aldridge: Copyright © 1992, *The Washington Post,* reprinted with permission.

"The First NBA Championship: Shining Moment": Reprinted courtesy of *Sports Illustrated* from the June 24, 1991, issue. Copyright © 1991, Time Inc. "Shining Moment" by Jack McCallum. All rights reserved.

"The Second NBA Championship": Reprinted courtesy of *Sports Illustrated* from the Special Collector's Edition of *Sports Illustrated Presents: The Chicago Bulls, Three Seasons to Savor.* Copyright © 1993, Time Inc. "That Championship Season Two" by Jack McCallum. All rights reserved.

"A Hero for the Wired World" by David Halberstam originally appeared in *Sports Illustrated* (December 23, 1991), and is reprinted with the permission of the author.

"The Dream Fulfilled" is reprinted from *America's Dream Team: The Quest for Olympic Gold* by Coach Chuck Daly with Alex Sachare with permission of Turner Publishing, Inc., a subsidiary of Turner Broadcasting System, Inc. and NBA Properties, Inc.

"The Third NBA Championship: They're History": Reprinted courtesy of *Sports Illustrated* from the June 28, 1993, issue. Copyright © 1993, Time Inc. "They're History" by Jack McCallum. All rights reserved.

"Youngsters Are Understanding of Basketball Hero's Decision" by Lisa Leff and Debbi Wilgoren originally appeared October 7, 1993 in the *Washington Post.* Copyright © 1993, *The Washington Post,* reprinted with permission.

"Hometown Reactions" by E.L. Rogers originally appeared in the *Wilmington Morning Star,* October 7, 1993, and is reprinted with permission.

"How to Guard Michael Jordan" by Jeff Weinstock was originally published under the title, "Five Players Share Their Thoughts on How to Defend Michael Jordan," from *Sport* magazine, Peterson Publications, June 1993. Copyright © 1993.

"Michael and Me" by Tim Brandhorst originally appeared in the new foreword of *Hang Time* by Bob Greene, copyright © 1993 by John Deadline Enterprises, Inc., St. Martin's Press, Inc., New York, NY.

"Magic Johnson on Michael Jordan" is extracted from "Isiah and Michael" from *My Life* by Earvin "Magic" Johnson, copyright © 1993 by June Bug Enterprises. Reprinted by permission of Random House, Inc.

"Shooting Star Retires at the Top of His Game" by Scott Whisnant originally appeared in the *Wilmington Star News,* October 7, 1993, and is reprinted with permission.

"The Unlikeliest Homeboy" by Curry Kirkpatrick: Reprinted courtesy of *Sports Illustrated* from the December 23, 1991, issue. Copyright © 1991, Time Inc. "The Unlikeliest Homeboy" by Curry Kirkpatrick. All rights reserved.

"Alone on the Mountaintop" by Jack McCallum: Reprinted courtesy of *Sports Illustrated* from the December 23, 1991, issue. Copyright © 1991, Time Inc. "Alone on the Mountaintop" by Jack McCallum. All rights reserved.

"Jordan's Top 10 'Kodak' Moments on Court" by Dan Bickley originally appeared in the *Chicago Sun-Times,* October 7, 1993, under the title, "Thanks for the Memories" and is reprinted by permission.

"Michael Jordan's Comprehensive Card Checklist," published in 1994, is used with permission of Beckett Publications, *Beckett Tribute: Michael Jordan.*